Language and Prejudice

TAMARA M. VALENTINE
University of South Carolina Spartanburg

PEARSON
Longman

New York   San Francisco   Boston
London   Toronto   Sydney   Tokyo   Singapore   Madrid
Mexico City   Munich   Paris   Cape Town   Hong Kong   Montreal

Senior Vice President and Publisher: Joseph Opiela
Acquisitions Editor: Susan Kunchandy
Marketing Manager: Deborah Murphy
Senior Production Manager: Bob Ginsberg
Project Coordination, Text Design, and Electronic Page Makeup:
    Sunflower Publishing Services
Cover Design Manager: Nancy Danahy
Cover Illustration/Photo: Punk Gear: The back of a leather clad Punk
    Rocker with "God Save the Queen", a swastika, and a Union
    Jack decorating the jacket. © Getty Images Inc.—Hulton Archive
    Photos
Manufacturing Buyer: Roy L. Pickering
Printer and Binder: RR Donnelley & Sons Company
Cover Printer: Coral Graphic Services, Inc.

For permission to use copyrighted material, grateful acknowledg-
ment is made to the copyright holders on pp. 260–262, which are
hereby made part of this copyright page.

Library of Congress Cataloging-in-Publication Data
Valentine, Tamara M.
    Language and prejudice/by Tamara M. Valentine.
        p. cm.—(Longman topics)
    ISBN 0-321-12236-4
    1. Language and culture. 2. Racism in language. 3. Sexism
in language. 4. Language and languages—Sex differences.
5. Prejudices. I. Title. II. Series

P35.V36 2003
306.44—dc22   2003053696

Copyright © 2004 by Pearson Education, Inc.

Please visit our website at http://www.ablongman.com

ISBN 0-321-12236-4

12345678910—DOH—06050403

CONTENTS

Narration

Illustration

Description

Division and Classification

Definition

Process

Persuasion and Argument

Humor and Satire

anguage is the essence of every culture of the world. It is the defining characteristic of humanness. It is the mirror of the soul. We tend to forget, however, the magic that language holds. We take for granted its power to name reality, its strength to empower its users, and its means to manipulate and control. Although Lewis Carroll's Humpty Dumpty proclaims to Alice that a word "means just what I choose it to mean," it is shared language that shapes our perception of the world and constructs our reality. Without language, how would we understand the world and our place within it? Examining language provides insights into the beliefs and attitudes of a community, the perceptions and stereotypes of its users, and the truth about ourselves.

A timely book, *Language and Prejudice* offers an overview of contemporary issues related to the power of language within the social and cultural contexts of ethnicity, gender, sexual orientation, age, and disability. A collection of authentic writings gathered from a wide range of sources, *Language and Prejudice* heightens students' appreciation for and understanding of language, sharpens their awareness of the language they use, and raises their sensitivity to how fundamental language is to perpetuating language stereotypes and in shaping cultural and personal identities. Students learn that their use of terms and expressions that exclude, dehumanize, and stereotype a group of people based on sex, race, ethnic origin, region, age, religion, physical ability, sexual orientation, or minority status perpetuates an inaccurate and unfair view of the world and the people who live in it. Language is a clear reflection of the prejudices that exist in a society and its users.

This book features an in-depth coverage of language and prejudice—topics that students think about and find relevant in their lives and important to their future goals. The book is arranged according to six socially based themes: language and society; language and ethnicity; language and gender; language and sexuality; language and age; and language and disability. Each chapter contains an introductory discussion on the specific theme related to language and prejudice and preliminary information about the readings within that chapter. Following the chapter introductions are prereading discussion questions and a variety of projects and other activities to advance students' reading, writing, and critical thinking skills. Each reading selection that follows is preceded by a headnote containing biographical information and a preliminary description of the reading, followed by questions and writing assignments. A set of guidelines follow Chapters 2 through 6 to help students make informed, thoughtful choices when writing and speaking and to help them avoid biased language.

Language and Prejudice is intended to challenge students to explore the interconnectedness of language and society. Serving as models for writing and composition, this reader exposes students to the variety of rhetorical strategies: narration, illustration, description, comparison and contrast, cause and effect, division and classification, definition, process, persuasion and argument, and humor and satire. This reader will also expose students to a range of genres: personal narratives, academic articles, newspaper articles, letters, poetry, opinion pieces, position papers, and reference entries, as well as numerous writing styles. As a springboard for stimulating discussion and writing, each reading invites students to delve into the complex nature of language by carrying out original library research, conducting fieldwork, studying film and other forms of mass media, and searching the Internet. Students are asked to write personal narratives, opinion papers, and letters, and to design individual language projects relevant to their personal lives and to their communities. Students are also encouraged to engage in practicing what they have learned.

For sociolinguists, like the author of this book, the study of language is a love and a passion. It is hoped that *Language and Prejudice* will inspire students to observe language, respect it, and appreciate it for its beauty to change the world.

ACKNOWLEDGMENTS

I wish to acknowledge the University of South Carolina at Spartanburg. Committed to nurturing a caring and sensitive environment in which to learn, teach, and work, this institution has endorsed a policy of non-biased language usage. And I am grateful to my students over the years whose enthusiasm for language study has kept me committed to the concept of this book.

I would like to dedicate this effort to my family. A special thanks goes to M. J. Del Missier, my supportive spouse, who never fails to light up my life with his wit and humor. I thank him for working into the late night hours proofreading, collating, and stapling, and making my computer life easier with his expertise as my MacGuru. And I thank my loving mother, Marie Valentine, who provided unfailing support and encouragement and kept me going with her treasure trove of told and untold stories.

TAMARA M. VALENTINE

Language
and Society

Language exerts hidden power, like a moon on the tides.
RITA MAE BROWN, *STARTING FROM SCRATCH,* 1988

Language is the heart and soul of a human society. It is the medium through which we communicate to one another, expressing who we are and what we think. Conveying our thoughts, feelings, and attitudes, language is central to our identity as an individual and as a member of a social group. It is the glue that binds us to each other as human beings and binds us to our particular cultures. Language and society are so intertwined that it is impossible to separate one from the other: Society cannot exist without language, and language cannot exist without society. When we talk about this relationship, we define society simply as a group of people who are drawn together for a certain common purpose. Depending on certain social and cultural factors, over which we often have no control—our age, our sex, our ethnicity, our race, our sexual orientation, or our geographical region—we derive a repertoire of social identities from our memberships in many social groups. The particular speech variety that we, the members of the society, share is our language.

Language takes different forms in different societies depending on the situation, participants, and topics. We shift our identities freely, easily, and naturally, not speaking the same way all the time. The use of a particular language variety not only identifies each of us as belonging to a particular social group, it also differentiates us from others who are not members but are seen as outsiders. We control many different styles of speaking, each and every style as important and worthy as the next.

Sociolinguists, scholars who study the relationship between language and society, hope that by closely studying language in social interaction, we can increase our awareness of the language we use, our responses and reactions to others who are not part of our speech community, and the attitudes associated with language and linguistic variation. Language specialists hope that as speaking human beings, we will look beyond the surface and appreciate each other for the diversity that exists within us and respect the many different social and ethnic groups that exist in the world today.

With an increasing emphasis on multiculturalism and diversity in the world today, it is our responsibility to be aware of how fundamental language is to our day-to-day existence. This chapter explores how language shapes our cultural and personal identity. It provides lively discussion on issues that are considered necessary reading in language studies classes, works that bring back childhood memories, and essays that provoke us into thinking about language differently. The collection of papers begins with a poignant article on the dehumanizing power of language, the "Introduction" from *The Language of Oppression* by Professor Haig A. Bosmajian. The nature of the relationship between language and thought is explained in the next reading "The Sapir-Whorf Hypothesis." Linguist David Crystal describes the claim that the structure of a language influences how its speakers view the world. Indian poet, Kamala Das, addresses the audience who criticizes her for writing in a language other than her mother tongue. Unlike Das, Eva Hoffman is *Lost in Translation* in "Exile," struggling to find a voice in a new language as she moves from Polish to English. The next reading is the story of Humpty Dumpty, from Lewis Carroll's *Through the Looking-Glass*, who insists that when he uses a word, it means just what he chooses it to mean. And the last reading, "Proud to be an American Means Speaking any Language, for Some" offers the advice from Dear Abby that speaking English is not a requirement to being an American.

These readings open the door to many fascinating topics related to the study of language. It is hoped that they will enhance our sensitivity, awareness, and appreciation of language and its use in today's complex, diverse social and linguistic world.

Discussion Questions

1. Think about *language*. What does it mean to know a language? Do we as human beings need language? How do we use it?

2. Famed linguist Noam Chomsky says, "It's about as likely that an ape will prove to have a language ability as that there is an island somewhere with a species of flightless birds waiting for human beings to teach them to fly." What do you think he means by this statement? Can you provide evidence to support or refute it?

3. There is much concern that the English language is on a path of decay. Its speakers pay little attention to detail and correct grammar, teenagers are creating their own slang, and words don't mean what they used to. Do you agree with these language purists, or do you think that language change is natural and inevitable?

4. It is estimated that there are between 5,000 and 8,000 different languages spoken in the world today. Nearly half these will not survive the next decade. What do you foresee to be the future of linguistic diversity? the future of the English language?

5. Define prejudice. Define stereotyping. What is the link between the two? Why is the study of prejudice and stereotyping important?

6. Explain how language is a means of maintaining and transmitting the cultural stereotypes of members of a culture. Think of specific proverbs, sayings, and social taboos to support your answer.

7. How do the words of a language reflect the underlying attitudes of a society? Since language changes over time, do the attitudes?

8. Some people argue that many ethnic and racial expressions that started out as insults have lost their impact and now apply to people in general. For example, to say "to welsh on a debt" or "to jew someone down" or "to pay dutch treat" no longer applies to one particular ethnic group. Do you agree or do you think that these expressions are still offensive?

9. View a film that deals directly with language. Discuss the relationship between language and society. Here are a few suggestions: *Nell* (1994) directed by Michael Apted, *Daughters of the Dust* (1992) directed by Julie Dash, *My Fair Lady* (1964) directed by George Cukor, *El Norte* (1983) directed by Gregory Nava, and *Children of a Lesser God* (1986) directed by Randa Haines.

Projects and Other Writing Activities

1. Conversation is viewed as a series of speech acts, organized and ordered to accomplish something. Tape-record a typical lecture, a radio talk show interview, or a telephone conversation. Describe the conversation. What rules do the speakers follow? How does each speaker use language to get his or her message across?

2. Research the history of names in your community. Go to the local library archives or newspaper obituaries. Can you identify what names have remained popular and which have died out? Are some of these names making a comeback?

3. Research any language issue or question that interests you. Write a paper explaining the issue and what you have learned in your research. What conclusion do you draw from the readings and research?

4. Spend a week critically examining how ethnic groups are represented in the media: television, movies, music, magazines, and the Internet. Keep a written record of who, what, when, and where. Be specific in your description. Write an analysis of your findings.

5. Proverbs are the collective voices of people, the rules and ideals governing their life and conduct, and the lessons to be learned. They are handed-down expressions of the customs, beliefs, and attitudes of one generation to the next. To get the flavor of a culture, simply look at its proverbs. Make a list of proverbs in a particular culture and analyze their significance.

6. Go through a telephone directory and examine the list of names. What can you glean about these speakers' nationality, ethnicity, religion, or even gender?

Introduction from
The Language of Oppression
Haig A. Bosmajian

Haig A. Bosmajian, professor emeritus, Stanford University, teaches and publishes in the areas of rhetoric and public address, with an emphasis on the freedoms guaranteed under the First Amendment. Bosmajian was honored in 1983 with the George

Orwell Award from the National Council of Teachers of English for his book *The Language of Oppression,* which explores the oppressive languages of anti-Semitism, White racism, Native-American derision, sexism, and war. Bosmajian's scholarly research began in the 1960s when he examined the speeches of Adolf Hitler and the Nazis. He believes that language has the power to dehumanize and perpetuate the oppression of people.

1. When you were a child, did you recite the rhyme "Sticks and stones"? Does the rhyme have different meanings to an adult and to a child? Explain the meaning of the rhyme. Give a personal example that refutes the rhyme.
2. "Our identities, who and what we are, how others see us, are greatly affected by the names we are called and the words with which we are labeled." The personal names we choose do more than name, they define our identities; they can assign respectability, status, intelligence, and tradition, as well as mockery and ugliness. Do parents choose names for their children based on their attitude toward, the history of, or the meaning of a name?
3. One of the most poignant statements in this article is "While names, words and language can be and are used to inspire us, to motivate us to humane acts, to liberate us, they can also be used to dehumanize human beings and to 'justify' their suppression and even their extermination." What do you think of this statement? Can you provide further evidence to support the power of naming?

Writing Assignments

1. Write an essay about your name. Do you like it? Would you ever change your name? Who named you and why? What images or qualities does your name conjure up?
2. Trace the history of your given name and your surname. What is the story of your family names? Write an essay on how your name has changed through the generations.
3. Are you called different names in different situations? How many names do you have? Why? Write an essay about the different names you have and how they reflect your different personalities.

4. Write a paper supporting Bosmajian's claim that names "can also be used to dehumanize human beings and to 'justify' their suppression and even their extermination."

————————— ✦ —————————

Sticks and stones may break my bones, but words can never hurt me." To accept this adage as valid is sheer folly. "What's in a name? that which we call a rose by any other name would smell as sweet." The answer to Juliet's question is "Plenty!" and to her own response to the question we can only say that this is by no means invariably true. The importance, significance, and ramifications of naming and defining people cannot be over-emphasized. From *Genesis* and beyond, to the present time, the power which comes from naming and defining people has had positive as well as negative effects on entire populations.

The magic of words and names has always been an integral part of both "primitive" and "civilized" societies. As Margaret Schlauch has observed, "from time immemorial men have thought there is some mysterious essential connection between a thing and the spoken name for it. You could use the name of your enemy, not only to designate him either passionately or dispassionately, but also to exercise a baleful influence."

Biblical passages abound in which names and naming are endowed with great power; from the very outset, in *Genesis*, naming and defining are attributed a significant potency: "And out of the ground the Lord God formed every beast of the field and every fowl of the air; and brought them unto Adam to see what he would call them: and whatsoever Adam called every living creature, that was the name thereof." Amidst the admonitions in *Leviticus* against theft, lying, and fraud is the warning: "And ye shall not swear my name falsely, neither shalt thou profane the name of thy God: I am the Lord." So important is the name that it must not be blasphemed; those who curse and blaspheme shall be stoned "and he that blasphemeth the name of the Lord, he shall surely be put to death, and all the congregation shall certainly stone him." So important is the name that the denial of it is considered a form of punishment: "But ye are they that foresake the Lord, that forget my holy mountain. . . . Therefore will I number you to the sword, and ye shall all bow down to the slaughter: because when I called, ye did not answer; when I spake, ye did not hear. . . . Therefore thus saith the Lord God, behold, my servants

[handwritten marginal note: Name calling leading to "sticks", "stones"]

shall eat, but ye shall be hungry. . . . And ye shall leave your name for a curse unto my chosen: for the Lord God shall slay thee, and call his servants by another name."

To be unnamed is to be unknown, to have no identity. William Saroyan has observed that "the word nameless, especially in poetry and in much prose, signifies an alien, unknown, and almost unwelcome condition, as when, for instance, a writer speaks of 'a nameless sorrow.' " "Human beings," continues Saroyan, "are for the fact of being named at all, however meaninglessly, lifted out of an area of mystery, doubt, or undesirability into an area in which belonging to everybody else is taken for granted, so that one of the first questions asked by new people, two-year-olds even, whether they are speaking to other new people or to people who have been around for a great many years, is 'What is your name?' "

To receive a name is to be elevated to the status of a human being; without a name one's identity is questionable. In stressing the importance of a name and the significance of having none, Joyce Hertzler has said that "among both primitives and moderns, an individual has no definition, no validity for himself, without a name. His name is his badge of individuality, the means whereby he identifies himself and enters upon a truly subjective existence. My own name, for example, stands for me, a person. Divesting me of it reduces me to a meaningless, even pathological, nonentity."

In his book *What Is In A Name?* Farhang Zabeeth reminds us that "the Roman slaves originally were without names. Only after being sold they took their master's praenomen in the genitive case followed by the suffix—'por' (boy), e.g., 'Marcipor,' which indicates that some men, so long as they were regarded by others as cattle, did not need a name. However, as soon as they became servants some designation was called forth." To this day one of the forms of punishment meted out to wrongdoers who are imprisoned is to take away their names and to give them numbers. In an increasingly computerized age people are becoming mere numbers— credit card numbers, insurance numbers, bank account numbers, student numbers, et cetera. Identification of human beings by numbers is a negation of their humanity and their existence.

Philologist Max Muller has pointed out that "if we examine the most ancient word for 'name,' we find it is *naman* in Sanskrit, *nomen* in Latin, *namo* in Gothic. This *naman* stands for gnaman and is derived from the root, *gna*, to know, and meant originally that by which we know a thing." In the course of the evolution of

[margin annotations: "5"; "What about Jr.'s, II, III... ?"; " "Name" in unrelated languages is the same"]

human society, R. P. Masani tells us, the early need for names "appears to have been felt almost simultaneously with the origin of speech. . . . personality and the rights and obligations connected with it would not exist without the name." In his classic work *The Golden Bough* James Frazer devotes several pages to tabooed names and words in ancient societies, taboos reflecting the power and magic people saw in names and words. Frazer notes, for example, that "the North American Indian regards his name, not as a mere label, but as a distinct part of his personality, just as much as are his eyes or his teeth, and believes that injury will result as surely from the malicious handling of his name as from a wound inflicted on any part of his physical organism."

A name can be used as a curse. A name can be blasphemed. Name-calling is so serious a matter that statutes and court decisions prohibit "fighting words" to be uttered. In 1942 the United States Supreme Court upheld the conviction of a person who had addressed a police officer as "a God damned racketeer" and "a damned Fascist." (*Chaplinsky v. New Hampshire*, 315 U.S. 568). Such namecalling, such epithets, said the Court, are not protected speech. So important is one's "good name" that the law prohibits libel.

History abounds with instances in which the mere utterance of a name was prohibited. In ancient Greece, according to Frazer, "the names of the priests and other high officials who had to do with the performance of the Eleusinian mysteries might not be uttered in their lifetime. To pronounce them was a legal offense." Jorgen Ruud reports in *Taboo: A Study of Malagasy Customs and Beliefs* that among the Antandroy people the father has absolute authority in his household and that "children are forbidden to mention the name of their father. They must call him father, daddy. . . . The children may not mention his house or the parts of his body by their ordinary names, but must use other terms, i.e., euphemisms."

It was Iago who said in *Othello*:

> Who steals my purse steals trash; 'tis something nothing;
> 'Twas mine, 'tis his, and has been slave to thousands;
> But he that filches from me my good name
> Robs me of that which not enriches him
> And makes me poor indeed.

Alice, in Lewis Carroll's *Through the Looking Glass*, had trepidations about entering the woods where things were nameless:

"This must be the wood," she said thoughtfully to herself, "where things have no names. I wonder what'll become of *my* name when I go in? I shouldn't like to lose it at all—because they'd have to give me another, and it would be almost certain to be an ugly one."

A Nazi decree of August 17, 1938 stipulated that "Jews may receive only those first names which are listed in the directives of the Ministry of the Interior concerning the use of first names." Further, the decree provided: "If Jews should bear first names other than those permitted . . . they must . . . adopt an additional name. For males, that name shall be Israel, for females Sara." Another Nazi decree forbade Jews in Germany "to show themselves in public without a Jew's star . . . [consisting] of a six-pointed star of yellow cloth with black borders, equivalent in size to the palm of the hand. The inscription is to read 'JEW' in black letters. It is to be sewn to the left breast of the garment, and to be worn visibly."

[handwritten margin note: Must be recognized as people by LABEL not NAME (dehumanizing)]

The power which comes from names and naming is related directly to the power to define others—individuals, races, sexes, ethnic groups. Our identities, who and what we are, how others see us, are greatly affected by the names we are called and the words with which we are labelled. The names, labels, and phrases employed to "identify" a people may in the end determine their survival. The word "define" comes from the Latin *definire*, meaning to limit. Through definition we restrict, we set boundaries, we name.

"When I use a word," said Humpty Dumpty in *Through the Looking Glass*, "it means just what I choose it to mean—neither more nor less." "The question is," said Alice, "whether you can make words mean so many different things." "The question is," said Humpty Dumpty, "which is to be master—that's all."

During his days as a civil rights-black power activist, Stokely   15
Carmichael accurately asserted: "It [definition] is very, very important because I believe that people who can define are masters. Self-determination must include self-definition, the ability and right to name oneself; the master-subject relationship is based partly on the master's power to name and define the subject.

While names, words and language can be and are used to inspire us, to motivate us to humane acts, to liberate us, they can *[handwritten margin note: HOW?]* also be used to dehumanize human beings and to "justify" their suppression and even their extermination. It is not a great step from the coercive suppression of dissent to the extermination of dissenters (as the United States Supreme Court declared in its 1943 compulsory flag salute opinion in *West Virginia State Board of Education v. Barnette);* nor is it a large step from defining a people as non-human or sub-human to their subjugation or annihilation. One of the first acts of an oppressor is to redefine the "enemy" so they will be looked upon as creatures warranting separation, suppression, and even eradication.

The Nazis redefined Jews as "bacilli," "parasites," "disease," "demon," and "plague." In his essay "The Hollow Miracle," George Steiner informs us that the Germans "who poured quicklime down the openings of the sewers in Warsaw to kill the living and stifle the stink of the dead wrote about it. They spoke of having to 'liquidate vermin'. . . . Gradually, words lost their original meaning and acquired nightmarish definitions. *Jude, Pole, Russe* came to mean two-legged lice, putrid vermin which good Aryans must squash, as a [Nazi] Party manual said, 'like roaches on a dirty wall.' 'Final solution,' *endgültige Lösung*, came to signify the death of six million human beings in gas ovens."

The language of white racism has for centuries been used to "keep the nigger in his place." Our sexist language has allowed men to define who and what a woman is and must be. Labels like "traitors," "saboteurs," "queers," and "obscene degenerates" were applied indiscriminately to students who protested the war in Vietnam or denounced injustices in the United States. Are such people to be listened to? Consulted? Argued with? Obviously not! One does not listen to, much less talk to, traitors and outlaws, sensualists and queers. One only punishes them or, as Spiro Agnew suggested in one of his 1970 speeches, there are some dissenters who should be separated "from our society with no more regret than we should feel over discarding rotten apples."

What does it mean to separate people? When the Japanese-Americans were rounded up in 1942 and sent off to "relocation camps" they were separated. The Jews in Nazi Germany were "separated." The Indians of the United States, the occupants of the New World before Columbus "discovered" it, have been systematically "separated." As "chattels" and slaves, the blacks in the United States were "separated"; legally a black person was a piece of property, although human enough to be counted as three-fifths of a person in computing the number of people represented by white legislators.

20   How is the forcible isolation of human beings from society at large justified? To make the separation process more palatable to the populace, what must the oppressor first do? How does he make the populace accept the separation of the "creatures," or, if not accept it, at least not protest it? Consideration of such questions is

not an academic exercise without practical implications. There is a close nexus between language and self-perception, self-awareness, self-identity, and self-esteem. Just as our thoughts affect our language, so does our language affect our thoughts and eventually our actions and behavior. As Edward Sapir has observed, we are all "at the mercy of the particular language which has become the medium of expression" in our society. The "real world," he points out, "is to a large extent unconsciously built up on the language habits of the group. . . . We see and hear and otherwise experience very largely as we do because the language habits of our community predispose certain choices of interpretation."

George Orwell has written in his famous essay "Politics and the English Language": "A man may take to drink because he feels himself to be a failure, and then fail all the more completely because he drinks. It is rather the same thing that is happening to the English language. It becomes ugly and inaccurate because our thoughts are foolish, but the slovenliness of our language makes it easier for us to have foolish thoughts." Orwell maintains that "the decadence in our language is probably curable" and that "silly words and expressions have often disappeared, not through any evolutionary process but owing to the conscious action of a minority." Wilma Scott Heide, speaking as president of the National Organization for Women several years ago, indicated that feminists were undertaking this conscious action: "In any social movement, when changes are effected, the language sooner or later reflects the change. Our approach is different. Instead of passively noting the change, we are changing language patterns to actively effect the changes, a significant part of which is the conceptual tool of thought, our language."

This then is our task—to identify the decadence in our language, the inhumane uses of language, the "silly words and expressions" which have been used to justify the unjustifiable, to make palatable the unpalatable, to make reasonable the unreasonable, to make decent the indecent. Hitler's "Final Solution" appeared reasonable once the Jews were successfully labelled by the Nazis as sub-humans, as "parasites," "vermin," and "bacilli." The segregation and suppression of blacks in the United States was justified once they were considered "chattels" and "inferiors." The subjugation of the "American Indians" was defensible since they were defined as "barbarians" and "savages." As Peter Farb has said, "cannibalism, torture, scalping, mutilation, adultery, incest, sodomy, rape, filth, drunkenness—such a catalogue of accusa-tions against a people is an indication not so much of their de-pravity as that their land is up for grabs." As long as adult women are "chicks," "girls," "dolls," "babes," and "ladies," their status in society will remain "inferior"; they will go on being treated as subjects in the subject-master relationship as long as the lan-guage of the law places them into the same class as children, mi-nors, and the insane.

It is my hope that an examination of the language of oppression will result in a conscious effort by the reader to help cure this deca-dence in our language, especially that language which leads to de-humanization of the human being. One way for us to curtail the use of the language of oppression is for those who find themselves being defined into subjugation to rebel against such linguistic suppres-sion. It isn't strange that those persons who insist on defining them-selves, who insist on this elemental privilege of self-naming, self-definition, and self-identity encounter vigorous resistance. Pre-dictably, the resistance usually comes from the oppressor or would-be oppressor and is a result of the fact that he or she does not want to re-linquish the power which comes from the ability to define others.

The Sapir-Whorf Hypothesis
DAVID CRYSTAL

In this article, "The Sapir-Whorf Hypothesis," linguist David Crystal summarizes the theory of linguistic determinism, a long-standing view advanced by the linguists Edward Sapir and Benjamin Whorf in the 1920s. This theory proposes that the way people think is determined by the structure of their language. Different languages represent different social realities. This hypothesis claims that people are prisoners of their language, and so speakers of different languages perceive the world differently.

1. According to Edward Sapir, we are all "at the mercy of the particular language which has become the medium of expres-sion" in our society. What does this statement mean? Do you agree that language affects our thoughts and our actions?
2. Two factors that illustrate the Sapir-Whorf hypothesis are cross-linguistic differences in vocabulary and grammatical

notions. For example, Eskimo languages have over 200 words for "snow"; East Asian cultures have many terms for "rice", South Asian languages have the same expressions for "yesterday" and "tomorrow", and the Hopi language structures the notion of time differently from Western time. Can you think of examples which support the position that language constrains our view of the world?

3. Many feminist scholars argue that as long as we use the generic "he" to refer to both a male and female and derogatory terms for females in our culture, we will continue to propagate the view that women are invisible, sexual beings, tasty dishes, and ineffectual leaders. What do you think of this idea? Does the use of certain terms support the Sapir-Whorf hypothesis that language confines the way we view others?

Writing Assignments

1. Write a paper critiquing the Sapir–Whorf hypothesis.

2. Provide examples which clearly show that one language makes more distinctions than another, for example, "snow" in Aleut, "rice" in Japanese. In an essay, explain the differences and the significance of these linguistic distinctions.

3. Nearly every culture has a story explaining the origin of language, often implying that everyone on earth at one time spoke a common language. Find a myth that includes an explanation of the origin of language or an illustration of the importance of language in a culture. Compare language mythologies across the cultures of the world.

4. Design an experiment to prove or disprove that humans cannot conceive of an idea or notion outside their language.

———————— ✦ ————————

The romantic idealism of the late 18th century, as encountered in the views of Johann Herder (1744–1803) and Wilhelm von Humboldt (1762–1835), placed great value on the diversity of the world's languages and cultures. The tradition was taken up by the American linguist and anthropologist Edward Sapir (1884–1939) and his pupil Benjamin Lee Whorf (1897–1941), and resulted in a view about the relation between language and thought which was widely influential in the middle decades of this century.

The "Sapir–Whorf hypothesis," as it came to be called, combines two principles. The first is known as *linguistic determinism:* it states that language determines the way we think. The second follows from this, and is known as *linguistic relativity:* it states that the distinctions encoded in one language are not found in any other language. In a much-quoted paragraph, Whorf propounds the view as follows:

> We dissect nature along lines laid down by our native languages. The categories and types that we isolate from the world of phenomena we do not find there because they stare every observer in the face; on the contrary, the world is presented in a kaleidoscopic flux of impressions which has to be organized by our minds–and this means largely by the linguistic systems in our minds. We cut nature up, organize it into concepts, and ascribe significances as we do, largely because we are parties to an agreement to organize it in this way–an agreement that holds throughout our speech community and is codified in the patterns of our language. The agreement is, of course, an implicit and unstated one, *but its terms are absolutely obligatory;* we cannot talk at all except by subscribing to the organization and classification of data which the agreement decrees.

[handwritten margin note: Necessary language conformity]

Whorf illustrated his view by taking examples from several languages, and in particular from Hopi, an Amerindian language. In Hopi, there is one word (*masa'ytaka*) for everything that flies except birds–which would include insects, aeroplanes and pilots. This seems alien to someone used to thinking in English, but, Whorf argues, it is no stranger than English-speakers having one word for many kinds of snow, in contrast to Eskimo, where there are different words for falling snow, snow on the ground, snow packed hard like ice, slushy snow (cf. English *slush*), and so on. In Aztec, a single word (with different endings) covers an even greater range of English notions–snow, cold and ice. When more abstract notions are considered (such as time, duration, velocity), the differences become yet more complex: Hopi, for instance, lacks a concept of time seen as a dimension; there are no forms corresponding to English tenses, but there are a series of forms which make it possible to talk about, various durations, from the speaker's point of view. It would be very difficult, Whorf argues, for a Hopi and an English physicist to understand each other's thinking, given the major differences between the languages.

[handwritten margin note: Environments in which the language develops]

Examples such as these made the Sapir–Whorf hypothesis very plausible; but in its strongest form it is unlikely to have any adherents now. The fact that successful translations between languages can be made is a major argument against it, as is the fact that the conceptual uniqueness of a language such as Hopi can nonetheless be explained using English. That there are some conceptual differences between cultures due to language is undeniable, but this is not to say that the differences are so great that mutual comprehension is impossible. One language may take many words to say what another language says in a single word, but in the end the circumlocution can make the point.

Similarly, it does not follow that, because a language lacks a word, its speakers therefore cannot grasp the concept. Several languages have few words for numerals: Australian aboriginal languages, for example, are often restricted to a few general words (such as "all", "many", "few"), "one" and "two". In such cases, it is sometimes said that the people lack the concept of number–that aborigines 'haven't the intelligence to count', as it was once put. But this is not so, as is shown when these speakers learn English as a second language: their ability to count and calculate is quite comparable to that of English native speakers.

However, a weaker version of the Sapir–Whorf hypothesis is generally accepted. Language may not determine the way we think, but it does influence the way we perceive and remember, and it affects the ease with which we perform mental tasks. Several experiments have shown that people recall things more easily if the things correspond to readily available words or phrases. And people certainly find it easier to make a conceptual distinction if it neatly corresponds to words available in their language. Some salvation for the Sapir–Whorf hypothesis can therefore be found in these studies, which are carried out within the developing field of psycholinguistics.

An Introduction
KAMALA DAS

Kamala Das, noted poet, short story writer, and novelist, was born March 31, 1934, in Malabar, southern India. Often cited as one of the earliest Indian women to write in English, Das's confessional poetry is often compared to that of Sylvia Plath and Anne Sexton. One of the most important features of her writing is that she chooses to write in Indian English without regard to conforming to the standards of native English varieties or to traditional Indian verse. In the following autobiographical poem, Das defends her use of "funny" English with its "distortions" and "queernesses."

1. Das, like the preceding author, talks of the power of language. Whom does she mean when she talks of "those in power?"
2. Can you point out instances in the poem of the Indianization of English and Das's nativizing English to fit Indian culture?

Writing Assignments

1. Although English was once considered to be the sole property of the native English-speaking users of of Great Britain, the United States, Australia, and Canada, it has become a second language to speakers whose first language is one other than English. Well-known varieties of the new Englishes include Indian English, Caribbean English, Singaporean English, and African English. Research how English is really not a single English but many Englishes. Research one of these varieties and discuss how it differs from standard American English.
2. Das introduces herself as a trilingual, who makes a distinction in the three languages she speaks. Although you may not be multilingual, write "My Language Story," giving a historical account of the language or languages that you speak.
3. Do you think that being multilingual is important in the world today? Write a paper arguing for bi/multilingual education in the schools.

——————— ✦ ———————

I don't know politics but I know the names
Of those in power, and can repeat them like
Days of week, or names of months, beginning with
Nehru. I am Indian, very brown, born in
Malabar, I speak three languages, write in   5
Two, dream in one. Don't write in English, they said,
English is not your mother-tongue. Why not leave
Me alone, critics, friends, visiting cousins,
Every one of you? Why not let me speak in

Any language I like? The language I speak   10
Becomes mine, its distortions, its queernesses
All mine, mine alone. It is half English, half
Indian, funny perhaps, but it is honest,
It is as human as I am human, don't
You see? It voices my joys, my longings, my   15
Hopes, and it is useful to me as cawing
Is to crows or roaring to the lions, it
Is human speech, the speech of the mind that is
Here and not there, a mind that sees and hears and
Is aware. Not the deaf, blind speech   20
Of trees in storm or of monsoon clouds or of rain or the
Incoherent mutterings of the blazing
Funeral pyre. I was child, and later they
Told me I grew, for I became tall, my limbs
Swelled and one or two places sprouted hair. When   25
I asked for love, not knowing what else to ask
For, he drew a youth of sixteen into the
Bedroom and closed the door. He did not beat me
But my sad woman-body felt so beaten.
The weight of my breasts and womb crushed me. I shrank 30
Pitifully. Then. . . . I wore a shirt and my
Brother's trousers, cut my hair short and ignored
My womanliness. Dress in sarees, be girl
Be wife, they said. Be embroiderer, be cook,
Be a quarreller with servants. Fit in. Oh,   35
Belong, cried the categorizers. Don't sit
On walls or peep in through our lace-draped windows.
Be Amy, or be Kamala. Or, better
Still, be Madhavikutty. It is time to
Choose a name, a role. Don't play pretending games.   40
Don't play at schizophrenia or be a
Nympho. Don't cry embarrassingly loud when
Jilted in love. . . . I met a man, loved him. Call
Him not by any name, he is every man
Who wants a woman, just as I am every   45
Woman who seeks love. In him. . . . the hungry haste
Of rivers, in me. . . . the oceans' tireless
Waiting. Who are you, I ask each and everyone,
The answer is, it is I. Anywhere and,
Everywhere, I see the one who calls himself   50
I in this world, he is tightly packed like the
Sword in its sheath. It is I who drink lonely

Drinks at twelve, midnight, in hotels of strange towns,
It is I who laugh, it is I who make love   55
And then, feel shame, it is I who lie dying
With a rattle in my throat. I am sinner,
I am saint. I am the beloved and the
Betrayed. I have no joys which are not yours, no
Aches which are not yours. I too call myself I.   60

Exile

Eva Hoffman

This excerpt from *Lost in Translation* tells the story of Eva Hoffman and her family's move to Canada from Poland in the late 1950s during the reign of hostility toward Jews during Communist rule. Her book deals with childhood, parting, and living a bicultural-bilingual identity. Struggling between two languages and two cultures, she asks the question, "What happens to language when a person changes her country"? The excerpt here describes her loss of language and her finding a voice in the English language.

1. Why is Hoffman frustrated with her language skills? What are her feelings toward the "foreign tongue, English"?
2. What does Hoffman mean when she says, "we want to be at home in our tongue"?
3. "If one is perpetually without words . . . that condition itself is bound to be an enraging frustration." Have you ever felt frustration at not being able to say what you want or what you mean? Explain.
4. Like Hoffman, do you associate certain values and attitudes with the different varieties and languages of the world? Confining yourself to the regional and social varieties of English that exist within the United States, what are your feelings toward African-American Vernacular English, Southern-American English, Appalachian English, Hispanic English, or New York English? Do you belong to any of these speech communities? What prejudices do these speakers experience?

Writing Assignments

1. Have you struggled with learning a second language? Write a paper describing your second language learning experiences.

2. Write about the language variety that you use. What do you sound like? What words do you use? What in your speech identifies your age, ethnicity, sex, class, and region?

3. Interview someone who has recently come to the United States from another country. Ask about his or her experiences learning a new language and culture.

4. In an interview, Hoffman said, "The main impact of immigration for me was my sense of the enormous importance of language. I think that for a while I was, in effect, without language, because Polish lost its relevance to this new world. . . . But that sense of losing language was a very, very powerful and potent lesson. . . . from then on, my struggle was for English to inhabit me and to acquire enough command of it so that it would articulate the world and so that it would express the world—both exterior and interior." Write a response to what she means by the importance of language.

5. Write a paper comparing Kamala Das's naturalness in writing in "foreign tongue" English with Eva Hoffman's struggles as she comes to terms with English.

———————— ◆ ————————

My voice is doing funny things. It does not seem to emerge from the same parts of my body as before. It comes out from somewhere in my throat, tight, thin, and mat—a voice without the modulations, dips, and rises that it had before, when it went from my stomach all the way through my head. There is, of course, the constraint and the self-consciousness of an accent that I hear but cannot control. Some of my high school peers accuse me of putting it on in order to appear more "interesting." In fact, I'd do anything to get rid of it, and when I'm alone, I practice sounds for which my speech organs have no intuitions, such as "th" (I do this by putting my tongue between my teeth) and "a," which is longer and more open in Polish (by shaping my mouth into a sort of arrested grin). It is simple words like "cat" or "tap" that give me the most trouble, because they have no context of other syllables, and so people often misunderstand them. Whenever I can, I do awkward little swerves to avoid them, or pause and try to say them very clearly. Still, when people—like salesladies—hear me speak without being prepared to listen carefully, they often don't understand me the first time around. "Girls' shoes," I say, and the "girls' " comes out as a sort of scramble. "Girls' shoes," I repeat, willing the syllable to form itself properly, and the saleslady usually smiles nicely, and sends my mother and me to the right part of the store. I say "Thank you" with a sweet smile, feeling as if I'm both claiming an unfair special privilege and being unfairly patronized. *If you cannot speak properly you are stupid.*

It's as important to me to speak well as to play a piece of music without mistakes. Hearing English distorted grates on me like chalk screeching on a blackboard, like all things botched and badly done, like all forms of gracelessness. The odd thing is that I know what is correct, fluent, good, long before I can execute it. The English spoken by our Polish acquaintances strikes me as jagged and thick, and I know that I shouldn't imitate it. I'm turned off by the intonations I hear on the TV sitcoms—by the expectation of laughter, like a dog's tail wagging in supplication, built into the actors' pauses, and by the curtailed, cutoff rhythms. I like the way Penny speaks, with an easy flow and a pleasure in giving words a fleshly fullness; I like what I hear in some movies; and once the Old Vic comes to Vancouver to perform *Macbeth*, and though I can hardly understand the particular words, I am riveted by the tones of sureness and command that mold the actors' speech into such majestic periods.

Sociolinguists might say that I receive these language messages as class signals, that I associate the sounds of correctness with the social status of the speaker. In part, this is undoubtedly true. The class-linked notion that I transfer wholesale from Poland is that belonging to a "better" class of people is absolutely dependent on speaking a "better" language. And in my situation especially, I know that language will be a crucial instrument, that I can overcome the stigma of my marginality, the weight of presumption against me, only if the reassuringly right sounds come out of my mouth.

Yes, speech is a class signifier. But I think that in hearing these varieties of speech around me, I'm sensitized to something else as well—something that is a matter of aesthetics, and even of psychological health. Apparently, skilled chefs can tell whether a dish from some foreign cuisine is well cooked even if they have never tasted it and don't know the genre of cooking it belongs to. There seem to be some deep-structure qualities—consistency, proportions of ingredients, smoothness of blending—that indicate culinary achievement to these educated eaters' taste buds. So each language has its own distinctive music, and even if one doesn't know its separate components, one can pretty quickly recognize the propriety of the patterns in which the components are put together, their harmonies and discords. Perpaps the crucial element that strikes the ear in listening to living speech is the degree of the speaker's self-assurance and control.

As I listen to people speaking that foreign tongue, English, I can   5
hear when they stumble or repeat the same phrases too many times, when their sentences trail off aimlessly—or, on the contrary, when their phrases have vigor and roundness, when they have the space and the breath to give a flourish at the end of a sentence, or make just the right pause before coming to a dramatic point. I can tell, in other words, the degree of their ease or disease, the extent of authority that shapes the rhythms of their speech. That authority—in whatever dialect, in whatever variant of the mainstream language—seems to me to be something we all desire. It's not that we all want to speak the King's English, but whether we speak Appalachian or Harlem English, or Cockney, or Jamaican Creole, we want to be at home in our tongue. We want to be able to give voice accurately and *to express* fully to ourselves and our sense of the world. John Fowles, in one of *who we* his stories in *The Ebony Tower,* has a young man cruelly violate an *are as* elderly writer and his manuscripts because the legacy of language *individuals* has not been passed on to the youthful vandal properly. This seems to me an entirely credible premise. Linguistic dispossession is a sufficient motive for violence, for it is close to the dispossession of one's self. Blind rage, helpless rage is rage that has no words—rage that overwhelms one with darkness. And if one is perpetually without words, if one exists in the entropy of inarticulateness, that condition itself is bound to be an enraging frustration. In my New York apartment, I listen almost nightly to fights that erupt like brushfire on the street below—and in their escalating fury of repetitious phrases ("Don't do this to me, man, you fucking bastard, I'll fucking kill you"), I hear not the pleasures of macho toughness but an infuriated beating against wordlessness, against the incapacity to make oneself understood, seen. Anger can be borne—it can even be satisfying—if it can gather into words and explode in a storm, or a rapier-sharp attack. But without this means of ventilation, it only turns back inward, building and swirling like a head of steam—building to an impotent, murderous rage. If all therapy is speaking therapy—a talking cure—then perhaps all neurosis is a speech dis-ease.

Humpty Dumpty

LEWIS CARROLL

Lewis Carroll (1832–1898) was in real life the Rev. Charles Lutwidge Dodgson, an Oxford mathematics lecturer (1855–1881), a scholar of mathematical treatises, and the writer of children's literature. As a child, Carroll showed an interest in parody, word play, and puzzles. He is best known for *Alice's Adventures in Wonderland* (1865) and *Through the Looking-Glass* (1872), in which the reader enters the surreal world of seven-year-old Alice where words take on new and different meanings and nothing is the way it seems. *Through the Looking-Glass* includes the characters Humpty Dumpty and Tweedledee and Tweedledum and the nonsense verses "Jabberwocky" and the "Walrus and the Carpenter."

1. What does Humpty Dumpty mean when he insists that a name must mean something? Does your name mean something?
2. "When I use a word . . . it means just what I choose it to mean—neither more nor less." Explain what Humpty Dumpty means by this statement.
3. Carroll is known for his word play and the coining and the blending of words. In "Jabberwocky" a popular poem recited by young children in school, he creates words and describes their meanings. Read the poem aloud. Can you figure out the word play? Is "Jabberwocky" really nonsense, or can you explain the poem's meaning by using your knowledge of language?
4. Is the interaction between Alice and Humpty Dumpty a *normal* conversation? Explain.

Writing Assignments

1. When you were a child, did you read the work of Lewis Carroll or any other wordsmiths? Describe what you remember about their writings?
2. The English language has more words than any other language in the world. One reason for this large number is the ability of English to add new nouns, verbs, and adjectives to its lexicon regularly and with ease. Although no speaker knows all the words of her or his language, every speaker can form new words and guess the meaning of unknown words simply by knowing the language. In this reading, Humpty Dumpty gives "un-words" meaning. Can you think of un-

words that have recently entered the English language or that you have used or heard which are not in the dictionary? Pretend you are writing a dictionary entry. Explain the meaning of each word.

3. Many times people legally change their names for religious or professional reasons. Some people change their names to disassociate themselves from an ethnic or religious identification. Famed boxer Mohammed Ali changed his name from Cassius Clay; basketball great Kareem Abdul-Jabbar changed his name from Lew Alcindor; and folk singer Bob Dylan was born Robert Zimmerman. Provide other examples of name changes and discuss why these people changed their names.

4. Taboo customs vary across the world. They reflect the power and magic of language. When a word takes on negative semantic features according to the way a particular culture feels about it, speakers replace it with a substitute word, known as a "euphemism." In the United States, for example, we avoid publicly talking about bodily functions, and at a very early age we are taught to substitute terms for private body parts and such normal activities as defecation and urination with euphemisms to lessen the discomfort level we have with the body and with bathroom functions. Can you think of other examples of cultural taboos? What do they say about the values and beliefs of a society?

───────────── ✦ ─────────────

However, the egg only got larger and larger, and more and more human: when she had come within a few yards of it, she saw that it had eyes and a nose and mouth; and when she had come close to it, she saw clearly that it was Humpty Dumpty himself. 'It can't be anybody else!' she said to herself. 'I'm as certain of it, as if his name were written all over his face!'

It might have been written a hundred times, easily, on that enormous face. Humpty Dumpty was sitting with his legs crossed, like a Turk, on the top of a high wall—such a narrow one that Alice quite wondered how he could keep his balance—and, as his eyes were steadily fixed in the opposite direction, and he didn't take the least notice of her, she thought he must be a stuffed figure after all.

'And how exactly like an egg he is!' she said aloud, standing with her hands ready to catch him, for she was every moment expecting him to fall.

'It's *very* provoking,' Humpty Dumpty said, after a long silence, looking away from Alice as he spoke, 'to be called an egg—*very!*'

5   'I said you *looked* like an egg, Sir,' Alice gently explained.

'And some eggs are very pretty, you know,' she added, hoping to turn her remark into a sort of compliment.

'Some people,' said Humpty Dumpty, looking away from her as usual, 'have no more sense than a baby!'

Alice didn't know what to say to this: it wasn't at all like conversation, she thought, as he never said anything to *her;* in fact, his last remark was evidently addressed to a tree—so she stood and softly repeated to herself:

> *'Humpty Dumpty sat on a wall:*
> *Humpty Dumpty had a great fall.*
> *All the King's horses and all the King's men*
> *Couldn't put Humpty Dumpty in his place again.'*

'That last line is much too long for the poetry,' she added almost out loud, forgetting that Humpty Dumpty would hear her.

10   'Don't stand chattering to yourself like that,' Humpty Dumpty said, looking at her for the first time, 'but tell me your name and your business.'

'My *name* is Alice, but—'

'It's a stupid name enough!' Humpty Dumpty interrupted impatiently. 'What does it mean?'

'*Must* a name mean something?' Alice asked doubtfully.

'Of course it must,' Humpty Dumpty said with a short laugh: '*my* name means the shape I am—and a good hand-me shape it is, too. With a name like yours, you might be any shape, almost.'

15   'Why do you sit out here all alone?' said Alice, not wishing to begin an argument.

'Why, because there's nobody with me!' cried Humpty Dumpty. 'Did you think I didn't know the answer to *that?* Ask another.'

'Don't you think you'd be safer down on the ground?' Alice went on, not with any idea of making another riddle, but simply in her good-natured anxiety for the queer creature. 'That wall is so *very* narrow!'

'What tremendously easy riddles you ask!' Humpty Dumpty growled out. 'Of course I don't think so! Why, if ever I *did* fall off—which there's no chance of—but *if* I did—' Here he pursed up his lips, and looked so solemn and grand that Alice could hardly help laughing. '*If* I *did* fall,' he went on, '*the King has promised me*—ah, you may turn pale, if you like! You didn't think I was going to say that, did you? *The King has promised me—with his very own mouth—to—to—*'

'To send all his horses and all his men,' Alice interrupted, rather unwisely.

'Now I declare that's too bad!' Humpty Dumpty cried, break- 20
ing into a sudden passion. 'You've been listening at doors—and behind trees—and down chimneys—or you couldn't have known it!'

'I haven't, indeed!' Alice said very gently. 'It's in a book.'

'Ah, well! They may write such things in a *book*,' Humpty Dumpty said in a calmer tone. 'That's what you call a History of England, that is. Now, take a good look at me! I'm one that has spoken to a King, *I* am: mayhap you'll never see such another: and to show you I'm not proud, you may shake hands with me!' And he grinned almost from ear to ear, as he leant forwards (and as nearly as possible fell off the wall in doing so) and offered Alice his hand. She watched him a little anxiously as she took it. 'If he smiled much more, the ends of his mouth might meet behind,' she thought: 'and then I don't know *what* would happen to his head! I'm afraid it would come off!'

'Yes, all his horses and all his men,' Humpty Dumpty went on. 'They'd pick me up again in a minute, *they* would! However, this conversation is going on a little too fast: let's go back to the last remark but one.'

'I'm afraid I can't quite remember it,' Alice said very politely.

'In that case we may start afresh,' said Humpty Dumpty, 'and 25
it's my turn to choose a subject——' ('He talks about it just as if it was a game!' thought Alice.) 'So here's a question for you. How old did you say you were?'

Alice made a short calculation, and said, 'Seven years and six months.'

'Wrong!' Humpty Dumpty exclaimed triumphantly. 'You never said a word like it.'

'I thought you meant "How old *are* you?" ' Alice explained.

'If I'd meant that, I'd have said it,' said Humpty Dumpty.

Alice didn't want to begin another argument, so she said 30
nothing.

'Seven years and six months!' Humpty Dumpty repeated thoughtfully. 'An uncomfortable sort of age. Now if you'd asked *my* advice, I'd have said, "Leave off at seven"—but it's too late now.'

'I never ask advice about growing,' Alice said indignantly.

'Too proud?' the other inquired.

Alice felt even more indignant at this suggestion. 'I mean,' she said, 'that one can't help growing older.'

35   '*One* can't, perhaps,' said Humpty Dumpty, 'but *two* can. With proper assistance, you might have left off at seven.'

'What a beautiful belt you've got on!' Alice suddenly re-marked. (They had had quite enough of the subject of age, she thought: and if they really were to take turns in choosing subjects, it was *her* turn now.) 'At least,' she corrected herself on second thoughts, 'a beautiful cravat, I should have said—no, a belt, I mean—I beg your pardon!' she added in dismay, for Humpty Dumpty looked thoroughly offended, and she began to wish she hadn't chosen that subject. 'If only I knew,' she thought to herself, 'which was neck and which was waist!'

Evidently Humpty Dumpty was very angry, though he said nothing for a minute or two. When he *did* speak again, it was in a deep growl.

'It is a—*most—provoking*—thing,' he said at last, 'when a person doesn't know a cravat from a belt!'

'I know it's very ignorant of me,' Alice said in so humble a tone that Humpty Dumpty relented.

40   'It's a cravat, child, and a beautiful one, as you say. It's a present from the White King and Queen. There now!'

'Is it really?' said Alice, quite pleased to find she *had* chosen a good subject after all.

'They gave it me,' Humpty Dumpty continued thoughtfully, as he crossed one knee over the other and clasped his hands round it, 'they gave it me—for an un-birthday present.'

'I beg your pardon?' Alice said, with a puzzled air.

'I'm not offended,' said Humpty Dumpty.

45   'I mean what *is* an un-birthday present?'

'A present given when it isn't your birthday, of course.'

Alice considered a little. 'I like birthday presents best,' she said at last.

'You don't know what you're talking about!' cried Humpty Dumpty. 'How many days are there in a year?'

'Three hundred and sixty-five,' said Alice.

50   'And how many birthdays have you?'

'One.'

'And if you take one from three hundred and sixty-five, what remains?'

'Three hundred and sixty-four, of course.'

Humpty Dumpty looked doubtful. 'I'd rather see that done on paper,' he said.

Alice couldn't help smiling as she took out her memorandum-   55
book, and worked the sum for him:—

$$\begin{array}{r} 365 \\ \underline{1} \\ 364 \end{array}$$

Humpty Dumpty took the book, and looked at it carefully.
'That seems to be done right——' he began.

'You're holding it upside down!' Alice interrupted.

'To be sure I was!' Humpty Dumpty said gaily, as she turned it
round for him. 'I thought it looked a little queer. As I was saying,
that *seems* to be done right—though I haven't time to look it over
thoroughly just now—and that shows that there are three hundred
and sixty-four days when you might get un-birthday presents——'

'Certainly,' said Alice.

'And only *one* for birthday presents, you know. There's glory   60
for you!'

'I don't know what you mean by "glory," ' Alice said.

Humpty Dumpty smiled contemptuously. 'Of course you
don't—till I tell you. I meant "there's a nice knock-down argument
for you!" '

'But "glory" doesn't mean "a nice knockdown-argument," ' Alice objected

'When I use a word,' Humpty Dumpty said in rather a
scornful tone, 'it means just what I choose it to mean—neither
more nor less.'

'The question is,' said Alice, 'whether you *can* make words   65
mean so many different things.'

'The question is,' said Humpty Dumpty, 'which is to be Master—that's all.'

Alice was too much puzzled to say anything, so after a minute
Humpty Dumpty began again. 'They've a temper, some of them—
particularly verbs, they're the proudest—adjectives you can do
anything with, but not verbs—however, *I* can manage the whole
lot of them! Impenetrability! That's what *I* say!'

'Would you tell me, please,' said Alice, 'what that means?'

'Now you talk like a reasonable child,' said Humpty Dumpty,
looking very much pleased. 'I meant by "impenetrability" that
we've had enough of that subject, and it would be just as well if
you'd mention what you mean to do next, as I suppose you don't
mean to stop here all the rest of your life.'

'That's a great deal to make one word mean,' Alice said in a   70
thoughtful tone.

'When I make a word to do a lot of work like that,' said Humpty Dumpty, 'I always pay it extra.'

'Oh!' said Alice. She was too much puzzled to make any other remark.

'Ah, you should see 'em come round me of a Saturday night,' Humpty Dumpty went on, wagging his head gravely from side to side: 'for to get their wages, you know.'

(Alice didn't venture to ask what he paid them with; and so you see I can't tell *you*.)

75   'You seem very clever at explaining words, Sir,' said Alice. 'Would you kindly tell me the meaning of the poem called "Jabberwocky"?'

'Let's hear it,' said Humpty Dumpty. 'I can explain all the poems that ever were invented—and a good many that haven't been invented just yet.'

This sounded very hopeful, so Alice repeated the first verse:

> *'Twas brillig, and the slithy toves*
>   *Did gyre and gimble in the wabe:*
> *All mimsy were the borogoves,*
>   *And the mome raths outgrabe.'*

'That's enough to begin with,' Humpty Dumpty interrupted: 'there are plenty of hard words there. "*Brillig*" means four o'clock in the afternoon—the time when you begin *broiling* things for dinner.'

'That'll do very well,' said Alice: 'and "*slithy*"?'

80   'Well, "*slithy*" means "lithe and slimy." "Lithe" is the same as "active." You see it's like a portmanteau—there are two meanings packed up into one word.'

'I see it now,' Alice remarked thoughtfully: 'and what are "*toves*"?'

'Well, "*toves*" are something like badgers—they're something like lizards—and they're something like corkscrews.'

'They must be very curious-looking creatures.'

'They are that,' said Humpty Dumpty: 'also they make their nests under sundials—also they live on cheese.'

85   'And what's to "*gyre*" and to "*gimble*"?'

'To "*gyre*" is to go round and round like a gyroscope. To "*gimble*" is to make holes like a gimlet.'

'And "*the wabe*," is the grass-plot round a sundial, I suppose?' said Alice, surprised at her own ingenuity.

'Of course it is. It's called "*wabe*," you know, because it goes a long way before it, and a long way behind it——'

'And a long way beyond it on each side,' Alice added.

'Exactly so. Well then *"mimsy"* is "flimsy and miserable"   90
(there's another portmanteau for you). And a *"borogove"* is a thin
shabby-looking bird with its feathers sticking out all round—
something like a live mop.'

'And then *"mome raths"*?' said Alice. 'I'm afraid I'm giving you
a great deal of trouble.'

'Well, a *"rath"* is a sort of green pig: but *"mome"* I'm not certain about. I think it's short "from home"—meaning that they'd
lost their way, you know.'

'And what does *"outgrabe"* mean?'

'Well, *"outgribing"* is something between bellowing and
whistling, with a kind of sneeze in the middle: however, you'll
hear it done, maybe—down in the wood yonder—and when
you've once heard it you'll be *quite* content. Who's been repeating
all that hard stuff to you?'

'I read it in a book,' said Alice. 'But I *had* some poetry re-   95
peated to me, much easier than that, by—Tweedledee, I think.'

'As to poetry, you know,' said Humpty Dumpty, stretching out
one of his great hands, '*I* can repeat poetry as well as other folk, if
it comes to that——'

'Oh, it needn't come to that!' Alice hastily said, hoping to keep
him from beginning.

'The piece I'm going to repeat,' he went on, without noticing
her remark, 'was written entirely for your amusement.'

Alice felt that in that case she really *ought* to listen to it, so
she sat down, and said, 'Thank you' rather sadly.

'In winter, when the fields are white,
I sing this song for your delight——

only I don't sing it,' he added, as an explanation.   100

'I see you don't,' said Alice.

'If you can *see* whether I'm singing or not, you've sharper eyes
than most,' Humpty Dumpty remarked severely. Alice was silent.

'In spring, when woods are getting green,
I'll try and tell you what I mean.'

'Thank you very much,' said Alice

'In summer, when the days are long,
Perhaps you'll understand the song:

In autumn, when the leaves are brown,
Take pen and ink, and write it down.'

'I will if I can remember it so long,' said Alice.

105   'You needn't go on making remarks like that,' Humpty
Dumpty said: 'they're not sensible, and they put me out.'

'I sent a message to the fish:
I told them "This is what I wish."

The little fishes of the sea
They sent an answer back to me.

The little fishes' answer was
"We cannot do it, Sir, because——" '

'I'm afraid I don't quite understand,' said Alice.
'It gets easier farther on,' Humpty Dumpty replied.

'I sent to them again to say
"It will be better to obey."

The fishes answered with a grin,
"Why, what a temper you are in!"

I told them once, I told them twice:
They would not listen to advice.

I took a kettle large and new,
Fit for the deed I had to do.

My heart went hop, my heart went thump;
I filled the kettle at the pump.

Then some one came to me and said,
"The little fishes are in bed."

I said to him, I said it plain,
"Then you must wake them up again."

I said it very loud and clear;
I went and shouted in his ear.'

Humpty Dumpty raised his voice almost to a scream as he repeated this verse, and Alice thought with a shudder, 'I wouldn't
have been the messenger for *anything!*'

'But he was very stiff and proud;
He said, "You needn't shout so loud!"

And he was very proud and stiff;
He said, "I'd go and wake them, if——"

I took a corkscrew from the shelf:
I went to wake them up myself.

And when I found the door was locked,
I pulled and pushed and kicked and knocked.

And when I found the door was shut,
I tried to turn the handle, but——'

There was a long pause.   110
'Is that all?' Alice timidly asked,
'That's all,' said Humpty Dumpty. 'Good-bye.'

This was rather sudden, Alice thought: but, after such a *very* strong hint that she ought to be going, she felt that it would hardly be civil to stay. So she got up, and held out her hand. 'Good-bye, till we meet again!' she said as cheerfully as she could.

'I shouldn't know you again if we *did* meet,' Humpty Dumpty replied in a discontented tone, giving her one of his fingers to shake; 'you're so exactly like other people.'

'The face is what one goes by, generally,' Alice remarked in a thoughtful tone.

'That's just what I complain of,' said Humpty Dumpty. 'Your face is the same as everbody has—the two eyes, so——' (marking their places in the air with his thumb), 'nose in the middle, mouth under. It's always the same. Now if you had the two eyes on the same side of the nose, for instance—or the mouth at the top—that would be *some* help.'

'It wouldn't look nice,' Alice objected. But Humpty Dumpty only shut his eyes and said, 'Wait till you've tried.'

Alice waited a minute to see if he would speak again, but as   115
he never opened his eyes or took any further notice of her, she said 'Good-bye!' once more, and getting no answer to this, she quietly walked away: but she couldn't help saying to herself as she went, 'Of all the unsatisfactory——' (she repeated this aloud, as it was a great comfort to have such a long word to say) 'of all the unsatisfactory people I *ever* met——' She never finished the sentence, for at this moment a heavy crash shook the forest from end to end.

Proud to Be an American Means Speaking Any Language, for Some

ABIGAIL VAN BUREN

Born Pauline Esther Friedman on July 4, 1918, Abigail Van Buren won the hearts of millions of readers as advice columnist "Dear Abby." Raised by Russian immigrant parents and twin to Ann Landers, Eppie, as Dear Abby was affectionately known, dispensed common-sense advice on topics related to sexuality, feminism, and personal relationships. Headstrong and liberal, Dear Abby cranked out columns for almost fifty years, until her death of multiple myeloma at age 83 on June 25, 2002. Editing and cowriting the column since 1987, her daughter Jeanne Phillips has assumed the spirit of her mother. Now the world's most widely syndicated columnist, Dear Abby appears in more than 1,400 newspapers worldwide and reaches more than 110 million readers each day. The following column, "Proud to be an American," is a series of letters to Dear Abby addressing the issue of language diversity in the United States.

1. Do you agree with the advice that Dear Abby gives in response to each letter?
2. Dear Abby is known for educating and entertaining its newspaper readers. What message is Abby sending to her readers in this column?
3. Why is the second letter writer offended when being asked "Where are you REALLY from?"
4. Do you agree with Abby's recommendation that every student in the United States should learn at least one foreign language?

Writing Assignments

1. Watch a non-English language television network. What observations can you make about this culture and language? How do these observations differ from your own culture and language?
2. Is there such a notion as "American"? Write an essay on what it means to be American.
3. Write an essay describing the diversity of life in the United States. Provide as many examples as you can to support the

idea that the United States is not a monolingual, monocultural nation.

4. Nowhere in the U.S. Constitution is there a provision that identifies English as the national language of the land. In recent years, a constitutional amendment has been proposed that would make English the only language of the United States. Write a letter to a government official or legislator arguing for or against making English the official language of the United States.

5. Write a letter to Dear Abby asking her advice on a language issue.

────────────── ✦ ──────────────

Dear Abby: You printed a letter from "Disillusioned American," who interceded when he saw a man in his 60s chastise a couple for speaking a foreign language outside a Kmart. You called it an example of xenophobia.

I do not share either the opinion of "Disillusioned" or you regarding people who refuse to learn English or at least speak it in public. There are two Spanish language TV networks in this country. Tell me another country that allows foreign language channels to operate, contributing to the fragmentation of that country.—**Lawrence in Avon Park, Fla.**

Dear Lawrence: Cable Network News (CNN) is an English-language network that is broadcast in more than 210 countries and territories in English. (In fact, someone recently told me she had seen me on "Larry King Live" while she was in Beijing—obviously not a nation that uses English as its primary language.)

Dear Abby: I am proud of being not only American, but a Chinese-American. I was raised bilingually and biculturally. Other than my Asian features, most people would be hard-pressed to find anything "un-American" about me.

However, occasional racist remarks are still thrown at me for   5
no other reason than my appearance. Fortunately, that type of bigotry is fading, but comments and actions like that man experienced at Kmart are common and should be stopped. White Americans should be sensitive about any treatment of nonwhite Americans as different.

For example, I am frequently asked where I am from. When I answer "Pittsburgh" (where I was born and raised), the response I often get is, "No, where are you REALLY from?" as if I couldn't be from America. I know people are curious about my heritage, but Caucasians (even ones with accents) are not treated thus, so why are those of us with Asian features, but nonaccented English, treated this way?—**Proud Chinese-American**

Dear Proud Chinese-American: Don't be so quick to assume that Caucasians with accents are not also asked where they are from. In this country, anyone with an accent is considered "exotic"—and as such, inspires curiosity. When people are curious, they ask questions. I know I'm right, because I have been guilty of it.

Dear Abby: I came to this country 20 years ago and attended college in the Midwest. I have also been accosted by such "patriots" on campus, in restaurants, and wherever I happened to be having a conversation in my language. My appearance does not give people any clue that I am not a "red-blooded American." I speak perfect, unaccented English, in addition to other languages, and I know there are many people like me.

Because I choose to speak another language does not mean I don't know English. I find it fascinating that Americans, when in other countries, expect people to accommodate their language needs, but do not afford the same courtesy to people who come to this country.—**Theresa B., Houston**

10　　**Dear Theresa:** Interesting point. And it's a good reason why U.S. students should learn at least one foreign language. Our world is shrinking, and it doesn't revolve around us.

Dear Abby: If that gentleman wants to be politically correct, perhaps he should be speaking an American-Indian dialect, since the Indians were here first and the Pilgrim fathers changed the language. (Only joking!)—**Sally in Willow Grove, Pa.**

Dear Sally: Mini-ha-ha!

Language
and Ethnicity

Language makes cultures, and we make a rotten culture when we abuse words.
CYNTHIA OZICK

It is estimated that between 5,000 and 8,000 languages exist in the world today. In the United States alone, there are approximately 230 different languages spoken. In New York City, at least 167 different languages are used. The explanations for the rich language diversity in the United States are varied: Settlement patterns and movements of people, geographical boundaries, and language contact help to contribute to language differences. Group reference and personal identity are important factors, as well, in maintaining language diversity and dialectal differences. From the times when indigenous populations struggled with the influx of the first European settlers and as new immigrants made their way to the United States within the last 500 years, multiethnic groups have brought to the linguistic table their own languages and cultures, ultimately contributing to a linguistic and cultural mosaic incomparable to that of any other nation.

The United States is an ethnically and racially diverse nation made up of more than 275 ethnic groups, including close to 170 Native-American nations. One-fourth of the United States is non-White, primarily comprised of African Americans, Latinos, Asian Americans, and American Indians. By 2020 these groups will represent more than 40 percent of the entire population.

Ethnologists, anthropologists, biologists, theologians, and other scientists have struggled to define the terms *race* and *ethnicity*. Throughout history, an individual's race has been assumed to be biological, fixed and natural: Differences were based

35

on assumed innate characteristics or visible physical appearances, such as the distribution of genes, skin color, hair type, body structure, head shape, or facial features. As a result of this belief, a racial typology had led to theories that certain races were inherently superior or inferior to one another—an unshakable belief among many people today who continue to classify multiracial individuals as Black or non-White. Geneticists claim that race is virtually a scientifically meaningless and useless term. Because scientists do not agree on the definition of race, sociologists have replaced the concept with terms that capture the dynamic social, rather than biological, distinctions which identify the variety of ethnic groups.

Difficult to differentiate from social factors, ethnicity is often the term used to classify ethnic groups in terms of national origin, religion, and cultural heritage. More important, ethnicity is the way a group of people define themselves; it is a sense of peoplehood. To reflect more accurately the nation's racial diversity, the 2000 United States Census forms allowed respondents, for the first time, the option of marking one or more choices out of many distinct race categories and ethnic combinations to describe themselves.

Prejudice and *discrimination* arise from our lack of understanding of the history, experiences, and cultural values of ethnic groups. As a result, we are quick to stereotype groups of people. The language we use often reflects our personal prejudices and the prejudices handed down through generations of our society. Unconscious of the bias embedded in the English language, we often use terms and expressions that we think have lost their potency. It is not that we are stupid or uncaring, but that we have become desensitized to the impact which language has on others. When we hear someone say, "I jewed someone down" or "The salesclerk gypped me" or "The cash register is nigger rigged" or "The dealer scalped the tickets," we often forget that the expressions "to jew," "to gyp," "to nigger rig," and "to scalp" communicate the deep-rooted prejudices that society has held for centuries about Jews as money-hungry business people, Romanies or gypsies as nomadic thieves, African Americans as shiftless workers, and Native Americans as savage warriors. Language is a powerful tool. It has the power to slant the way we perceive and respond to the world, prejudicing the way we think of others. The language we choose does more than name or describe; it can assign respect, status, and value as well as insult, mock, and discriminate. We must choose our language wisely, otherwise, we perpetuate an inaccurate and unfair view of the world and the people who live in it.

In the following chapter we will read about the many forms of prejudicial acts and behaviors that are reflected in our language. To begin to help us understand prejudices, their impact on others, and how we can reduce prejudicial behavior, "Prejudice Quiz" assesses our knowledge of the dynamics of prejudices. Following the quiz, herstorian Amoja Three Rivers provides "Cultural Etiquette: A Guide for the Well-Intentioned" to individuals who are motivated to refine their behavior and attitudes in this fast-paced, changing world of diverse cultures, languages, and histories.

The next three readings address the controversies surrounding language and African American ethnic identity. Famed actor Ossie Davis wages war on the English language in "The English Language Is My Enemy!" by drawing our attention to the ways in which English words reflect negative stereotypes about African Americans. Professor Randall Kennedy in his book *nigger* traces the earliest use of the word, examines its legal history, and discusses the attempts to eradicate its existence. In the final chapter from that book entitled, "How Are We Doing with *Nigger?*" he notes that although the N-word still stirs intense emotions, its increasing social acceptance in mainstream culture assures its future for many years to come. In contrast, college student Rob Nelson argues in "The Word 'Nigga' Is Only for Slaves and Sambos" that the N-word "conjures up images of sweaty slaves and singin' Sambos," and as long as African Americans continue to use the word, they perpetuate an unshakable image of racism. The word is offensive and acts as a reminder of its ugly history.

The next two selections address issues related to the power of naming and particularly the practice of naming professional and college sports teams after Native-American nations. First, in the short piece "Ordinary Words Cause Extraordinary Pain," Clara Standing Soldier describes her pain on hearing a racial slur directed at the Native American heritage. The next reading, "The Indian Wars," published in *Sports Illustrated,* responds to the question of whether the use of names for team mascots is an act of offense or pride.

The selection that follows takes a historical look at the prejudicial language used against Jews. Thomas Friedmann in "Heard Any Good Jews Lately?" describes how Jews have suffered from linguistic discrimination throughout history. The next selection, "Term Limits: Hispanic? Latino? A National Debate Proves No One Name Pleases Everyone" by Mark McDonald, explores the challenge of group naming. Addressing the Hispanic or Latin populations in the United States, McDonald presents an overview of the multiple factors involved when groups of several ethnic origins name themselves.

The last two readings focus on the lack of understanding we have about other cultures. Although South Asians in Asia have experienced similar histories, South Asian Americans are differentiated by their relationships with their home countries. Indian Anita Vasudeva's poem "Can You Talk Mexican?" recreates a childhood game from her country of birth, the United States. And reporter Aparisim Ghosh delves into the mind of a racist in his article "Subcontinental Drift: The Mind of a Racist."

The chapter ends with suggested "Guidelines for Avoiding Racist Language." To achieve a more bias-free society, we must heighten our sensitivity to the pervasive power of prejudicial language. To do so is a statement of respect for the cultural diversity that exists in the world today.

Discussion Questions

1. One change in the 2000 United States Census was in the category of race. Since 1977, respondents had been required to identify themselves by only one racial group: Black, White, American Indian, Alaskan Native, Asian, or Pacific Islander. Now, multiracial individuals may list all categories that apply—126 possible racial combinations. Why was this change made? What are your views on the "multiracial debate"?

2. In what ways do the media and advertising perpetuate the stereotypical images of people from different parts of the world, different regions of the United States. Different ethnic and racial groups, different genders, different sexual orientations, different classes, and other social and regional groups?

3. There are certain stereotypes about dialects and prejudice toward the users of particular regional and social varieties of English in the United States. What are your attitudes toward the speech of particular regional, ethnic, or social groups? Consider New York City English, Southern American English, African American Vernacular English, Appalachian English, and other varieties.

4. The language we use often reflects our personal prejudices and the prejudices handed down through generations of our society. Can you think of examples where we as users of a language have become desensitized to the impact that language has on others?

5. According to the following equation, only those persons and groups who hold a dominant position of power can be sexist, racist, or homophobic. Do you agree with this equation? Explain.

    prejudice + power = ism (sexism, racism, classism, homophobism)

6. The famous crayon brand Crayola celebrated its 100th birthday in 2003. As the attitudes toward race and culture changed, so did the names of the colors of the crayons. "Flesh" became "peach" in 1962, and "Indian red" became "chestnut" in 1999. What is your reaction to Crayola's sensitivity of the changing times?

7. View a film that deals directly with language. Discuss the relationship between language and ethnicity. Here are a few suggestions: *Smoke Signals* (1998) directed by Chris Eyre; *Daughters of the Dust* (1992) directed by Julie Dash; *A Great Wall* (1986) directed by Peter Wang; *Monsoon Wedding* (2002) directed by Sean Chavel; and any of the films directed by Spike Lee.

Projects and Other Writing Activities

1. Examine the results of the most recent United States Census. In particular, pay attention to the questions on the form relating to the social variables of gender, age, ethnicity, region, religion, and language. Discuss how ethnically, linguistically, and socially diverse the United States is. Examine how people living in the United States define themselves racially.

2. Research the history of your community. Discuss the ways in which settlement patterns, population movements, physical geography, and other factors have influenced the speech of the area.

3. A great deal of research has been devoted to the study of African American Vernacular English (AAVE), a complete linguistic system with its own rules. Research this topic and explore the relationship between AAVE and Anglo-American vernacular varieties.

4. In 1996 the Board of Education in Oakland, California, unanimously passed a resolution on Black English, known as Ebonics, in the school system. In announcing its policy, the board affirmed the legitimacy of AAVE as a language system and stated that African Americans speak a language distinct from English. Write a paper explaining the so-called Ebonics controversy and the report's major recommendations.

ne of the following Internet sources and write a report review-
scussion of prejudice.

an Psychological Associations	www.apa.org/pubinfo/hate
ʌacism Net	www.igc.org/igc/gateway/arnindex.html
National Association of Colored People	www.naacp.org
Anti-Defamation League	www.adl.org
American Civil Liberties Union	www.aclu.org

Prejudice Quiz

Use this quiz to test your knowledge concerning the origins and
prevalence of prejudice in our society as well as the viability of
various antidotes and solutions. After taking the quiz, discuss
each question and answer in a group. Compare your answers to
those that follow at the end of this "Prejudice Quiz." Which answers surprised you? Is there an interesting issue that you would
like to explore in the library and write a paper on?

1. Punishing those who behave in prejudiced ways is:
   A. the quickest solution to ending the problems of preju-
      diced behavior.
   B. a response that is impossible since most prejudiced be-
      havior is difficult to observe or prove.
   C. unlikely to make a major difference since those who are
      the most prejudiced tend to have already received more
      punishment than most of us have received.
   D. Both B and C.
2. If one thinks prejudiced thoughts, one should suppress them
   or avoid thinking them.
   A. Yes. Thoughts are very close to actions and one should
      avoid thinking negative thoughts about other groups of
      people.
   B. No. One should not suppress the thoughts, but should in-
      stead actively replace them with more positive images of
      the group members.
   C. No. Prejudiced thoughts are normal and harmless; they
      are part of being in a group.

D. D. Yes. If we don't start on a personal level to reduce prejudiced thinking, then the problems will simply grow.

3. Prejudices don't cost our society and therefore are really only a problem to those who are the victims of prejudiced behavior.
   A. To discuss the monetary cost of prejudiced behavior is impossible.
   B. The cost of prejudiced behavior is a human cost and is not a national economic issue.
   C. The costs of sexism and racism alone have been estimated at over a half trillion dollars per year.
   D. Both A and B are true.

4. Most people are not prejudiced.
   A. Surveys show that well over 75 percent of people in the United States do not consider themselves to be racist.
   B. Those who discriminate represent a very small proportion of the U.S. population.
   C. Research has shown that those who identify themselves as low in prejudiced beliefs still discriminate.
   D. Both A and C are true.

5. There are no inexpensive methods of managing prejudiced behavior.
   A. This is true because prejudiced behavior is so widespread, but we still need to try.
   B. There are ways of managing prejudiced behavior that cost next to nothing.
   C. While the training might be expensive, the long-term savings are worth the investment.

6. Those who risked their lives to save Jewish people in Western Europe during the period that the Nazis were practicing genocide were more religious than those who did not try to save Jewish people.
   A. True
   B. False

7. Those who saved Jewish people from Hitler's genocide had more resources than those who did not.
   A. True; they had larger attics or larger basements.
   B. False; they had no more resources.

8. Those who are in positions of authority can do a great deal to manage prejudice within the ranks of an organization.
   A. True
   B. False

9. Being strongly prejudiced has little to do with a person's intellectual functioning or ability to make other types of judgments.
   A. True
   B. False

10. The motivation of a strongly prejudiced person who is committing an overtly prejudiced act is basically the same as that of a person with lower levels of prejudiced behavior who is functioning out of a stereotyped perception.
    A. True
    B. False

11. When a person who does not hold prejudiced beliefs behaves in a prejudiced way, he or she often feels a personal sense of discomfort.
    A. True
    B. False

12. Those who are most strongly prejudiced toward a target group generally know no more negative stereotypes about those they are prejudiced toward than those who are low in prejudiced behavior toward the same group.
    A. True
    B. False

13. When the leading scientists of the world look at the issues that threaten our future, they look at environmental concerns, not prejudiced behavior.
    A. Scientists have little agreement about the things that threaten our future and there is nothing that even resembles a consensus.
    B. There is clear consensus among the majority of leading scientists in the world about what threatens our future, and it includes concerns about prejudiced behavior.
    C. There is clear consensus among the majority of the leading scientists in the world about what threatens our future and it includes concerns about prejudiced behavior, specifically sexism.

14. Sexism, racism, ageism, xenophobia, homophobia, and prejudices toward those with disabilities all have basically the same dynamics.
    A. They are all basically the same except for homophobia, which functions very differently from the others.
    B. Each is different and has its own set of dynamics.

C. They are all basically the same except for prejudices toward those with disabilities, which function very differently from the others.
D. They are all basically the same.

ANSWERS TO PREJUDICE QUIZ

1. **D:** Punishing those who behave in prejudiced ways is impossible because most prejudiced behavior is difficult to observe or prove. Research has shown that those who are most prejudiced generally have received more punishment than most of us.

2. **B:** If one thinks prejudiced thoughts, one should not suppress them. One should actively replace prejudiced thoughts with more positive images of the group members about whom one has had prejudiced thoughts.

3. **C:** Prejudices cost our society and therefore are a real economic problem for all of us, not just those who are the victims of the prejudiced behavior. The cost of sexism and racism alone have been estimated at over a half trillion dollars per year.

4. **D:** Most people are not prejudiced. Surveys show that well over 75 percent of people in the United States do not consider themselves to be racist. Research has shown that those who identify themselves as low in prejudiced beliefs still discriminate.

5. **B:** There are inexpensive methods of managing prejudiced behavior; in fact, there are ways of managing prejudiced behavior that cost next to nothing.

6. **B:** Those who risked their own lives to save Jewish people in Western Europe during the period that the Nazis were practicing genocide were no more religious than those who did not try to save Jewish people.

7. **B:** Those who saved Jewish people from Hitler's genocide had no more resources than those who did not attempt to save Jewish people.

8. **A:** Those who are in positions of authority can do a great deal to reduce prejudices within the ranks of an organization. People in positions of authority often have more leverage with those who are strongly prejudiced than they realize.

9. **B:** Being strongly prejudiced has much to do with a person's intellectual functioning and ability to make other types of judgments.

10. **B:** The motivation of a strongly prejudiced person who is committing an overtly prejudiced act is basically different than that of a person with lower levels of prejudiced behavior who is functioning out of a stereotyped perception.

11. **A:** When a person who is low in prejudiced beliefs behaves in a prejudiced way, he or she generally feels a personal sense of discomfort following the behavior.

12. **A:** Those who are most strongly prejudiced toward a target group generally know no more negative stereotypes about those toward whom they are prejudiced than those who are low in prejudiced behavior toward the same group.

13. **C:** When the leading scientists of the world look at the issues that threaten our future there is clear consensus. The concerns of a majority of the leading scientists in the world about what threatens our future include concerns about prejudiced behavior, specifically sexism.

14. **D:** Sexism, racism, ageism, xenophobia, homophobia, and the prejudices toward those with disabilities all have basically the same dynamics.

Cultural Etiquette: A Guide for the Well-Intentioned

AMOJA THREE RIVERS

Amoja Three Rivers, a cofounder of the Accessible African Herstory Project, is a lecturer, herstorian, and craftswoman. In "Cultural Etiquette," she provides the reader with a model for identifying the unwritten social rules that operate in our society—a guide to help well-meaning people not fall in the trap of uttering words that may be deemed racist or anti-Semitic.

1. The author defines *ethnocentrism, exotic,* and *ethnic.* Do you agree with her definitions? Are you guilty of using words that show ethnocentric and racist attitudes?

2. Amoja Three Rivers states that "no person of color can be a racist as long as white people maintain power. . . . 'reverse racism,' . . . is a contradiction in terms." Do you agree with her argument?

3. The author argues that people of color sometimes need time and space apart from the dominant White group. What do you think she means by this statement? Do you agree?

Writing Assignments

1. Design a brochure that outlines some of the rules of cultural etiquette.

2. Have you ever been insensitive to someone's feelings? Write this person a letter apologizing for your insensitivity.

3. Write a paper arguing for the respect of cultural diversity or design a project to heighten the awareness of language.

4. In a group, write your own set of rules of etiquette based on gender, sexual orientation, or any group identity.

5. How do you handle prejudice with a close friend? family member? boss? Dramatize such a situation. Pretend one of these people publicly makes an offensive comment about a particular ethnic group. How would you respond to this situation?

Racism and the racial stereotypes it spawns are so subtly interwoven into the fabric of Western society that very often, even those with the best of intentions will display bad cultural manners. This does not necessarily mean one is a bad person. Sometimes people just don't know any better.

This guide is to help people avoid some of the obvious as well as not so obvious pitfalls of unwitting racism and anti-Semitism. This does not try to talk anyone out of being racist or anti-Semitic. Rather it seeks to help those with good and righteous intentions to refine behavior and attitudes bred in cultural ignorance.

Ethnocentrism, according to the *Random House Dictionary* of the English language, means "a tendency to view alien groups or cultures in terms of one's own" and "the belief in the inherent superiority of one's own group and culture, accompanied by a feeling of contempt for other groups and cultures."

The term "exotic," when applied to human beings, is ethnocentric and racist. It defines people of color only as we relate to white people. It implies a state of other-ness, or foreign origin, apart from the norm. It is not a compliment.

5 "Ethnic" refers to nationality or race. Everyone's nationality or race. Margaret Thatcher, Susan B. Anthony, and Bach are just as "ethnic" as Miriam Makeba, Indira Gandhi, and Johnny Colon. While it is true that most citizens of the United States are white, at least four-fifths of the world's population consists of people of color. Therefore, it is statistically incorrect as well as ethnocentrist to refer to us as minorities. The term "minority" is used to reinforce the idea of people of color as "other."

Within the cultures of many people, more value is placed on relationships, and on the maintenance of tradition and spirituality than on the development and acquisition of machinery. It is ethnocentric and racist to apply words like backward, primitive, uncivilized, savage, barbaric, or undeveloped to people whose technology does not include plumbing, microwaves, and microchips. Are people somehow more human or more humane if they have more technological toys?

Monotheism is not more "advanced" than polytheism. It is simply another kind of spirituality, and both have equal validity. The notion of "one true god, one true faith" is often used to invalidate the ancient and complex religious traditions of millions of people.

"Fetish" is a term that means object of spiritual veneration, but in Western society, it is mainly applied to religious items of people of color in an effort to diminish their depth and importance. One never hears a crucifix referred to as a fetish, even though it basically serves the same purpose as an Acuaba or even the ancient Asherah.

Native Americans and Native American cultures are alive and thriving, thank you. In fact, you are on our land.

10 White people have not always been "white," nor will they always be "white." It is a political alliance. Things will change.

No person of color can be a racist as long as white people maintain power. This is because racism is "power over." A person of color may have race prejudice, but until most of Congress, state, provincial, and local governments, the Pentagon, the FBI, CIA, all major industries, the Stock Exchange, Fortune 500 members, the educational system, health care system, the International Monetary Fund, the armed forces, and the police force are all operated and controlled by people of color and their cultural values, we do not have the kind of power that it takes to be racist toward anyone. Similarly, "reverse racism," within the context of present society, is a contradiction in terms.

The media images we see of poor, miserable, starving, disease-ridden "third world" people of color are distorted and misleading. Nowhere among the tearful appeals for aid do they discuss the conditions that created and continue to create such hopeless poverty. In point of fact, these countries, even after they threw off the stranglehold of colonialism, have been subjected to a constant barrage of resource plundering, political meddling, and brutal economic manipulation by European and American interests. Most non-Western countries could function quite adequately and feed themselves quite well if they were permitted political and economic self-determination. People do not have a hard time because of their race or cultural background. No one is attacked, abused, oppressed, pogromed upon, or enslaved because of their race, creed, or cultural background. People are attacked, abused, oppressed, pogromed upon, or enslaved because of racism and anti-Semitism! There is a subtle but important difference in the focus here. The first implies some inherent fault or shortcoming within the oppressed person or group. The second redirects the responsibility back to the real source of the problem.

The neighborhoods of urban people of color are sometimes run down because of poverty, depression, and hopelessness, and the racist behavior of banks, city planners, and government and industry. But before anyone again sighs, "There goes the neighborhood," one should consider this: before white people invaded these lands, the air was clean, the water was pure, and the earth was unspoiled.

In 500 years of African cultures, we never had a drug problem until we were brought here. Everyone speaks with an accent. Language is a fluid, flexible tool that naturally reflects the life and culture of the speaker, and always changes with the situation. All "accents" and "dialects" are legitimate, proper, and equal in value. Many people of color value and consciously choose to keep their "accents" because it is an affirmation of our respective cultural identities.

JUST DON'T DO THIS, OKAY?

It is not a compliment to tell someone: "I don't think of you as   15
Jewish." ". . . Black." ". . . Asian." ". . . Latina." ". . . Middle Eastern" ". . . Native American." Or, "I think of you as white."

Do not use a Jewish person or person of color to hear your confession of past racist transgressions. If you have offended a particular person, then apologize to that person. But don't (please don't) just pick some person of color or Jewish person at random, or who is unrelated to the incident, to confess to and beg forgiveness from. Find a priest or a therapist.

Is this really racism or just use of the word: which came first?

Do not equate bad, depressing, or negative things with darkness. Observe how language reflects racism: a black mood, a dark day, a black heart. *when it's cloudy for instance*

The meaning of the word "denigrate" is to demean by darkening. Be creative. There's thousands of adjectives in the English language that do not equate evil with the way people of color look. How about instead of "the pot calling the kettle black," you say, "the pus calling the maggot white"? Think of and use positive dark and black imagery. Dark can be rich and deep and cool and sweet.

As an exercise, pretend you are from another planet and you want examples of typical human beings for your photo album. Having never heard of racism, you'd probably pick someone who represents the majority of the people on the planet: an Asian woman.

20   It is not "racism in reverse" or "segregation" for Jews or people of color to come together in affinity groups for mutual support. Sometimes we need some time and space apart from the dominant group just to relax and be ourselves. It's like family time. Most of the U.S.A. is white and gentile with white, gentile rules and values prevailing. Sometimes we need to be in control of our own space, time, and values, to shape our own reality or turf. Sometimes we need to be alone to commiserate with each other about racism and anti-Semitism, and to formulate plans and strategies for dealing with it. Sometimes we need time and space to explore who we are, free from outsider definitions, influences, and ethnocentric imagery. Sometimes we just need an environment that is totally free from even the possibility of racism and anti-Semitism. So when you see: "Native American Conference," "Jewish Caucus," "Womyn of Color Tent" . . . please know that we are not being against anybody by being for ourselves.

The various cultures of people of color often seem very attractive to white people. (Yes, we are wonderful, we can't deny it.) But white people should not make a playground out of other people's cultures. We are not quaint. We are not exotic. We are not cool. Our music, art, and spiritualities are but small, isolated parts of integrated and meaningful ancient traditions. They were developed within each group, for that group, by the deities and teach-

& can be used only by that group?

ers of that group, according to their own particular conditions
and connections to the cosmos, and their own particular histories
and philosophies. In addition, our cultural expressions carry all
the pain, joy, bitterness, and hope that reflect our lives and our
struggles in dealing with so-called Western civilization. While
most philosophies can have universal application, it has been the
habit of many non-people of color to select unconnected pieces of
our cultures for fads and fashion, taking them totally out of context and robbing them of all meaning and power.

It's like we take all the beautiful old things from our own cultures. And we take the shit and blood and pain that whites have
heaped upon us too,

And we deal with all of that,
Mix it up,
Compost it,   25
Plow it under,
Work the soil,
Pull the weeds,
Nurture the seedlings,
And finally   30
Here it is, our garden
These fruits,
These songs and dances,
These visions.
Then here YOU come,   35
Fresh from the Big House,
Having neither sowed nor plowed
But fully expecting to reap.

Now it is perfectly natural for human beings to share and
blend cultures, but let us face a hard reality: 20th century white
society is culturally addicted to exploitation. Cultivate an awareness of your own personal motivations. Do not simply take and
consume. If you are white and you find yourself drawn to Native
American spirituality, Middle Eastern religion, African drum-
ming, Asian philosophies, or Latin rhythms, make an effort to
maintain some kind of balance. Don't just learn the fun and excit-
ing things about us and then go home to your safe, isolated,
white, privileged life. Learn about the history of the people whose
culture you're dabbling in. Learn how our history relates to your
own, how your privilege connects and contributes to our oppression and exploitation. And most importantly, make it a fair exchange—give something back. If you want to pick the fruit, then
carry some manure and plow some fields. Give your land back to

the Indians and the Mexicans. Make reparations to the Africans. Work for Native peoples' autonomy and Puerto Rican independence. Send relief money to Middle Eastern and Asian disaster victims. Lobby Congress for fair immigration laws. Provide rides for Elders of color or single mothers who need to get to the market. Quietly contribute money to the African National Congress, *Akwe sasne Notes*, and LaRaza. Then take your drum lesson and your dance class. Then burn your sage and cedar.

40   Sometimes white people who are drawn to other people's cultures are hungry for a way of life with more depth and meaning than what we find in 20th-century Western society. Don't forget that every white person alive today is also descended from tribal peoples. If you are white, don't neglect your own ancient traditions. They are as valid as anybody else's, and the ways of your own ancestors need to be honored, remembered, and carried on into the future.

     "Race" is an arbitrary and meaningless concept. Races among humans don't exist. If there ever was such a thing as race (which there isn't), there has been so much constant criss-crossing of genes for the last 500,000 years, that it would have lost all meaning anyway. There are no real divisions between us, only a continuum of variations that constantly change, as we come together and separate according to the flow and movement of human populations.

The English Language Is My Enemy!
OSSIE DAVIS

Ossie Davis was born on December 18, 1917, in Cogdell, Georgia, and attended Howard University from 1935 to 1939. An African-American actor of stage and screen, Davis is also known for his writing and directing ability. He was a leading activist during the civil rights era, joining Dr. Martin Luther King, Jr. in his crusade for equal rights and freedom. He eulogized King and later Malcolm X at their funerals. In his words, "The profoundest commitment possible to a black creator in this country today—beyond all creeds, crafts, classes and ideologies whatsoever—is to bring before his people the scent of freedom." In this reading from the *Negro Story Bulletin*. Davis argues that the English language is the enemy of the Black person.

1. What does Davis mean when he says, "The English language is my enemy!"
2. According to Davis, the synonyms for "whiteness" are favorable and those for "blackness" are unfavorable. As a result, an African American child "born into the English Language" will learn to despise him or herself, and a White child using these same terms only assists the African American child in this self-debasing process. What do you think of this argument?
3. Look up words related to "whiteness" and "blackness" in the dictionary or a thesaurus. Do you come up with the same conclusions as the author?

Writing Assignments

1. Write an essay relating "The English Language Is My Enemy!" to the Sapir–Whorf hypothesis.
2. Write an essay showing the link between language and ethnic identity.
3. One of the most useful tools for studying the history of words in the English language is the twenty-volume *Oxford English Dictionary (OED)*. Make a list of racially or ethnically-charged terms. Choose one and examine its history in the *OED*. Write a report outlining the history of the word.

———————————— ✦ ————————————

A superficial examination of *Roget's Thesaurus of the English Language* reveals the following facts; the word WHITENESS has 134 synonyms; 44 of which are favorable and pleasing to contemplate, i.e. purity, cleanness, immaculateness, bright, shining, ivory, fair, blonde, stainless, clean, clear, chaste, unblemished, unsullied, innocent, honorable, upright, just, straight-forward, fair, genuine, trustworthy, (a white man-colloquialism). Only ten synonyms for WHITENESS appear to me have negative implications—and these only in the mildest sense: gloss over, whitewash, gray, wan, pale, ashen, etc.

The word BLACKNESS has 120 synonyms, 60 of which are distinctly unfavorable, and none of them even mildly positive. Among the offending 60 were such words as: blot, blotch, smut, smudge, sully, begrime, soot, becloud, obscure, dingy, murky, low-toned, threatening, frowning, foreboding, forbidden, sinister, baneful, dismal, thundery, evil, wicked, malignant, deadly, un-

Which came first: Was white language's use of "dark" words or [crossed out: its] its introduction to "dark" people.

clean, dirty, unwashed, foul, etc. . . . not to mention 20 synonyms directly related to race, such as: Negro, Negress, nigger, darky, blackamoor, etc.

When you consider the fact that *thinking* itself is sub-vocal speech—in other words, one must use *words* in order to think at all—you will appreciate the enormous heritage of racial prejudgement that lies in wait for any child born into the English Language. Any teacher good or bad, white or black, Jew or Gentile, who uses the English Language as a medium of communication is forced, willy-nilly, to teach the Negro child 60 ways to despise himself, and the white child 60 ways to aid and abet him in the crime.

Who speaks to me in my Mother Tongue damns me indeed! . . . the English Language—in which I cannot conceive myself as a black man without, at the same time, debasing myself . . . my enemy, with which to survive at all I must continually be at war.

How Are We Doing with *Nigger?*
RANDALL KENNEDY

Born in Columbia, South Carolina, Harvard law professor Randall Kennedy teaches courses on freedom of expression and the regulation of race relations. He served as a law clerk for Justice Thurgood Marshall of the United States Supreme Court. In his 2002 book *nigger,* Kennedy examines "the strange career of a troublesome word." In it, he attempts to "put a tracer on nigger, report on its use, and assess the controversies to which it gives rise." As pervasive as the word was and still is, in the excerpt here Kennedy reminds us that one thing is for sure: The word is so deeply ingrained in the culture of the United States, it is here to stay.

1. After reading this article, were you offended by the word "nigger"? Is the *N-word* a euphemism for it?
2. How is the use of this term a paradox in modern society? Do you think that the use of the N-word is ever okay? Is it always used to offend? Is the term moving beyond negative connotations and becoming a term with a broader use?
3. In *Through the Looking-Glass* Humpty Dumpty says to Alice, "When I use a word . . . it means just what I choose it to mean—neither more nor less." Do you think that this idea ap-

plies to words such as the N-word with a long history of racist use? Can people take a word and make it mean whatever they want it to mean?

Writing Assignments

1. Write a letter to Randall Kennedy arguing either that the N-word is a term that is racist and demeaning under any circumstances, or that the N-word is a term of endearment and liberation among African Americans.

2. In recent years, dictionaries and books such as Mark Twain's *Huckleberry Finn* have come under attack for including the word "nigger." Do you think that dictionaries should remove the N-word or other racist or sexist terms, or that literary works containing the N-word should be banned from schools and libraries? Write an essay to support your view.

3. Many politicians have made embarrassing racial "slips of the tongue." For example, in 2002 Mississippi Republican Senator Trent Lott said that if Dixiecrat Strom Thurmond had become president in 1948 "we wouldn't have had all of these problems"; in 2001 West Virginia Democrat Senator Robert C. Byrd used the racial slur "white nigger"; and in the 1970s former Vice President Spiro Agnew called Polish Americans "polacks." Find other examples in which politicians have had to publicly apologize for their insensitive comments. Do you think that such comments reveal the user's true attitudes and feelings about race and ethnicity? Are such people out of touch with the changing times? Do you think that they can ever redeem themselves in the eyes of the public?

4. Many celebrities and public figures such as former Cincinnati Reds owner Marge Schott and former football analyst Jimmy "The Greek" Snyder have been pressured to resign from their positions of leadership because each of them had made insensitive racial remarks. Schott was permenently suspended from baseball for remarking that Hitler did good things for Germany until he went "nuts" and calling African American baseball plays "her niggers"; Snyder was fired from CBS for stating that the African American athlete is "bred to be the better athlete because, this goes all the way to the Civil War when . . . the slave owner would breed his big woman so that he would have a big black kid." Do you think

that the inappropriate use of language matters? Although all these highly visible figures apologized for their insensitivity, they were fired. Is inappropriate language justification for a firing?

———————— ✦ ————————

Although references to *nigger* continue to cause social eruptions, major institutions of American life are handling this combustible word about right. Where the most powerful and respected political and professional positions are at stake, public opinion has effectively stigmatized *nigger*-as-insult. Anyone with ambitions to occupy a high public post, for example, had better refrain from *ever* using *nigger* in any of its various senses, because the N-word rankles so many people so deeply. Political prudence counsels strict avoidance. We now know that a man can become president of the United States even if he is overheard calling someone an asshole, but the same is no longer true of a person who refers to another as a nigger: too many voters view such conduct as utterly disqualifying. It is precisely because seasoned politicians know better than ever to utter the word *nigger* publicly that mouths dropped open when, during a television appearance in March 2001, Senator Robert C. Byrd of West Virginia talked about having seen "a lot of white niggers in [his] time"—a remark for which he quickly apologized.

Reinforcing public opinion is the coercive power of government as manifested in tort law and antidiscrimination statutes. As we have seen, in certain situations victims of racial harassment can obtain money damages and other relief from their tormentors or from employers who fail to address harassment that is brought to their attention.

Various forces prevent the complete eradication of *nigger*-as-insult. Some of these are negative, such as vestigial racism and toleration of it; in many settings it is still the case that a habit of using *nigger*-as-insult does not much hurt one's reputation. It is also true, however, that positive forces militate in favor of the survival of *nigger*-as-insult. One such is libertarianism in matters of linguistic expression. Protecting foul, disgusting, hateful, unpopular speech against governmental censorship is a great achievement of American political culture.

As a linguistic landmark, *nigger* is being renovated. Blacks use the term with novel ease to refer to other blacks, even in the presence of those who are not African American. Whites are increasingly referring to other whites as niggers, and indeed, the term both as an insult and as a sign of affection is being affixed to people of all sorts. In some settings, its usage is so routine as to have become virtually standard. *Nigger* as a harbinger of hatred, fear, contempt, and violence remains current, to be sure. But more than ever before, *nigger* also signals other meanings and generates other reactions, depending on the circumstances. This complexity has its costs. Miscues are bound to proliferate as speakers and audiences misjudge one another. The latina singing star Jennifer Lopez said that she was surprised when some African Americans accused her of bigotry on account of lyrics in one of her songs that referred to *niggers.* Maybe she was merely posturing; controversy is often good for record sales. But maybe she was expressing genuine astonishment; after all, many African American female entertainers sing lyrics containing *nigger* without raising eyebrows. Perhaps a dual misunderstanding was at work, as Lopez mistook how she would be perceived and disappointed listeners mistook her sentiments. The popular film *Rush Hour* spoofs this reality. In one of its scenes, a black character (played by Chris Tucker) is warmly received after saluting a black acquaintance as "my nigger," while a Chinese man (played by Jackie Chan) sparks fisticuffs when he innocently mimics Tucker's use of the N-word.

A diminished ability to stigmatize the word is another cost. As *nigger* is more widely disseminated and its complexity is more widely appreciated, censuring its use—even its use as an insult—will become more difficult. The more aware judges and other officials become of the ambiguity surrounding *nigger,* the less likely they will be to automatically condemn the actions taken by whites who voice the N-word. This tendency will doubtless, in certain instances, lead to unfortunate results, as decision makers show undue solicitude toward racists who use the rhetoric of complexity to cover their misconduct.

Still, despite these costs, there is much to be gained by allowing people of all backgrounds to yank *nigger* away from white supremacists, to subvert its ugliest denotation, and to convert the N-word from a negative into a positive appellation. This process is already well under way, led in the main by African American innovators who are taming, civilizing, and transmuting "the filthiest, dirtiest, nastiest word in the English language." For bad and for good, *nigger* is thus destined to remain with us for many years to come—a reminder of the ironies and dilemmas, the tragedies and glories, of the American experience.

The Word "Nigga" Is Only for Slaves and Sambos

ROB NELSON

In this article published by *The Daily Tar Heel,* the student newspaper of the University of North Carolina, Rob Nelson argues that the word "nigger" is so racially charged that the everyday use of it among African Americans does not erase the long history of racism. According to Nelson, African Americans must "wake up and realize what a damaging step backwards using the word really is."

1. The author is offended by the racist term "nigger" under any circumstances uttered by any individual. Why is he offended?
2. The author argues that when African Americans use the N-word among themselves, it is a "damaging step backwards." What does he mean by this? Do you agree?
3. What does the title mean? Why does the author use the pronunciation "nigga" rather than "nigger" in the title? What does the author mean when he refers to the expression "only for slaves and sambos"?

Writing Assignments

1. This article was written by a student for a university student paper. Who is the intended audience? Write a reply.
2. Interview a person of color and ask him or her what their views are on the use of a word like "nigger." Write about your results.

——————— ◆ ———————

To hell with political correctness; it's not "the N-word." It's nigger. And perhaps no other word in the English language has remained so racially explosive. There's just something about those two little syllables strung together that, for most blacks, evokes anger and conjures up images of sweaty slaves and singin' Sambos. Out of the many racial slurs that still run rampant throughout society, the word nigger seems overarching; it has withstood the test of time in that, for most blacks, there is still no greater insult than to be referred to by that word.

But while most blacks, of course, understand the implications and the racist history of the word nigger, it has somehow dangerously and disturbingly found its way into everyday language. I can't begin to count the number of times I've heard some of my own refer to themselves and other blacks as niggers.

"Yo, what up, nigga?"

"Hey, you goin' to the Great Hall party tonight, nigga?"

"Did you see the game last night, nigga?"

A former black suitemate of mine would come back from working out, stand shirtless in front of the mirror, and admire his physique by saying "This nigga is gettin' big, yo!" A black colleague of mine told me I should point out a certain subtlety in all of this racist banter. He explained that there was a difference between "nigger" and "nigga." While "nigger" was the full-blown racial epithet, "nigga" was more of an affectionate term used among close friends. In a phrase—nigga, please.

No matter what's done with the last syllable of the word, it doesn't make it any less offensive or demeaning. It doesn't soften the blow of a word that has been used for centuries to ostracize, humiliate, and dehumanize blacks. It doesn't erase the scars of the word's slavery-laden meanings or lessen the severity of its racism. It doesn't do a damn thing except prove that, after decades of progress in civil rights, blacks are still shackled. And, this time, by their very own lock and key.

For blacks to refer to themselves and each other as niggas is, at best, self-defeating. It is hypocritical and, quite frankly, absurd. Blacks talk about how they still want equality, how racism still runs true and deep in this country, and how important it is to maintain their culture and their identity. But to preach about such ideals and still refer to themselves with the most notoriously racist word in our language is a sad contradiction.

More important, the everyday use of the word nigger creates an atmosphere of acceptance—as if it's perfectly fine for others to now see and call blacks niggers. After all, if blacks themselves do it, why can't others?

10   In fact, since if we insist upon referring to ourselves with that word, let's not stop there. Let's go all the way and live up to every other stereotype in the book. Starting today, let's parade around campus with watermelon slices dangling from our lips, a box of fried chicken under our arms, and some cotton still stuck under our fingernails. Let's shine all the white students' shoes and sing them a little ditty about all of the good days we had out there in the field. And when those shoes are all shined, let's follow them around campus all day in case they need their trash taken out or their asses wiped. Wouldn't it be grand?

Granted my exaggeration, but it shocks me that more blacks don't realize that by using the word nigger and thus exacerbating its entire racist connotation, the above image is exactly the one we are perpetrating. A hell of a price to pay for an "affectionate term."

Langston Hughes once wrote, "I look ahead, and I see my race blossoming like the rose. . . ." But until blacks wake up and realize what an incredibly damaging step backwards using the word nigger really is, that rose is nothing but a dying weed thirsty for self-respect.

Ordinary Words Cause Extraordinary Pain
CLARA STANDING SOLDIER

In this story, Clara Standing Soldier is emotionally overwhelmed and offended when a passerby makes a racial comment about her Native American husband. As a result of this insult, her life is changed forever.

1. Explain what the author means when she compares the images of Native American sports mascots with the "propagandistic caricatures of Jews in Nazi Germany, African Americans during certain eras in United States history and American images of the Japanese during World War II."
2. How does the offensive comment alter the author's life and world view forever?
3. Do you think the passerby meant to be racially insensitive by his remark?

Writing Assignments

1. Have you ever been confronted with a similar situation that has affected your life? Dramatize this situation with a classmate. Write an essay about this experience.

2. View the film *In Whose Honor: American Indian Mascots in Sports* (1997) directed by Jay Rosenstein. Write a report on the pain and humiliation that Native American activist Charlene Teters felt after watching the University of Illinois mascot, Chief Illiniwek, dance in front of thousands of non-American Indian fans. Write about the most memorable moment in the film.

◆

On the morning of March 15, something ordinary happened in St. Louis.

My husband and I got up at 5:30 a.m. to jog on the bike trail in Forest Park along Lindell Boulevard. Cooling down, we walked toward about 10 men and one or two women running in a group. And as we moved off the pavement to make room for the group to pass, we clearly heard one man say to another, "Here comes Chief Illiniwek."

It was an obvious reference to my husband, a tall Native American man with traditional long hair. Chief Illiniwek, of course, is a University of Illinois athletic team mascot whom we'd learned about through an excellent documentary on PBS called *In Whose Honor.*

The part of the film I remember best was Charlene Teters, formerly a graduate student at the University of Illinois, telling of her first encounter with Chief Illiniwek. Teters, a Native American, attended a game and the appearance of Chief Illiniwek at halftime was a complete shock. She described the pain and humiliation she felt as she watched.

On a University of Illinois Web site, I found a wealth of information about Chief Illiniwek. A photo shows the "chief" in buckskin regalia, arms outstretched in a stereotypical gesture. And I found these words: "One of the most dramatic and dignified traditions in college athletics is the performance of Chief Illiniwek. Since 1926, this symbol has stirred pride and respect in audiences."

What if a student dressed up as a priest or a rabbi—or as an African American or an Asian-American—and strutted about "in character" at halftime? Would it be considered "dramatic and dignified?" Would it stir "pride and respect?"

The fact is, mockery and ridicule are not an honor.

On a recent trip to Cleveland I saw images of Chief Wahoo, the mascot of the Cleveland Indians, plastered all over town. I was struck by the similarity of Chief Wahoo to propagandistic caricatures of Jews in Nazi Germany, African-Americans during certain eras in U.S. history and American images of the Japanese during World War II. If the Cleveland baseball team were named the "Negroes" and the mascot were a racist caricature of a slave, people would be shocked and outraged—with good reason.

The comment we heard on the bike trail was offensive because it was racially based. But it was doubly offensive because it equated my dignified, well-educated, professional husband with a mascot we find despicable. It would be like announcing, as an African-American passes on the bike trail, "Here comes Black Sambo."

10   Those ordinary words we heard on the bike trail ruined March 15 for the whole family. My husband and I were crabby to our children, who were then grumpy with their friends. I felt alienated at work and had trouble looking my boss in the eye.

More important, however, is that since March 15 we have not been back to the bike trail. We used to run there every day and we loved the towering trees, the stately homes and the serenity of the park. But now it just brings back bad memories.

This event was ordinary because it's the kind of remark made in passing every day. It was ordinary because apparently the speaker didn't think twice about the words he uttered.

But that simple remark had—and continues to have—extraordinary effects on me and on my family.

The Indian Wars
S. L. Price

"The Indian Wars," written for the readers of *Sports Illustrated*, discusses the slippery issue surrounding the use of Native American names and mascots by high school, college, and professional sports teams: insult or tribute? The results of a survey are very surprising.

1. A recent poll conducted by *Sports Illustrated* shows that the general Native American population does not oppose the use of American Indian nicknames and mascots in sports,

whereas Native American activists consider their use dishonorable and disrespectful to indigenous people. Why do you think there is such a difference of opinion?

2. Explain how using terms such as "savage," "scalpers," and "Redskins" dehumanizes a whole population of people?

3. What are the two sides of the mascot-naming argument? Provide arguments for either continuing or eliminating the use of American Indian nicknames and mascots in sports. Which side is more convincing?

Writing Assignment

1. Write a letter to the officials of a professional sports team that uses Native American nicknames, for example, Atlanta Braves, Chicago Blackhawks, Cleveland Indians, Washington Redskins. Using the evidence from previous readings in this book, argue that the use of such mascots is racist and offensive to Native Americans.

2. As children, did you play cowboys and Indians? Write a paper about childhood games that perpetuate a clash between two cultures.

3. View some old westerns. Compare the language and cultures of the Western frontier and the American Indian. Describe how these films portrayed stereotypes.

4. Many states have enacted legislation to banish the use of racial stereotypes such as American Indians or other ethnic groups as sports mascots, and to eliminate other racially offensive behavior such as the tomahawk chop. Are there sports teams in your state that continue to identify themselves with racial mascots? Write a letter to your legislator arguing that this practice should be abolished.

---- ◆ ----

Solve this word problem: Billy Mills, the former runner who won the gold medal in the 10,000 meters at the 1964 Olympics, is on a commercial airliner hurtling somewhere over the U.S. It is August 2001. Because Mills's father and mother were three-quarters and one-quarter Native American, respectively, he grew up being called half-breed until that was no longer socially acceptable. As sensibilities shifted over the years, he heard a variety of words and phrases describing his ethnic background, from Indian to Sioux to Native American to the one with which he is most comfortable, the age-old name of his tribal nation: Lakota.

Mills is sitting in first class. A flight attendant—the words steward and stewardess are frowned upon today—checks on him every so often. The man is African-American, the preferred designation for his racial background; before that, society called him black or colored or Negro. The man is friendly, doing his job. Each time he addresses Mills, he calls him Chief. Mills doesn't know if the flight attendant realizes that he is Lakota. Maybe he calls everyone Chief. Maybe he means it as a compliment. Mills motions him over.

"I want to tell you something," Mills says. The man leans in. "I'm Native American, and you calling me Chief, it turns my stomach. It'd be very similar to somebody calling you Nigger." The flight attendant looks at Mills. He says, "Calling you Chief doesn't bother me . . . Chief."

Who is right and who is wrong? Whose feelings take precedence? Most important, who gets to decide what we call one another?

5   If you've figured out an answer, don't celebrate yet. The above confrontation is only a warmup for sport's thorniest word problem: the use of Native American names (and mascots that represent them) by high school, college and professional teams. For more than 30 years the debate has been raging over whether names such as Redskins, Braves, Chiefs and Indians honor or defile Native Americans, whether clownish figures like the Cleveland Indians' Chief Wahoo have any place in today's racially sensitive climate and whether the sight of thousands of non-Native Americans doing the tomahawk chop at Atlanta's Turner Field is mindless fun or mass bigotry. It's an argument that, because it mixes mere sports with the sensitivities of a people who were nearly exterminated, seems both trivial and profound—and it's further complicated by the fact that for three out of four Native Americans, even a nickname such as Redskins, which many whites consider racist, isn't objectionable.

Indeed, some Native Americans—even those who purportedly object to Indian team nicknames—wear Washington Redskins paraphernalia with pride. Two such men showed up in late January at Augustana College in Sioux Falls, S. Dak., for a conference on race relations. "They were speaking against the Indian nicknames, but they were wearing Redskins sweatshirts, and one had on a Redskins cap," says Betty Ann Gross, a member of the Sisseton-Wahpeton Sioux tribe. "No one asked them about it. They looked pretty militant."

Gross's own case illustrates how slippery the issue can be. She grew up on a reservation in South Dakota and went to Sisseton High, a public school on the reservation whose teams are called the Redmen. Gross, 49, can't recall a time when people on the reservation weren't arguing about the team name, evenly divided between those who were proud of it and those who were ashamed. Gross recently completed a study that led the South Dakota state government to change the names of 38 places and landmarks around the state, yet she has mixed feelings on the sports issue. She wants Indian mascots and the tomahawk chop discarded, but she has no problem with team names like the Fighting Sioux (University of North Dakota) or even the Redskins. "There's a lot of division," Gross says. "We're confused, and if we're confused, you guys should be really confused."

Indeed, a recent SI poll . . . suggests that although Native American activists are virtually united in opposition to the use of Indian nicknames and mascots, the Native American population sees the issue far differently. Asked if high school and college teams should stop using Indian nicknames, 81% of Native American respondents said no. As for pro sports, 83% of Native American respondents said teams should not stop using Indian nicknames, mascots, characters and symbols. Opinion is far more divided on reservations, yet a majority (67%) there said the usage by pro teams should not cease, while 32% said it should.

"I take the middle ground," says Leigh J. Kuwanwisiwma, 51, director of the Hopi Cultural Preservation Office in Kykotsmovi, Ariz., and an avid devotee of the Atlanta Braves. "I don't see anything wrong with Indian nicknames as long as they're not meant to be derogatory. Some tribal schools on Arizona reservations use Indians as a nickname themselves. The Phoenix Indian High School's newspaper is The Redskin. I don't mind the tomahawk chop. It's all in good fun. This is sports, after all. In my living room, I'll be watching a Braves game and occasionally do the chop."

Native American activists dismiss such opinion as misguided   10 ("There are happy campers on every plantation," says Suzan Harjo, president of the Morning Star Institute, an Indian-rights organization based in Washington, D.C.) or as evidence that Native Americans' self-esteem has fallen so low that they don't even know when they're being insulted. American Indians—unlike, say, the Irish Catholics who founded Notre Dame and named its teams the Fighting Irish—had no hand in creating most of the teams that use their names, their identities were plucked from them wholesale and used for frivolous purposes, like firing up fans at ball games.

"This is no honor," says Michael Yellow Bird, an associate professor of social work at Arizona State. "We lost our land, we lost our languages, we lost our children. Proportionately speaking, indigenous peoples [in the U.S.] are incarcerated more than any other group, we have more racial violence perpetrated upon us, and we are forgotten. If people think this is how to honor us, then colonization has really taken hold."

Regardless, the campaign to erase Indian team names and symbols nationwide has been a success. Though Native American activists have made little progress at the highest level of pro sports—officials of the Atlanta Braves, Chicago Blackhawks, Cleveland Indians and Washington Redskins, for example, say they have no intention of changing their teams' names or mascots—their single-minded pursuit of the issue has literally changed the face of sports in the U.S. Since 1969, when Oklahoma disavowed its mascot Little Red (a student wearing an Indian war bonnet, buckskin costume and moccasins), more than 600 school teams and minor league professional clubs have dropped nicknames deemed offensive by Native American groups.

What's more, the movement continues. On Jan. 9 the Metropolitan Washington Council of Governments, which represents 17 local governments in D.C., southern Maryland and northern Virginia, voted 11-2 to adopt a resolution calling the Redskins name "demeaning and dehumanizing" and asking team owner Dan Snyder to change it by next season. A week earlier former Redskins fullback Dale Atkeson had been told by the California Department of Motor Vehicles to remove his vanity plates reading 1 REDSKN. The word Redskin was banned on plates by the DMV in 1999.

"We consider ourselves racially sensitive," says D.C. council member Carol Schwartz, who introduced the resolution against the Redskins, "yet in this one area we are so hypocritical. Since when is a sports team's name more important than the sensitivities of our fellow human beings? For decades we had the Washington Bullets, and [owner] Abe Pollin on his own changed the name [in 1997, because of the high murder rate in D.C.]. Guess what? The world did not stop spinning. Why we would keep this racist term is beyond me."

15   While those who support names such as Seminoles (Florida State) and Braves can argue that the words celebrate Native American traditions, applying that claim to the Redskins is absurd. Nevertheless, Redskins vice president Karl Swanson says the name "symbolizes courage, dignity and leadership and has al-

ways been employed in that manner"—conveniently ignoring the fact that in popular usage dating back four centuries, the word has been a slur based on skin color. Swanson trots out research that traces the term redskin to Native Americans' custom of daubing on red paint before battle. Many experts on Native American history point out that the red paint was used not for war but for burial, and that the word redskin was first used by whites who paid and received bounties for dead Indians. "If you research the origin of redskin, no one would want that associated with his team," says pro golfer Notah Begay III, who is half Navajo and half Pueblo. "Trading-post owners used to offer rewards for Indian scalps. Signs would say something like, 'Redskin scalps, worth so much.' "

However, what's most important, Swanson counters, is intent: Because the Redskins and their fans mean nothing racist by using the nickname, it isn't racist or offensive. "This has been the name of our organization for 70 years," Swanson says. "We believe it has taken on a meaning independent of the word itself—and it's positive."

Not so, says Harjo: "There's no more derogatory word that's used against us, about us, in the English language. Even if it didn't have such heinous origins, everyone knows that it has never been an honorific. It's a terrible insult."

Harjo is not alone in her thinking. A slew of dictionaries agree that redskin is contemptuous, and so do Native American academics, nearly every Native American organization and three judges on the U.S. Trademark Trial and Appeal Board. In April 1999, responding to a lawsuit brought by Harjo and six other Indian leaders, the board stripped the Washington Redskins of federal protection on their seven trademarks. If the decision stands up under appeal, the team and the NFL could lose an estimated $5 million annually on sales of licensed merchandise.

Even though no team name is under more sustained attack, there's evidence that for the Redskins, a name change would be good for business. In 1996, after much pressure from alumni threatening to withdraw their financial support, Miami (Ohio) University acceded to the Miami tribe's request that it change its team names from Redskins to Redhawks. The following year alumni gave a record $25 million to the school. "Someday it will change," Miami spokesman Richard Little says of the Washington Redskins name. "And you know what? There'll still be a football team there, and there'll still be those ugly fat guys in dresses cheering for it."

20   Swanson says the vast majority of Redskins fans like the name, and indeed, beyond the protests of politicians, there's no groundswell of outrage against it in D.C. In a city so racially sensitive that an aide to mayor Anthony Williams was forced to resign in 1999 for correctly using the nonracial term niggardly, there's nothing hotter than the mass pilgrimage of 80,000 fans to Landover, Md., on Sundays in autumn to sing Hail to the Redskins at FedEx Field. Williams mentioned changing the name at a press conference once, but "no one really paid attention," says his aide Tony Bullock. "It's not something that anyone is really talking about." Nevertheless, Bullock says, "the mayor believes it is time to change the name."

     That the name is offensive to Native Americans is easy for non-Natives to presume. It resonates when an Olympic hero and former Marine Corps captain such as Mills, who speaks out against Indian names and mascots at schools around the country, insists that a team named Redskins in the capital of the nation that committed genocide against Native Americans is the equivalent of a soccer team in Germany being called the Berlin Kikes. Says Mills, "Our truth is, redskin is tied to the murder of indigenous people."

     Somehow that message is lost on most of Mills's fellow Native Americans. Asked if they were offended by the name Redskins, 75% of Native American respondents in SI's poll said they were not, and even on reservations, where Native American culture and influence are perhaps felt most intensely, 62% said they weren't offended. Overall, 69% of Native American respondents—and 57% of those living on reservations—feel it's O.K. for the Washington Redskins to continue using the name. "I like the name Redskins," says Mark Timentwa, 50, a member of the Colville Confederated Tribes in Washington State who lives on the tribes' reservation. "A few elders find it offensive, but my mother loves the Redskins."

     Only 29% of Native Americans, and 40% living on reservations, thought Snyder should change his team's name. Such indifference implies a near total disconnect between Native American activists and the general Native American population on this issue. "To a lot of the younger folks the name Redskins is tied to the football team, and it doesn't represent anything more than the team," says Roland McCook, a member of the tribal council of the Ute tribe in Fort Duchesne, Utah.

     The Utes' experience with the University of Utah might serve as a model for successful resolution of conflicts over Indian nick-

Permission given by Native Americans.

names. Four years ago the council met with university officials, who made it clear that they would change their teams' name, the Running Utes, if the tribe found it objectionable. (The university had retired its cartoonish Indian mascot years before.) The council was perfectly happy to have the Ute name continue to circulate in the nation's sports pages, but council members said they intended to keep a close eye on its use. "We came away with an understanding that as long as the university used the Ute name in a positive manner that preserved the integrity of the Ute tribe, we would allow the use of the name and the Ute logo [two eagle feathers and a drum]," says McCook. Florida State, likewise, uses the name Seminoles for its teams with the express approval of the Seminole nation.

*Doesn't
It already
degrade
their
integrity*

Like the Ute tribe, most Native Americans have no problem 25 with teams using names like Indians and Fighting Illini—or even imposed names like Sioux. "People get upset about the Fighting Sioux, but why?" Gross says. "We're not Sioux people, anyway. The French and the Ojibway tribe gave us that name, and they're our hereditary enemies. We're not braves, and we're not really Indians. I know the history. For me those names are not a problem." Many Native Americans are offended, however, by mascots such as Illinois's Chief Illiniwek and others that dress up in feathers and so-called war paint. "Just do away with the imagery—the dancing, the pageantry," says Gross.

Which brings us to the point at which the word problem becomes a number problem. Say you are a team owner. You kiss Chief Wahoo goodbye. Stop the chop. Dump the fake Indian garb, the turkey feathers and the war paint. Get rid of, say, the Redskins name because it's got a sullied history and just sounds wrong. Rename the team the Washington Warriors—without the Indianhead logo—and watch the new team hats and jackets hit the stores. Money is going to pour in, you see, and someone will have to count it.

Heard Any Good Jews Lately?

Thomas Friedmann

When the persecution of the Jews began in Nazi Germany, they were described as a lower species of life; they were called "parasites" and "cholera germs." Emphasizing Haig A. Bosmajian's words, "This metaphoric language was essential for dehumanizing the 'enemy.'" Thomas Friedmann examines how Jews have suffered from linguistic discrimination to the extent that this manipulation of language helped to justify the "final solution."

1. What words have been used throughout history to relegate Jews to subhuman status?
2. The author lists a number of English words related to "Jew" and Yiddish expressions that have pejorative connotations. Can you think of other anti-Semitic insults that are in use today?
3. What message about the nature of Jews does the use of such anti-Semitic language send?
4. What lesson do you think the author wants to teach the reader?

Writing Assignments

1. Jews are not the only social group that is the object of ridicule in jokes. Consider other jokes that target blondes, Poles, and other groups. Write a paper about the stereotyping of certain groups in humor.
2. It has been argued that Hollywood does not fairly represent minority ethnic groups on the screen. Do you think it is the responsibility of Hollywood to include more positive images of ethnic minorities?

———————— ◆ ————————

The horrors of mass murder can be made bearable if the intended victim is made to appear an object that deserves extermination. The Nazis understood this. Thus, while their bureaucrats searched for the means by which the wholesale destruction of Europe's Jews could be carried out, their propagandists primed the populace to accept psychologically the annihilation of those Jews. In their manipulation of language to justify the "Final Solution," the Nazis resorted to terminology that had been utilized earlier to render Jews subhuman. Martin Luther, urging the expulsion of Jews, had written about them as "a plague and a pestilence." In 1895, three and a half centuries after Luther, a deputy in the German *Reichstag* made clear that Luther's characterization had not been forgotten.

He described Jews as "parasites" and "cholera germs." Hitler's propagandists preserved the tradition. They continued to disseminate the notion that Jews were a lower species of life, designating them "vermin," "lice," and "bacilli."

Then, in an act that might be considered almost poetic were it not so horrifying and grotesque, the Nazi administrative apparatus captured the spirit of the metaphor its propagandists had devised. It contacted the chemical industries of the *Reich*, specifically the firms that specialized in "combating vermin." Simply, it requested that these manufacturers of insecticides produce another delousing agent, one a bit stronger than the product used for household ticks and flies, but one that would be used for essentially the same purpose. The companies complied. Thus was *Zyklon B* created. The gas, used in a milder form for occasionally fumigating the disease-ridden barracks where other victims were penned, killed millions of men, women, and children. Obscenely clinging to the metaphor they had accepted, the Nazis herded their Jewish victims into gas chambers of death that were disguised as "showers" and "disinfectant centers."

What the bureaucrats accomplished, the propagandists had made psychologically possible. How could anyone object when, with the whiff of invisible gas from the crackling blue crystals of *Zyklon B*, millions of Jews were exterminated? Is not extermination the deserved fate of all vermin?

But that was Nazi Germany, people tend to say. The mass murder of so many people was an aberration, an accident of history. That artificial, created language that made it possible for participants to accept the horror of the Holocaust would not have the power again. Surely, that manufactured imagery, that inhuman metaphor, no matter how traditional, can never again conceal that these are Jews that are being threatened, not subhuman creatures. Call them by their name—Jew—and you could never forget that they are people. Certainly the name is an affirmation. *Jew*, by way of Middle English *Giu*, Old French *juiu*, Latin *Judäeus*, and Hebrew *Yehudi*, derives from Judah, the foremost of the Twelve Tribes of Israel. Its name means "praised," its emblem is the lion, it has borne a line of kings. Surely the name itself can withstand the ravages of prejudice!

But the King's English has not retained the proud heritage of the name. Eric Partridge, in *A Dictionary of Slang and Unconventional English*, lists *Jew* as a verb meaning "to drive a hard bargain," or "to overreach or cheat." In addition, *Jew* as prefix yields to *Jew-*

down, meaning to haggle unfairly, *Jew-bail,* meaning "worthless bail," *Jew-balance,* a name for the hammerhead shark, *Jew-food,* mockingly ham, the food forbidden to Jews, *Jew's harp,* whose French origin has nothing to do with Jews but whose sound was picked up by English dramatists to mean Jew and hence an instrument of lesser value, and finally, two astounding phrases, *worth a Jew's eye* and *a Jüdische compliment* or *a Jew's compliment.* As with the slur *sheeny,* which is probably a perversion of the flattering *shaine* (Yiddish) or *schön* (German), meaning "beautiful," both of these apparent phrases of flattery are, in fact, derogatory. To receive *a Jew's compliment* is apparently to be blessed with the misfortune of having "a large penis but little money." The great worth of *a Jew's eye* exists because that was the organ removed when a Jew failed to pay his levy or tax. Another source suggests that it was the teeth that would be threatened with removal. Because Jews invariably paid up, the expression became popular, as in, "If a Jew is willing to pay that much for his teeth, imagine the worth of a Jew's eye."

Jew also figures in the acronym JAP, applied to certain young women. A JAP, Jewish American Princess, is meant to describe a pampered, snobbish, money-conscious female who is princess in her parents' household. *Jew* is also a pejorative when used in *Jewess.* Why is there no *Protestantess?* Feminists find it doubly offensive, since the *-ess* generally reduces the worth of the noun, as in *poetess.* And, when accounting is dubbed *Jewish engineering,* a cash register a *Jewish piano,* and a dollar bill the *Jewish flag,* the term *Jew* is unmistakably being used as an insult. One thinks of the Greeks for whom anyone not Greek was a foreigner and hence primitive and uncivilized, a barbarian. Imagine the Jew whose very name is a negative term. Naming himself, he excludes himself from mankind.

Only the use of *Indian* comes to mind in this context. As *Jew. Indian* is often found as a damning prefix in such compounds as *Indian-cholera, Indian giver,* and *Indian tobacco,* this last the name given to a poisonous North American plant. And while the negative use of *Indian* is at least partially mitigated by positive *(Indian summer)* and neutral uses (Indian pipe, Indian bread), no balance exists for *Jew.*

Given the derision attached to *Jew* itself, one can imagine the multiplied power of the slur in the slang versions of *Jew: Jew-boy, geese, kike, mockie,* and *sheeny. Sheeny,* incidentally, is thought by some sources to have come from "shiny," a comment on the brilliantined hair of many young British Jews. The coinage of *kike,* the most familiar of these slurs, is attributed by some writers, rather gleefully perhaps and without documentation, to Jews. According to Ernest Von Den Haag, German Jewish immigrants, the earlier arrivals to the United States, were the ones who formulated *kike* to identify their Eastern-European brethren, whom they considered their inferiors. The term is thought to have been derived from *-ki* or *-ky,* the final syllable of many Polish and Russian names. More plausible seems Leo Rosten's suggestion that *kike* comes from "kikel," the Yiddish word for circle. This was the mark with which Jewish immigrants would sign their names when they could not write, preferring it to the commonly used *X* which they thought resembled a cross. Whatever the origin of the term, there is no question that it is a pejorative. At Queen Victoria's court Prime Minister Disraeli wryly defined the name. "A kike," he said, "is a Jewish gentleman who has just left the room."

In addition to these opprobations, American English has accepted a great many Yiddish words which are used as insults. A partial list would include: *gonif* (thief), *gunsel* (catamite), *dreck* (feces, junk), *kibbitzer* (irritating bystander), and a host of *sch* words: *schnook, schmuck, schlep, schlock, schmaltzy, schlemiel, schlamazel, schwantz, schnorrer,* and possibly *shyster* (by way of *schiess*—shit). While such easy adoption of foreign words might be considered a sign of the pluralistic nature of the English language and a source of its astonishing variety, the terms cannot help but remind users of their source. Were they not, after all, insults applied by Jews to other Jews in their own tongue?

A few words, finally, about Jewish jokes or more precisely, jokes about Jews. One of the more bizarre aspects of Nazi propaganda was its utilization of toys, games, and jokes. German children played with "Jews Get Out," a board game produced by Fabricus Co., and their elders had the opportunity to laugh at caricatures of Jews. A typical one shows a hooknosed Jew in the form of a snake, being crushed under the boot of a National Social German Workers' Party (Nazi) member. Other cartoons, particularly political appeals, contained messages about the acquisitive nature of Jews, and hence, their exploitation of Germans. Below is an update indicating that jokes with a similar message have been reinvented in this country. Note that each of the jokes reproduced below is American, containing either an American locale or an American idiom. These are "Made in USA," not imported and translated.

QUESTION:	How was the Grand Canyon formed?
ANSWER:	A Jew lost a nickel in a crack.
QUESTION:	Why do Jews have big noses?
ANSWER:	Air is free.
QUESTION:	Why are few Jews in jail?
ANSWER:	Crime doesn't pay.

The message in each case is clear. What is the basic nature of Jews? They are money-hungry creatures with no moral restraints who will go to great lengths for financial gain. Just jokes, right? Professor Harvey Mindess, who organized the International Conference on Humor at Antioch College, suggested that jokes are good, that laughter "lets out a little of the devil inside all of us." What about the great big devil jokes let in, allowing people to make subtle distinctions between "them" and "us," using laughter as the great divider? Jokes about Jews, about any ethnic group, communicate negative stereotypes that become just a little bit more credible with each telling.

A rather self-deprecating joke Israelis tell about themselves points out the increasingly secular nature of their country. The anecdote is about the immigrant Israeli mother who wanted her son to learn Yiddish so he would remember that he was Jewish. But the typical news commentator fails to see the distinction the joke makes. Israel is inevitably "the Jewish State," her neighbors "Arab countries." Why not "Moslem countries"? Why not the "Hebrew State"?

And it is similarly good for a laugh when the Mary Tyler Moore character in the film *Ordinary People* responds with a raised eyebrow and an unhappy face upon being informed that her son is not only seeing a psychiatrist but that this psychiatrist is named *Berger*. One of *those* people, of course. Even when they change their names, thanks to Archie Bunker their secret identities as Jews can be penetrated. It's all in the first name, Archie has explained. "They" may be named Smith or Jones, but one knows who they really are when their first names are Moe, and Iz, and Ben, unmistakably Jewish first names, right, Abe Lincoln? Oh yes, those Jewish lawyers, they're not always such smart Ginsbergs!

Personally, Archie, I have suffered from reverse discrimination. To this day, it is my first name that draws questions from Jew and Gentile alike. "Tom? What kind of a name is that for a Jewish boy?" And the little jokes go on with their work. Like maggots and earthworms they grind the ground in the quiet, preparing the soil for another little seed of prejudice.

Term Limits: Hispanic? Latino? A National Debate Proves No One Name Pleases Everyone
Mark McDonald

The debate over racial and ethnic terminology continues, especially among the members of one particular ethnic population. In "Term Limits" Mark McDonald asks what we should call the fastest-growing ethnic group in the United States. Hispanic? Latino? Chicano? Mexican American? The 29 million people of the United States can't seem to agree on one single term, arguing that there are many factors that differentiate them.

1. What are the arguments for and against the use of *Hispanic, Latino, Chicano,* and *Mexican American*? How does each term differ?
2. Why do you think ethnic terms differ regionally across the United States?

Writing Assignment

1. One argument against the label "Hispanic" is that it obscures the diversity among people who come from many countries and whose ancestry differs. It is estimated that approximately seventeen major Hispanic/Latino subcultures in the United States can be identified. Research the population shift of this group and explain how ethnologists determine each subculture.
2. Do you believe that changing the language is the key to changing attitudes? If dictionaries remove the word "jew" or "nigger" or "spic" from the English language, then do you think that we would see less anti-Semitic and racial violence and aggression?

———————— ◆ ————————

Use Domingo Garcia as the appropriate metaphor.

"When I was a kid growing up I was 'Spanish-surnamed,'" says the Dallas City Council member.

"Then I was Latin-American, then Chicano, then Mexican-American, then Hispanic.

"And now," he says, "I'm Latino."

15   Such has been the progression of the debate, a debate still percolating, over the collective, politically correct term for more than 22 million people in the United States.

Are they Hispanic? Or are they Latino?

And should one-fourth of the people in Texas be called Chicanos? Or is Mexican-American the better term?

The debate can get complicated, but one thing is clear: In the 1990 census, 22.4 million people said they were of "Spanish/Hispanic origin." What to call them—as a group—has intrigued and exasperated any number of academics, activists, demographers, linguists and historians.

Although Hispanic was used in the '90 census, not everyone whom the government considered to be part of this amorphous group spoke Spanish. Nor did they all have Spanish surnames.

10   The word *Hispanic* was chosen by default. "It really came right out of the dictionary," says one census official.

The word doesn't please everyone, of course, and it doesn't even exist in the Spanish language. Further, it conjures up images of colonial domination by Spain and Portugal while denying the people's Indian and African heritages.

"Latino" is gaining currency as an umbrella term, especially on the East and West coasts, although some still find it too limiting.

"The word Hispanic got its play among the middle class, but it's really a relic of the Reagan era," says Mr. Garcia. "Latino is more inclusive now. I use it when I speak in national terms, and you hear Henry Cisneros using Latino now.

"In reference to Americans of Mexican descent, I prefer Chicano. Locally, I say 'Chicano community,' or '*Mejicano*.'"

15   The word *Chicano* apparently comes from the shortening of a colloquial pronunciation of "Mexicano," in which the first syllable sounds like "Metch."

In modern usage, "Chicano" has come to mean American citizens or residents with Mexican heritage. It has been most widely used in California and Texas, although some Mexican-

Americans, especially the elderly, still find the word crude and offensive.

"Chicano" also has political connotations left over from the '60s, when it was the term of choice among left-wing activists.

"Chicano has always been the most predominant word here, especially in the barrios," says Mr. Garcia. "Go to a high school or into the community—especially among those 35 and older, the word is Chicano. Or among the older crowd, Mejicano."

So the debate goes—locally, nationally, politically, academically—and the opinions can be as challenging as they are diverse.

"PROCESSED MILK"

Although Martha Cotera publishes the *Austin Hispanic Directory*,   20
she doesn't care too much for the adjective.

"*Hispanic* is a generic term that doesn't express a national heritage or any ethnic pride," she says. "It tends to homogenize us, like processed milk. It's sanitized. It only acknowledges our European roots and denies our Indian roots. A more apt term might be *Indo-Hispanic*.

"I don't know where this argument for *Latino* comes from. It's false, especially for Texans. The word goes back to the Latin conquest of Spain and Portugal. It is so remotely connected to us.

"*Hispanic* blends us into mush. And *Latino*—it's such an old term—just makes us into an *older* mush.

"Neither *Latino* nor *Hispanic* are satisfactory terms, although I might use them publicly. I always use *Mexican-American* in official documents. There is very seldom the choice of *Chicano*, but my gut reaction would be to mark *Chicana* if they had it.

"In Texas we're very practical. *Latino, Chicano, Hispanic*—we   25
don't give a damn what we're called, just as long as we're doing okay."

GEOPOLITICS

The National Council of La Raza uses "Hispanic" and "Latino" interchangeably. "It's a very fluid situation," says Lisa Navarrete, an NCLR spokesperson. "It depends a lot on where you are."

"Latino hasn't caught on in Texas, but it's the preferred term in Chicago, New York and California. It's a bad thing to say 'Hispanic' in California.

"The exception (to Latino) is the Southwest and Florida. The Cuban-American community feels less connection with national Hispanic groups. They see themselves as an exile community, and they have more tenuous ties.

"We deal so much with census data we use 'Hispanic' a lot. But the direction seems to be toward 'Latino.' It's the more progressive movement. We don't trash people who use one or the other. It's clearly something people are thinking about."

"SLAVE NAME"

30 Sandra Cisneros, 38, is the author of *Woman Hollering Creek, The House on Mango Street* and *My Wicked, Wicked Ways.* She grew up in a Mexican-American family in Chicago, now owns a home in San Antonio and has described herself as "a Chicana feminist."

Ms. Cisneros, no relation to the former San Antonio mayor, does not allow her work to be included in anthologies or collections that use the word *Hispanic,* a term she says is "a repulsive slave name." "'Hispanic' is English for a person of Latino origin who wants to be accepted by the white status quo," she said recently in an interview in *The New York Times.*

"*Latino* is the word we have always used for ourselves. . . . To say 'Latino' is to say you come to my culture in a manner of respect."

↳ how is this different?

"BENITO JUAREZ FACES"

Guillermo Galindo is a Spanish-English interpreter, a longtime political activist and a member of the Dallas Park Board.

"To most gringos, I'll say I'm Chicano. If it's a Mexican-American, maybe an older person or conservative, I'll say I'm Mexican-American. It's more comfortable for them.

35 "*Hispanic* is a term that identifies us with Spain. But up until the last century, Spain and Portugal were two of the most backward countries in the world. Nothing in the entire history of Spain makes me proud. Why would I want to claim or belong to a country that created the Inquisition?

"Some people say, 'The Spanish gave us culture and language.' They didn't give us anything. They *imposed* it on us.

"As Mexicans we are a conquered people. I speak a conquered language. As Roman Catholics we practice a conquered religion. We have an imposed culture.

"And Latinos—they all want to be descended from the motherland, from Spain. If you call yourself Latino, you're trying to escape from the existential reality as to what you really are.

"Mexican-Americans are always denying our Indian heritage. You can have 20 Mexican-Americans sitting around talking about 'Hispanics' and they all have these Indian Benito Juarez faces. It's a joke."

NUANCE AND INSULT

Author Earl Shorris titled his new book *Latinos: A Biography of* 40
the People. "To many Latinos, drawing the distinctions among the nationalities constitutes a kind of game, like a quiz program," he writes. "Everyone has a theory about everyone else. Some are amusing, all are accurate, and every nuance is important."

Mr. Shorris grew up in El Paso, became a novelist, and for the last 20 years has been a contributing editor at *Harper's* magazine.

Laborers and the very poor in Mexico were known as Chicanos, he says, and although the word was derogatory, "it was the mildest of insults."

"Nevertheless, many older people continue to be appalled at the use of the term. . . . The Chicano generation began in the late 1960s and lasted about six or eight years. Some people call themselves Chicanos but the definition is vague and the word has lost its fire."

"DISTINCT POPULATIONS"

Dr. Rodolfo de la Garza had some ideas about what he and his colleagues might find in their now widely quoted Latino National Political Survey. Not all those ideas worked out, however.

"One thing that was surprising to us: We thought 'Latino' was 45
more popular. It's absolutely not. More people call themselves American than Latino.

"People don't come here with a Latino identity," says Dr. de la Garza, the Mike Hogg professor of community affairs at the University of Texas. "They come as Bolivians, Venezuelans, Colombians. They might *become* Latino or Hispanic in the United States, but they don't have that sort of identity when they arrive."

The survey also showed a sort of hierarchy of terms that people prefer when describing themselves.

"The first labels are national origin, such as 'Mexican' or 'Mexican-American,' 'Puerto Rican' or 'Cuban.' Then depending on the national origin, people prefer pan-ethnic terms such as *Hispanic, Latino, Spanish,* or *Hispano.* Then comes the nonethnic label which is American."

Dr. de la Garza knows well the objections to Hispanic. "Some say that Hispanic eliminates the indigenous people and I used to make that left-wing radical position myself. I used to participate in this debate on the side of Latino. No more. *Mea culpa.* I've gone back to being Mexican."

Can You Talk Mexican?
AMITA VASUDEVA

In the poem "Can You Talk Mexican," Amita Vasudeva, a self-proclaimed American Born Confused Desi or ABCD, illustrates the ethnocentrism of the United States' culture.

1. What is the point of the poem?
2. What stereotypes do people from the United States harbor about Mexicans, American Indians, and South Asian Indians?
3. Many times we hear people say, "I talk American." What does that mean? Can you talk Mexican or Indian?

Writing Assignments

1. Recently, a controversy arose concerning designer Abercrombie and Fitch T-shirts featuring caricatured faces of Asians. Abercrombie and Fitch argued that the T-shirts are designed to appeal to young Asian shoppers with a sense of humor. However, many Asian groups have protested the T-shirt,

claiming that it depicts old stereotypes and trivializes the tradition, religion, and philosophy of Asian cultures and have demanded an apology from Abercrombie and Fitch. Write an essay addressing this issue.

2. Examine how Asians and Asian Americans are represented in the media around you. Bring to class television clips, movies, musical lyrics, magazine articles, advertisements, and information from Internet Web sites. Discuss and write about the different images of Asians and Asian Americans.

———————— ✦ ————————

"Can you talk Mexican?"
        They used to ask me.
"No, I'm not Mexican I'm Indian, and besides they speak
   Spanish,"
        I used to reply, waiting listlessly for their best
        attempt at doing a "raindance."
"Owwow ooh ow ow." Smacking outstretched palms to their   5
   little mouths and hopping around.
"Not THAT kind of Indian—Indian from India,"
        I would correct, as soon as they finished whooping.
"Oh . . . Can you talk Indian?"

Subcontinental Drift: The Mind of a Racist

Aparisim Ghosh

In this humorous and thought-provoking essay, *Time* Senior Editor Aparisim Ghosh meets a real-life racist at lunch. Mistaking Ghosh for a Muslim and an Arab, the racist accuses Ghosh of practicing a "medieval" religion, among other things.

1. How did Ghosh's image of a racist differ from the real-life racist he met in a London café?
2. List all the racially insensitive comments the "racist" makes to Ghosh. What makes these comments offensive?

3. Why was it insulting to Ghosh when the racist requested to be addressed as "Sir"?

Writing Assignments

1. Describe a time when you confronted someone who clearly showed him or herself to be a bigot. What did you do or regret not doing?
2. When you picture a racist, what do you see? Write a paper describing this image.
3. How does Ghosh "play along" with the racist? Have you ever played along with someone who has made assumptions about you, just as Ghosh does with the real-life racist? With a partner, dramatize such an interaction, then write about this experience.
4. Research the legal definition of "hate crime." What constitutes a hate crime? Do you think that the legal definition is too broad or too narrow?

————————— ✦ —————————

When called upon to picture a racist, my mind usually runs to the stereotype: I envision a big, ugly brute in a Leeds United T-shirt, smelling of lager and sweat, spewing obscenities from a mouthful of rotting teeth as he advances towards me with harmful intent. The scene is so familiar, played out ad nauseum in Hollywood potboilers and in my imagination, it's no longer scary. It's also, I discovered yesterday, no preparation for the real thing.

I met my first real-life racist at lunchtime in a central London café. He was wearing a dark blue suit and a fawn felt overcoat, crisp white shirt and a brick-red tie. He was a small, wiry figure, with a wide forehead, thinning blond hair and grey eyes behind rimless glasses. He was well-spoken, uttered not a single obscenity and had good teeth. And he didn't raise a hand towards me in anger. He sat down on the stool next to me, balancing his lunch tray on his lap. My sandwich, salad and soft drink were taking up most of the space on the table, so I mumbled an apology and made room for his tray. "Well, Ramadan's obviously over," he said, abruptly.

"Sorry?"

"Ramadan," he said, pointing his chin towards my multiple plates. "It's over, isn't it?"

"Looks like it," was the best I could do.   5

"You people eat so much the rest of the year," he continued, "it's a wonder you can skip lunch for an entire month."

This was getting odder and odder. And his tone—it had initially seemed jokey, but now sounded harsh and snide—was even more puzzling. He was looking at me, expecting a reply. Nonplussed, I could only shrug.

"So what happens during the rest of the year, do you pray only four times a day to make time for lunch?"

The penny dropped: he had taken me for an Muslim. I might have corrected him at this point, but my mouth was full. By the time I'd finished swallowing, I was not sure I wanted to continue a conversation. We ate quietly for a while, before he spoke up again.

"It must be a hard time to be an Arab in the West." he said.   10
(No surprise there: I've been mistaken for an Arab before.) "After Sept. 11, it must be quite frightening for you."

I decided to play along: it would be easy enough. I didn't feel in any danger. It was a very public place, and he didn't look the violent sort. Besides, I was twice as big as he.

"I don't feel frightened," I said.

"Oh, come on!" he said, jerking his head away in disbelief, then looking at me again with the smile of a mischievous boy. "The whole world is coming after you and you have no friends anywhere. And you know, you've been asking for it, for a long, long time."

His directness was so surprising, it took me a while to come back. "Why do you say that?" I asked.

"Look," he said, now taking on a conciliatory tone, "for all I   15
know, you're a perfectly nice fellow. You were probably educated in this country, and you are Westernized. But your religion. . . ." He shook his head.

"What about it?" I asked.

"Well, it's savage and medieval and . . . savage," he said. "It's not polite to say these things these days, but they need to be said. And after what happened in America, it can't be hidden any longer."

"Why is it savage?"

"It's full of hate, isn't it? It teaches your people to be hostile, towards us, towards anybody who disagrees with you. And women, too, your own women." He then favored me with his thesis on Islam. Muslims, in his view, allowed their clergy ("the Imams," he called them) to run their lives. They—we—were brainwashed to be unquestioning and unthinking, to aspire to a medieval way of life. He liked the word "medieval," and used it re-peatedly. Islam, he added, had failed to "snap out of its medieval trance and recognize that the world has moved on."

20 He spoke in a quiet voice that would have been polite if it hadn't been so filled with hatred. The words came in short bursts, and he frequently ran out of breath midway through sentences. I wondered if this was his normal speech, a function of small lungs—or was his throat so compressed with hate that it was somehow constricting his oxygen supply. Despite his low tone, he was obviously deeply angry, at me, at all Arabs. Maybe this rage had come from something that had happened to him recently, some specific event, like the loss of a job or a contract (or a wife?) to an Arab. Or did he carry his loathing with him all the time, coiled up in his gut like a wounded rattlesnake, ready to lash out at anybody. I wanted to ask, but didn't know how.

"You seem to have done some reading on Islam," I said.

"A lot more than you think," he replied. "I've read a lot of religious books." He looked pleased with himself, rather like a debater who had just scored a point. "And I have been to your countries."

I noted the plural. "Which ones?"

"Lots of them. Dubai, and others. I used to be in oil."

25 "What did you think of Dubai?" I asked, almost reflexively. "Quite nice, isn't it?"

"I suppose so. But that's because of the Americans, isn't it? It's ironic. The Americans and the British helped you build your countries—or God knows what you'd have done with that oil. And still your lot hate us. Come on, surely you can see there's something wrong with the religion if it makes you hate the people who helped you? I mean, you look like an educated man. You can see how your religion has no place in the 20th century, can't you?"

"The 21st century. . ." Immediately, I regretted saying it.

"Oh alright, you've got me there," he said impatiently, as if to an impudent child. "But I'm right about the rest, aren't I? It's not polite to say these things nowadays," he repeated this phrase two more times, like he was setting up the taboo before smashing it. "But it's got to be said: in the 21st century," he paused and mock-bowed to me, "some religions are just too far behind the modern world."

I didn't much feel like clashing theological swords with him, and anyway I can't claim to be an expert on Islam. I tried to change the subject. He said he had worked in oil. I asked him what he did. "I work near here," he said, flicking a wrist in the direction of the Strand outside. I felt he was not really being eva-sive, he just didn't think it worth his while to tell me about himself. "Where do you work?" he asked, instead.

"I work for *Time* Magazine," I said. I wondered if he would be mortified at the thought of talking so openly with a journalist. But he simply didn't believe me.

"No, really, what do you do?" 30

"I work for *Time* Magazine."

"I don't believe you." His tone was not hostile or condescending, but strangely patient and paternalistic; my father used to talk to me that way when he knew I was lying about something and wanted to coax the truth out of me.

I gave him my business card. He looked at it carefully, then exclaimed, with some satisfaction: "It says Time Asia. That's not the real *Time* Magazine."

"It's the Asian edition," I said.

"No it's not; you're just using the Time name to give your 35 magazine some credibility, aren't you?"

"Why is it hard for you to believe that I work for the real *Time* Magazine?" I asked, exasperated.

"Well, they're American, aren't they? They'd never hire you. Not after Sept. 11." This was getting so absurd, I let it drop. He looked at my card again. "What do your parents feel about your using a Christian name?" (My nickname, Bobby, is supplied on the card, for the benefit of those who find Aparisim hard to pronounce.)

"They game me the nickname," I said.

"Oooh, that must have gone down well with the Imam," he said.

The sarcasm was clearly intended to get a rise out of me. I let 40 the bait dangle for a few moments as we chewed on our lunches. Then I asked for his name. "You can call me Sir."

Again, this was so directly offensive, I had to pause before responding. "That's not fair," I said, lamely. "After all, you know my name."

"You can call me Sir," he said again, with that small boy's smile.

I didn't know where to take the conversation next. We continued eating in silence, until he had finished his sandwich. As he got up to leave, he said, suddenly and surprisingly: "Have a nice day." No smile this time, just a quick nod of the head. My mouth full of food, I was only able to grunt back at him before he strode out.

Then, as I watched the fawn felt overcoat merge into the crowd of pedestrians outside the café, I felt a rage rise in me. I was angry at myself, and ashamed. Throughout our conversation, I had not once challenged this man, not told him to his face that he was a racist nut and that his notions about Arabs and Muslims were all warped and ugly and wrong. As a journalist, I'm so used to holding my own opinions while seeking out those of others that I sometimes let nonsense go unchallenged. Or—and this was the shameful part—perhaps it was because, not being an Arab or a Muslim, I was unable to take his bigotry personally. And finally, coming from such an incongruous figure, his words had seemed more amusing than offensive—at the time. But now I felt like chasing after him on the crowded pavement and confronting him in the street, humiliating him in public.

45   The moment passed. I told myself it would serve no purpose, because his mind was closed. Besides, he had given me something valuable, an insight into his prejudices. And, probably more precious, a real face to put on my mental image of a racist. I will never forget it.

Guidelines for Avoiding Racist Language

Racist language is the use of words or expressions that stereotype and demean a group of people based on color, race, ethnicity, or national origin. Racist language is a form of discrimination against a group of people judged to be different based on color, race, ethnicity, or national origin.

Rule 1. Do not refer to a person's *race, ethnicity*, or *national origin* unless it is relevant.

Rule 2. Avoid phrases that are outdated.

Terms "colored" and "Negro," common in the 1960s, are now offensive and obsolete. Conveying the dual heritage of Blacks born in the United States, "African American" is the currently preferred term.

Rule 3. Avoid using hyphens in multiword names.

Some people object to hyphenated naming on the grounds that hyphenation characterizes a person as less fully a member of society than a person whose name is unhyphenated. Delete the hyphen in most cases unless the first term cannot stand alone, for example, "Anglo-American" or "Ibero-American" but "Asian American" or "Latin American."

Rule 4. Do not assume "White."

As with other *isms*, do not assume that the reader or listener shares the same racial or ethnic identity. Avoid talking about "we/us" and "they/them," making

What about that article all w/us? you

generalizations such as "we behave like this" and "they behave like that." Emphasizing the differences between people often implies that some groups are superior to others.

Rule 5. Avoid racial and ethnic stereotyping.

Avoid such disparaging expressions as "Latin lover," "Sicilian mafia," "Jewish mother," "Indian burn," "Indian file," "Indian giver," "on the warpath," "Mexican standoff," and "Chinese fire drill." Although many of these terms have lost their original impact and are applied to people in general, the expressions are derogatory. References to ethnicity and race, when irrelevant, should be avoided.

Rule 6. Use the currently preferred term when referring to a particular ethnic group.

Naming patterns change as the times change. Be aware of the way particular groups want to be identified. Generally, people prefer terms that include their ancestry, region, or religion rather than their color.

Meaning of Ethnic/Racial Term

African American or Black	U.S. citizen of Black African ancestry
Afro-American, colored, Negro	Terms no longer used to refer to African Americans or Blacks.
American/Americans	Term referring specifically to peoples of both North America and South America. Avoid using this term to refer only to people of the United States.
American Indian, Native American	Indigenous peoples of North and South Americas and their descendants. Use the precise name of the specific group if possible, for example, "Cherokee," "Crow." Unless used in their proper culturally specific context, avoid American Indian terms such as "papoose," "squaw," and "wampum."
Anglo, Anglo-American	A person of English origin or descent, or whose language and culture are English. Historically, this term does not refer to any White person.
Asian	A person of or from Asia. Use the correct regional term or precise name of the group: "Southeast

Meaning of Ethnic/Racial Term   *(continued)*

	Asian," "Central Asian," "East Asian," "South Asian" or the specific country when possible: "Japanese," "Chinese," "Malaysian."
Caucasian	An outdated term referring to the Caucasoid race of people. White is the accepted term when referring to White persons of non-Latin extraction.
Chicana/Chicano	Offensive term used to refer to Mexican Americans. Although used in the 1960s and 1970s to refer to political activists, Chicano has been replaced with Mexican American.
Eskimo	Not the preferred term. Use "Inuit" to refer to the group of peoples of northern Canada, Greenland, Alaska, and eastern Siberia.
Gypsy/Gypsies	A term not acceptable to the Romani/Romanies, a traveling population throughout Europe.
Hispanic	Spanish-speaking or descended from Spanish-speaking peoples from Mexico, Central or South America, or the Caribbean.
Hispanic American	U. S. residents who speak Spanish as a first language or those who are one or two generations removed from the Hispanic Spanish-speaking regions. Mexican American and Latin American are sometimes preferred. Use the more specific term when possible: "Central American," "South American," "Brazilian."
Indian	A person from India. A person whose religion is "Hinduism" is called a "Hindu"; a major language of India is "Hindi." Although this term is

Meaning of Ethnic/Racial Term   *(continued)*

	sometimes used to refer to indigenous peoples of North America and South America, the preferred terms for the indigenous people of the Americas are American Indian or Native American.
Jew	A person whose religion is Judaism or cultural heritage is Jewish. Jew describes an ethnicity, not a race. "Israeli" refers to a citizen of Israel.
Latin American	Citizens of Latin American countries. Commonly used to refer to U. S. residents who are Spanish-speaking and/or are of Mexican, Central American, South American, or Caribbean ancestry.
Latina/Latino	An adjective, meaning Spanish-speaking or those descended from Spanish-speaking people from Mexico, Central or South America, or the Caribbean. Sometimes these terms are used to refer only to those of Latin American ancestry, excluding Mexican Americans.
Mexican American	The preferred term when referring to U. S. residents of Mexican origin or ancestry.
Muslim	A person whose religion is Islam or a term to designate something of or pertaining to Islam. This term is preferred to "Moslem" and "Mohammedan," but not interchangeable with "Arab" or "Arabian." Not all Muslims are Arab, and not all Arabs are Muslim.
Native American	Indigenous North and South American peoples and their descendants.

Meaning of Ethnic/Racial Term *(continued)*

	American Indian is now the generally preferred term. Use the precise name of the specific group if possible, for example, "Cherokee," "Crow."
Negro	Dated term, unless used in a historical context. The preferred terms are African American and Black.
Oriental	Dated term referring to people from East Asia. Asian or a more specific term is preferred.
People of color	Term used to refer to persons who are non-White.
Spanish	A person from Spain; one of the Romance languages.
White	Accepted term when referring to any White person of non-Latin extraction, that is, non-African descent, non-American Indian descent, non-Asian descent, non-Hispanic descent, etc.

CHAPTER 3

Language and Gender

Language is magic. It makes people and things appear and disappear.
NICOLE BROSSARD, 1984

The moment a baby is born, the first question we ask is, "Is it a girl or a boy?" We swaddle her in pink and him in blue; we call her "kitten" and "sweetheart" and him "tiger" and "toughie." We rock her soothingly in our arms and gently throw him in the air. What separates the boys from the girls? What makes women women and men men? In most world cultures, gender matters. And through language, we learn to communicate our gender and understand the world around us. "Doing gender," of course, is only part of the social repertoire of our total identity, but it is a big part of letting others know who we are.

Although females and males are much more alike than different, a popular view held by most of the world is that the two genders are categorically and fundamentally different based on their natural sex determined at birth. For the most part, Western science and thought have led the world in the assumption of what is known as biological essentialism: One's gender is identical to one's sex. Based on socially agreed upon characteristics rooted in biology: chromosomal factors (XX for female and XY for male), genetic explanations, reproductive capacity, genital appearance, and hormonal differences, humans are assigned the label of either *female* or *male* at birth. Although there is no standard legal or medical definition of the term, according to the *Oxford English Dictionary, sex* has retained its original meaning of "either of the two divisions of organic beings distinguished as male and female, respectively." And we in compliance have

89

accepted the natural bipolarity of human beings. In fact, we even pit men and women against each other: "war of the sexes," "the opposite sexes," and girls against boys.

By accepting essentialism, we assume that there is one single way of being female and being male and ignore the many different cultural systems, communities, and expressions of feminism that exist in the world. If biology alone were the exclusive determiner of sex and predictor of behaviors, then we would not find such great cultural diversity and fluidity of gender in the world today. Many world cultures recognize more than two genders and accept a person's ability to change his or her sex or gender within a lifetime. For example, the ambiguous gender roles of the Xanith in Oman of Saudi Arabia, the Berdache of northwestern American Indian societies, and the Mahu of Tahiti are often cited as alternative sex and gender roles institutionalized and sanctioned within their cultural systems. Among the sexually ambiguous community of hijras of North India, men dress and act like women but describe themselves as "neither man nor woman." Margaret Mead's work in Papua, New Guinea, reports both Arapesh men and women displaying "feminine" behaviors by Western standards. Examples of multiple gender systems abound in societies around the world.

In our initial effort to understand gender and its relationship to language, we need to tread carefully in explaining language differences as sex differences. There are other social factors that determine our gender. The term *gender* has come to refer to the social, cultural, and psychological phenomena related to sex. Sex is natural, biological, and fixed; gender is sociocultural and variable. To illustrate, men do not breastfeed because it is biologically impossible. But the fact that men have traditionally not worked as nurses, teachers, or secretaries in the United States is a cultural limitation society has placed on being male. According to Western society, then, biological sex becomes the organizing principle of social structure that determines gender, one's social roles and behaviors.

Language is an important facet to understanding ourselves as gendered beings. In this chapter, we will examine the role of language in our gendered lives. In the first selection, "A Script of Their Own," Laura Hutchison introduces us to Nu Shu, the secret language of the women of southern China during the Tang Dynasty (618–907). It is followed by Pamela Perry's poem "The Secret Language of Women," a description of how the words of women can not be silenced. Alleen Pace Nilsen's "Sexism in English: Embodiment and Language" demonstrates the linguistic bias against women and campaigns for language reform with respect to English, for language has not served all its speakers equally, especially in a male-dominated system where women's thoughts and ideas have been muted and silenced. The next selection, an excerpt of "Words on a Feminist Dictionary" from Cheris Kramarae and Paula Treichler's book *A Feminist Dictionary*, describes how dictionary making has been primarily a male exercise. As a result, recording the history of a language's words has excluded women's contributions to the shaping and reshaping of the English language. In the fifth selection "Marked Women," sociolinguist Deborah Tannen identifies women as the marked gender. According to Tannen, there is no unmarked woman. Not only does a woman's clothing, hairstyle, and behavior convey additional meaning, but a woman's markedness is expressed in language as well.

The next two readings take a cross-cultural look at language and gender. In "Small Ads: Matrimonials," Ashwini Dhongde offers a description of the ideal bride in the marriage ads of Indian newspapers. Mark Magnier's essay "In Japan, Women Fight for the Last Word on Last Names" discusses the issue of Japanese women's right to keep their birth name after marriage.

At the chapter's end suggested "Guidelines for Gender-Neutral Language or Nonsexist Language" are provided to heighten our awareness of the importance of language in constructing gender identity.

Discussion Questions

1. What is *gender*? How are gender differences learned? How do you "do gender"?

2. When you were young, were you socialized to speak like a male or a female? How did your early experience affect the way you use language today?

3. Do you agree with the *androcentric rule* that men are the yardstick by which women are measured?

4. Do you think that language mirrors gender structures, attitudes, and ideas?

5. Are attitudes toward males and females revealed in the way we use language? Give examples of situations where language does not treat certain groups fairly and equally?

6. Studies show that the English language contains far more degrading terms for women than for men. Come up with a list of such terms. What do these ways of referring to men and women demonstrate about the value and behaviors associated with the two sexes?

7. In what ways do males and females speak differently? Do you think that miscommunication leads to the high rate of divorce in the United States?

8. Do males and females talk to children differently? to animals? to objects?

9. Make a list of stereotypes of men's and women's speech in a language with which you are familiar. Do you notice any patterns? How do these stereotypes relate to the way men and women actually talk?

Projects and Other Writing Activities

1. Go to the library. Examine any issue on language and gender that interests you. Write a paper explaining the issue and what you have learned in your research study. What conclusions can you draw from the readings and research?

2. There is considerable literature on gender and language in other world cultures. Examine a culture of your choice and explore the issue of language and gender.

3. Go to your local greeting card store. Examine greeting cards addressed to persons of a particular gender, for example, "To my favorite uncle." What messages are sent about the roles, activities, or behaviors of men and women in our society? Do the designs and images on the card reflect a gendered society?

4. Examine photographs and advertisements in magazines and other print materials. What differences in power between women and men are conveyed in the ads?

5. Gather examples from a language other than English that demonstrate the values and behaviors associated with women and men in that culture.

6. What can be done to promote gender equity in language use?

7. Examine the following celebrity quotes. Discuss how these quotes make you feel. Are they inspiring, consciousness-raising, exasperating, maddening, or validating? Do you think that persons of celebrity status should be more conscious of their language? Should they refrain from public displays of prejudice and bigotry?

   "A man can be called ruthless if he bombs a country into oblivion. A woman can be called ruthless if she puts you on hold." Gloria Steinem, Founding Editor of *Ms. Magazine*

"Be quiet. Didn't your husband teach you not to interrupt when a man is talking?" Pieter Botha, President of South Africa, in response to a female heckler

"You know how women are. They get crazy at times and yell a lot." Jim Brown, Football Hall of Famer

"I enjoy getting dressed as a Barbie doll." Vanna White, co-host of the TV show *Wheel of Fortune*

"One need not be married to achieve status." Miss Piggy, Muppet

"When men do dishes, it's called helping. When women do dishes, it's called life." Anna Quindlen, columnist for the *New York Times*

"They are trying to prove their manhood." Ross Perot, former third-party presidential candidate, responding to why women reporters ask him tough questions

"I never thought of myself as a boss. I'm just a chick singer." Wynonna Judd, country-western singer

8. The following nursery rhyme appears in many Mother Goose books. Read it aloud, then comment on what this rhyme means to you. Examine other children's rhymes for cultural messages. What messages are we sending children who read such rhymes?

> What are little boys made of?
> Snips and snails,
> And puppy dog tails,
> That's what little boys are made of.
>
> What are little girls made of?
> Sugar and spice,
> And everything nice,
> That's what little girls are made of.

9. There are many periodicals directly related to gender and language studies. Consult the journal *Women and Language*. Write a review of one of its articles.

10. Consult one of the following feminist and women's organizations and write a report reviewing its approach toward gender issues.

American Association of University Women (AAUW), www.aauw.org

Center for Women's Global Leadership (CWGL), www.cwgl.rutgers.edu

Feminists for Animal Rights, www.farinc.org

Ms. Foundation for Women, www.ms.foundation.org

NARAL Pro-Choice America (formerly The National Abortion and Reproductive Rights Action League), www.naral.org

National Organization for Women (NOW), www.now.org

Older Women's League (OWL), www.owl-national.org

Planned Parenthood Federation of America (PPFA),
www.plannedparenthood.org

Third Wave Foundation, www.thirdwavefoundation.org

Women's Environment and Development Organization (WEDO),
www.wedo.org

A Script of Their Own
Laura Hutchison

As long ago as two to three centuries in the villages of southern China, women had developed a secret language, Nu Shu, or "female writing." In "A Script of Their Own," Laura Hutchison describes Nu Shu, the dying secret language of a minority group of Yao women in Hunan, China. As long ago as the seventh century, as a powerful act of resistance to male domination, these women found their voice in writing and singing in Nu Shu about their harsh existence. Surviving in its written form, Nu Shu has its own unique script written with curves and tilted lines. Instead of being read, Nu Shu is sung in a call-response style while women perform their daily activities of embroidery and weaving. In the past, women often wove Nu Shu characters into cloth and embroidered the characters as patterns. Industrialization, government policies, and urbanization have dealt a near-fatal blow to Nu Shu; today, only a few surviving speakers remain in Hunan province.

1. Why is Nu Shu such an interesting language for linguists and other language specialists?
2. According to the author, why did the women of southern China create their own language? Was creating their own language an act of subversive resistance? How has Nu Shu survived throughout the centuries?

3. Why do you think that Nu Shu is dismissed and not taken seriously by the men of the community and by Chinese scholars?

Writing Assignments

1. Many anthropological accounts from the seventeenth century identify gender-exclusive languages in American Indian societies and in traditional African and Asian cultures. Research male and female language varieties around the world. Write a report on one of these cultures.

2. There have seen many efforts to *create* an artificial language: Esperanto, "a universal language to combat global mistrust and miscommunication"; Laadan, a language for women conceived by a woman to express the perceptions of women; and Klingon, the language of aliens in *Star Trek*. Research an artificial language of your choice. Write an essay describing the future of such a language.

3. Nu Shu was created in resistance to such oppressive practices as foot binding, segregation, and illiteracy in China. What are some other ways that societies, both Western and non-Western, condone the oppression of women? Write a paper about the oppression of women in cultures around the world.

4. Write about a "secret" language you created as a child.

5. View the 1999 videotape *Nu Shu: A Hidden Language of Women In China* by Yue-Qing Yang. What did you learn from this documentary? Write an essay arguing for the preservation of this dying language.

───────────── ◆ ─────────────

For sister, the attic
For brother, the great hall and study
We embroider a thousand patterns
Younger brother reads a thousand books

Translations of Nu Shu writings

When the men of Shangjiangxu township banished their wives and daughters to the upstairs rooms of their houses as early as the Tang Dynasty (618–907), little did they know that the women would take the opportunity to create a whole new language, kept secret from the men, through which they could discuss their restricted situation, and celebrate the birth of a sisterhood.

Crippled by their bound feet, and barred access to the wider community, women in a remote corner of Hunan's Jiangyong county developed their own script, called *nu shu* (女书, or women's writing). While nu shu had a spoken form, it closely mimicked local dialects, and was intelligible to the men. But in its written form, it evolved into its own independent language—an impenetrable alternative to hieroglyphic Chinese, embodying a spirit of freedom and equality.

Although only four speakers of the language are still alive, three of whom are over the age of 80, its importance today is as historic evidence of the important contribution of women to the advancement of China's civilization, and a snapshot into the hard and often abusive lives of women in traditional societies.

WORDS OF WISDOM

The precise origins of nu shu are lost in the mists of time. One legend tells of the invention of the language by one of the Emperor's concubines, named Hu Yuxin. "She was taken from her home village of Jingtian and found herself lonely in the palace," explains Yang Yueqing, producer and director of the documentary *Nu Shu: A Hidden Script of Women in China*. "She missed home terribly, but was afraid of bringing shame on the Emperor by writing home about her desolate life, so she embroidered her feelings onto cloth and sent them home to her sisters."

5   Several other variations on this theme exist, but all have one thing in common: a gifted young girl at the center who creates *nu shu*.

The language takes the form of an alphabet of approximately 600 characters based on highly simplified Chinese characters. Words with the same pronunciation used the same character, cutting down the total numbers of characters employed and replacing semantic meanings with syllabic ones.

Chinese characters studied by the men in the community were probably memorized by the daughters and sisters of those men, and while some characters such as *tian* appear frequently, no accurate count exists. "The script was never codified or institutionalized," explains Cathy Silber, assistant professor of Chinese at Williams College in the U.S. "Given the fact that usage of the script was never strictly uniform, these decisions will always, to some degree, be arbitrary."

The language was associated primarily with the practice of creating *san chao shu*, or third day missives—cloth booklets presented to a bride by her mother and sisters. The books contained songs and poems about the sorrow of being parted, and wishing her happiness. *Nu shu* was also written on fans, cloth, or in notebooks.

"Some people presume it would be mothers who taught their daughters *nu shu*," says Professor Zhao Liming, an academic at Beijing's Qinghua University. "This is not always the case. It was often transmitted from a grandmother to a granddaughter through daily activities, such as sewing and cooking, playing, and singing. Or it was taught to the child by a hired tutor."

Many *nu shu* women were seen as "cultured" and "educated,"   10
and this facilitated the hiring of *nu shu* tutors for young girls. Families would invest in a tutor to teach a child songs, and how to embroider and write the 600-plus characters. Four or five families would arrange for their daughters to study the language together, consequently supplying numerous local women with an income and independence.

CULTURAL CROSSROADS

Why such a rural outpost should become a hotbed of feminine independence at a time when Confucian patriarchal values ruled the roost is a matter of mere speculation. Prof. Zhao believes the reasons lie partly in the geography of the region: "Jiangyong is the focal point of Hunan, Guangxi, and Guangdong. This meant that there were influences coming in from all these regions, which facilitated cultural change."

The confluence of two rivers in Jiangyong—the Yangtze from the north, bringing in Han culture, and the Zhu from the south, bringing ethic cultures—meant that the area became the focal point for the south's resistance to northern Confucianism in the late Ming and early Qing Dynasties.

The Emperor took the region as a military base, forcing Yao women to flee to the mountains. The new society was a shock to the Yao, whose women had previously refused to adopt the practice of foot binding, and who lived a life relatively integrated with the men. Women would often choose their own spouses through singing, which was in strict opposition of the incoming Han culture and its saying that it was "better to have a dog than a daughter: a dog will guard your house, but a daughter will leave it."

The region was also exceptionally fertile, and women's labor was not required in the fields. This had the effect of creating a division of labor that had women pursuing *nu hong*—the womanly arts of textile arts and crafts. In many cases, the women would gather in one home, working together at needlepoint, singing, and talking.

15   These tea parties gradually became sworn sisterhoods, or *jiebai zhimei*. "There was no official ceremony when it came to sisterhood," says Zhao. "Writing letters was enough."

Most of the sisterhoods contained four to six women of roughly the same age, and women would seek out companions for their daughters at a young age, selecting girls from a similar social background to play together—and who would later communicate in *nu shu*. "A woman's social identity changed when she moved into the home of her husband," says documentary producer Yang. "She was ultimately just someone's wife. Combined with the fact that, in most cases, she would be transported from her home village to the man's town, this contributed to a great sense of loneliness."

In turn, this sense of loneliness sparked a surprising degree of political activism among the women. "In some of the scripts," says Prof. Zhao, "we see that women say 'The Emperor has made the wrong rules', and, 'How could we run from the invading forces of Japan when our feet are bound?' "

Comments were couched as opinion and statement rather than an incitement to action, however. "The texts show both accommodation and resistance in a variety of ways," says U.S. academic Silber. Comic elements are incorporated, such as the well-known story of Zhu Yingtai, who fled her hometown and family, dressed as a male scholar, and attended class with male classmates who were oblivious to her gender.

Hot issues of the day, such as the Taiping Rebellion, Kuomintang conscription practices, and the Anti-Japanese war were also debated.

SPREADING THE WORDS

20   Scripts were passed between women on the few legitimate occasions they were permitted beyond their houses, such as at visits to temples. Women would use *nu shu* to write their prayers to the Gods, leaving them as offerings in temples. Subsequent women would pick up the books, and pour over the characters.

The men, is seems, were oblivious to the subversive activities that were taking place among them. "It didn't really register with the men what these women were doing," says documentary maker Yang. "They never really acknowledged that it was actually writing, and the bottom line was that what women did was not important, so they believed it would never be dangerous for them."

In producing her documentary, there was a basic consensus among the inhabitants of Jiangyong county. "The women said that men got their own written language with the arrival of Han culture," Yang recalls. "Women wanted a language too. This was just their way of seeing things as being equal."

One woman interviewed in Yang's documentary, surnamed Zhou, recalls a conversation with a local scholar, Nian Huayi: "She told me her father was hiring a private tutor to teach her brother *nan shu* (male script). She remembered standing beside a desk, watching her brother study, and realized that she was not included. So she decided that if she could not learn *nan shu*, she would learn *nu shu* instead."

A surprising side effect of the sisterhood was a relatively low suicide rate in the region among women—something which Prof. Zhao of Qinghua has no doubt is directly related to the existence of *nu shu*. "Women were encouraged to speak out and share their hardships," she explains. "This made it easier to deal with life. When one woman cried, another cried with her. This is just a type of therapy."

She quotes a line from a *nu shu* verse: "Beside a well, one won't thirst. Beside a sister, one won't despair." 25

Reasons for despair were plentiful, however. A *nu shu* autobiography from the 1930s describes horrific levels of domestic violence, including almost being bitten to death by her husband on several occasions. Eventually, tottering on bound feet and suffering from brutal injuries, she made her way to the county authorities and filed for a divorce.

SPEAKING OUT

Nu shu remained hidden from view until the 1930s, when Zhou Shuoyi, an officer from the Jiangyong county cultural bureau, saw some *nu shu* in his father's papers. "Zhou tried to interest provincial level authorities in the script in the 1950s but failed," says U.S. academic Silber. The Cultural Revolution intervened, and it was only after rehabilitation that he could continue to study the language.

The language also resurfaced in the 1950s when a Hunan policeman found an injured woman at a train station in Shaoyang. Officials, unable to understand the writing she carried with her, suspected her of being a spy who had been parachuted into China.

Fear and confusion escalated through the Cultural Revolution, and *nu shu* books were burned wholesale as part of the task to destroy the "four olds" of culture, ideas, customs, and habits. "Many of these women were burned along with their books," says Zhao. "They were seen to represent feudal superstitions."

30   Feudal their society may have been, but they were also highly progressive. "This was very brave behavior for women at that time," says Zhao. "This is the history of a civilization, of old society."

With no evidence of male participation in its creation or transmittance, that makes *nu shu* a truly unique language. The only other women-only texts use male literati tradition to convey their messages. There is little other evidence of what life was like at that time for women, and the relics offer a glimpse straight to the heart of the most private sphere of life in former times.

"I think *nu shu* is truly a manifestation of the great spirit of the Chinese people," writes Chinese literature scholar Ji Xianlinin the preface to Zhao's book on the subject, titled *A Collection of Chinese Nu Shu*. "In the former society, people were oppressed and exploited. They were deprived of the right to education. . . . Women lived as slaves, and some were not even given the right to have a name of their own. . . . So imagine the persevering spirit that created this calligraphy, so grand that it forces us men to accord it the greatest admiration."

Not surprisingly, with the onset of language reform, and modernization of the society, however, *nu shu* is dying an inevitable death. "The teaching of the script when none of its uses are practiced anymore makes for a strange situation," says Silber. "From a strictly preservationist point of view, you could say it's good that knowledge of the writing system hasn't died out. But from any other point of view you have to acknowledge that a script is more than a tool for rendering the sounds of language on a page, and unless these new learners find *nu shu* texts meaningful, it may well be the case that they are only learning the script in anticipation of becoming the next tourist attraction."

Professor Zhao agrees. "There are only four women remaining who are authentic speakers and writers of *nu shu*, and their future is in tourism," she explains. Although 94-year-old *nu shu* writer Yang Huanyi featured in Yang's documentary conducts classes, they are primarily for tourist purposes.

As women leave rural areas in search of work in urban regions where pay is higher and the opportunity is greater for a better life, the odd child who studies *nu shu* today in Hunan province will be an asset to her community in her ability to draw tourists to the region. And although Yang Huanyi brought *nu shu* into the public eye again when she appeared as a delegate at the 1995 Women's Conference held in Beijing, the highlight of her trip to the capital was not showing the world her secret language. "She was more excited about seeing Tian'anmen," says Zhao. "All she had ever wanted was to see Chairman Mao."

35

The Secret Language of Women
Pamela Perry

In the poem "The Secret Language of Women," Pamela Perry describes the cycle of death and rebirth of womanhood symbolized by the Phoenix. Just as the ancient voices and wisdom of the women of southern China live on in the secret language Nu Shu, so, too, does the phoenix always rise from the ashes.

1. Why does Perry begin her poem with a Nu Shu saying?
2. How does the title relate to the meaning of the poem?
3. Describe the evolutionary stages of the birds described in the poem.
4. What does the last line, "she carries wisdom in ashes from a funeral pyre," mean?

Writing Assignments

1. Research the myth of the phoenix. Explain the symbolism of the phoenix in the cultures of the world.
2. Analyze the poem making associations to the previous reading, "A Script of Their Own," by Laura Hutchison.

beside a well one does not thirst
beside sisters one does not despair

A Nu Shu saying

as a small hummingbird her skipping rhymes
took flight on the feathers of milkweeds

as a beautiful crane her guileless pipa notes
were bound into new moons that she might

skim the tops of golden lilies in tiny slippers
forget song in the sun of the three-legged raven

still the vermillion bird rises again

to weave her words into persimmon cloths
embroider solace in curves and canted lines

she blows poems to sisters from the folds of her fan
she carries wisdom in ashes from a funeral pyre

Sexism in English: Embodiment and Language
ALLEEN PACE NILSEN

Alleen Pace Nilsen is a professor of English education at Arizona
State University, Tempe. Nilsen has written several books, particularly in the area of literature for young adults. In the selection
"Sexism in English," Nilsen criticizes how we dichotomize the
gender world into two absolute categories: male and female. After
scanning a dictionary, she finds that the English language reflects
an artificial division of the sexes.

1. What did Nilsen learn about the English language while reading through the dictionary entries related to males and females? What observations does she make?

2. Nilsen provides a number of examples that support how slowly language change keeps up with sociological change. Discuss a few of these examples and provide some evidence of your own.

3. Show how the language of naming, the language of marriage, the language of religion, and the language of metaphor treat men and women differently.

4. Do you agree with Nilsen when she states, "new language customs will cause a new generation of speakers to grow up with different expectations"? Support your answer.

Writing Assignments

1. Nilsen provides examples of how language sexualizes females as animals, playthings, food, and inanimate objects, identifies females as passive and dependent, and narrows and disparages female terms and broadens and glorifies male terms. Write a convincing essay that shows how the asymmetry in male and female terms preserves gender hierarchy and male control.

2. Select an excerpt from a traditional cultural document, such as the Bible, the Declaration of Independence, or the United States Constitution, which is heavily laden with biased terms and references. Transform the excerpt into a nonsexist document. Write a paper explaining the changes in meaning between the two versions.

3. Write a convincing letter to a school board suggesting that American English is sexist (or racist, ageist, or homophobic) and that biased language needs to be removed from all written documents, textbooks, teaching materials, and lecture matter. Explain why biased language is detrimental to all students and presents an unbalanced view of society.

4. The Sapir–Whorf hypothesis of linguistic determinism states that human thought is determined by the nature and structure of the language. Comment on the following quote by Alma Graham. Write a paper relating such quotes to the Sapir–Whorf hypothesis.

If a woman is swept off a ship into the water, the cry is "Man overboard!" If she is killed by a hit-and-run driver, the charge is "manslaughter." If she is injured on the job, the coverage is "workmen's compensation." But if she arrives at a threshold marked "Men Only," she knows the admonition is not intended to bar animals or plants or inanimate objects. It is meant for her.

Alma Graham

———————————— ✦ ————————————

During the late 1960s, I lived with my husband and three young children in Kabul, Afghanistan. This was before the Russian invasion, the Afghan civil war, and the eventual taking over of the country by the Taleban Islamic movement and its resolve to return the country to a strict Islamic dynasty, in which females are not allowed to attend school or work outside their homes.

But even when we were there and the country was considered moderate rather than extremist, I was shocked to observe how different were the roles assigned to males and females. The Afghan version of the *chaderi* prescribed for Moslem women was particularly confining. Women in religious families were required to wear it whenever they were outside their family home, with the result being that most of them didn't venture outside.

The household help we hired were made up of men, because women could not be employed by foreigners. Afghan folk stories and jokes were blatantly sexist, as in this proverb: "If you see an old man, sit down and take a lesson; if you see an old woman, throw a stone."

But it wasn't only the native culture that made me question women's roles, it was also the American community within Afghanistan.

Most of the American women were like myself—wives and mothers whose husbands were either career diplomats, employees of USAID, or college professors who had been recruited to work on various contract teams. We were suddenly bereft of our traditional roles. The local economy provided few jobs for women and certainly none for foreigners; we were isolated from former friends and the social goals we had grown up with. Some of us became alcoholics, others got very good at bridge, while still others searched desperately for ways to contribute either to our families or to the Afghans.

5   When we returned in the fall of 1969 to the University of Michigan in Ann Arbor, I was surprised to find that many other women were also questioning the expectations they had grown up with. Since I had been an English major when I was in college, I decided that for my part in the feminist movement I would study the English language and see what it could tell me about sexism. I

started reading a desk dictionary and making note cards on every entry that seemed to tell something different about male and female. I soon had a dog-eared dictionary, along with a collection of note cards filling two shoe boxes.

The first thing I learned was that I couldn't study the language without getting involved in social issues. Language and society are as intertwined as a chicken and an egg. The language a culture uses is telltale evidence of the values and beliefs of that culture. And because there is a lag in how fast a language changes—new words can easily be introduced, but it takes a long time for old words and usages to disappear—a careful look at English will reveal the attitudes that our ancestors held and that we as a culture are therefore predisposed to hold. My note cards revealed three main points. While friends have offered the opinion that I didn't need to read a dictionary to learn such obvious facts, the linguistic evidence lends credibility to the sociologic observations.

WOMEN ARE SEXY; MEN ARE SUCCESSFUL

First, in American culture a woman is valued for the attractiveness and sexiness of her body, while a man is valued for his physical strength and accomplishments. A woman is sexy. A man is successful.

A persuasive piece of evidence supporting this view are the eponyms—words that have come from someone's name—found in English. I had a two-and-a-half-inch stack of cards taken from men's names but less than a half-inch stack from women's names, and most of those came from Greek mythology. In the words that came into American English since we separated from Britain, there are many eponyms based on the names of famous American men: Bartlett pear, boysenberry, Franklin stove, Ferris wheel, Gatling gun, mason jar, sideburns, sousaphone, Schick test, and Winchester rifle. The only common eponyms that I found taken from American women's names are Alice blue (after Alice Roosevelt Longworth), bloomers (after Amelia Jenks Bloomer), and Mae West jacket (after the buxom actress). Two out of the three feminine eponyms relate closely to a woman's physical anatomy, while the masculine eponyms (except for "sideburns" after General Burnsides) have nothing to do with the namesake's body, but, instead, honor the man for an accomplishment of some kind.

In Greek mythology women played a bigger role than they did in the biblical stories of the Judeo-Christian cultures, and so the names of goddesses are accepted parts of the language in such place names as Pomona, from the goddess of fruit, and Athens, from Athena, and in such common words as *cerea* from Ceres, *psychology* from Psyche, and *arachnoid* from Arachne. However there is the same tendency to think of women in relation to sexuality as shown through the eponyms "aphrodisiac" from Aphrodite, the Greek name for the goddess of love and beauty, and "venereal disease" from Venus, the Roman name for Aphrodite.

10   Another interesting word from Greek mythology is *Amazon.* According to Greek folk etymology, the *a-* means "without," as in *atypical* or *amoral,* while *-mazon* comes from "mazos," meaning "breast," as still seen in *mastectomy.* In the Greek legend, Amazon women cut off their right breasts so they could better shoot their bows. Apparently, the storytellers had a feeling that for women to play the active, "masculine" role the Amazons adopted for themselves, they had to trade in part of their femininity.

This preoccupation with women's breasts is not limited to the Greeks; it's what inspired the definition and the name for "mammals" (from Indo-European "mammae" for "breasts"). As a volunteer for the University of Wisconsin's *Dictionary of American Regional English (DARE),* I read a western trapper's diary from the 1830s. I was to make notes of any unusual usages or language patterns. My most interesting finding was that the trapper referred to a range of mountains as "The Teats," a metaphor based on the similarity between the shapes of the mountains and women's breasts. Because today we use the French wording "The Grand Tetons," the metaphor isn't as obvious, but I wrote to mapmakers and found the following listings: Nipple Top and Little Nipple Top near Mount Marcy in the Adirondacks; Nipple Mountain in Archuleta County, Colorado; Nipple Peak in Coke County, Texas; Nipple Butte in Pennington, South Dakota; Squaw Peak in Placer County, California (and many other locations); Maiden's Peak and Squaw Tit (they're the same mountain) in the Cascade Range in Oregon; Mary's Nipple near Salt Lake City, Utah; and Jane Russell Peaks near Stark, New Hampshire.

Except for the movie star Jane Russell, the women being referred to are anonymous—it's only a sexual part of their body that is mentioned. When topographical features are named after men, it's probably not going to be to draw attention to a sexual part of their bodies but instead to honor individuals for an accomplishment.

Going back to what I learned from my dictionary cards, I was surprised to realize how many pairs of words we have in which the feminine word has acquired sexual connotations while the masculine word retains a serious businesslike aura. For example, a callboy is the person who calls actors when it is time for them to go on stage, but a callgirl is a prostitute. Compare sir and madam. *Sir* is a term of respect, while *madam* has acquired the specialized meaning of a brothel manager. Something similar has happened to master and mistress. Would you rather have a painting "by an old master" or "by an old mistress"?

It's because the word *woman* had sexual connotations, as in "She's his woman," that people began avoiding its use, hence such terminology as ladies' room, lady of the house, and girl's school or school for young ladies. Those of us who in the 1970s began asking that speakers use the term *woman* rather than *girl* or *lady* were rejecting the idea that *woman* is primarily a sexual term.

I found two-hundred pairs of words with masculine and feminine forms; for example, *heir-heiress, hero-heroine, steward/stewardess, usher/usherette.* In nearly all such pairs, the masculine word is considered the base, with some kind of a feminine suffix being added. The masculine form is the one from which compounds are made; for example, from king/queen comes kingdom but not queendom, from sportsman/sportslady comes sportsmanship but not sportsladyship. There is one—and only one—semantic area in which the masculine word is not the base or more powerful word. This is in the area dealing with sex, marriage, and motherhood. When someone refers to a virgin, a listener will probably think of a female unless the speaker specifies male or uses a masculine pronoun. The same is true for prostitute.

In relation to marriage, linguistic evidence shows that weddings are more important to women than to men. A woman cherishes the wedding and is considered a bride for a whole year, but a man is referred to as a groom only on the day of the wedding. The word *bride* appears in *bridal attendant, bridal gown, bridesmaid, bridal shower,* and even *bridegroom. Groom* comes from Old Middle English *grom,* meaning "man," and in that sense is seldom used outside of the wedding. With most pairs of male/female words, people habitually put the masculine word first: *Mr. and Mrs., his and hers, boys and girls, men and women, kings and queens, brothers and sisters, guys and dolls,* and *host and hostess.* But it is the bride and groom who are talked about, not the groom a bride.

The importance of marriage to a woman is also shown by the fact that when a marriage ends in death, the woman gets the title of widow. A man gets the derived title of widower. This term is not used in other phrases or contexts, but widow is seen in *widowhood, widow's peak,* and *widow's walk.* A widow in a card game is an extra hand of cards, while in typesetting it is a leftover line of type.

Changing cultural ideas bring changes to language, and since I did my dictionary study three decades ago the word *singles* has largely replaced such gender-specific and value-laden terms as *bachelor, old maid, spinster, divorcée, widow,* and *widower.* In 1970 I wrote that when people hear a man called "a professional," they usually think of him as a doctor or a lawyer, but when people hear a woman referred to as "a professional," they are likely to think of her as a prostitute. That's not as true today because so many women have become doctors and lawyers, it's no longer incongruous to think of women in those professional roles.

Another change that has taken place is in wedding announcements. They used to be sent out from the bride's parents and did not even give the names of the groom's parents. Today, most couples choose to list either all or none of the parents' names. Also it is now much more likely that both the bride and groom's picture will be in the newspaper, while twenty years ago only the bride's picture was published on the "Women's" or the "Society" page. In the weddings I have recently attended, the official has pronounced the couple "husband and wife" instead of the traditional "man and wife," and the bride has been asked if she promises to "love, honor, and cherish," instead of to "love, honor, and obey."

[handwritten margin note: changes in wedding vows]

WOMEN ARE PASSIVE; MEN ARE ACTIVE

20 However, other wording in the wedding ceremony relates to a second point that my cards showed, which is that women are expected to play a passive or weak role while men plan an active or strong role. In the traditional ceremony the official asks, "Who gives the bride away?" and the father answers, "I do." Some fathers answer, "Her mother and I do," but that doesn't solve the problem inherent in the question. The idea that a bride is something to be handed over from one man to another bothers people because it goes back to the days when a man's servants, his children, and his wife were all considered to be his property. They were known by his name because they belonged to him, and he was responsible for their actions and their debts.

The grammar used in talking or writing about weddings as well as other sexual relationships shows the expectation of men playing the active role. Men *wed* women while women *become* brides of men. A man *possesses* a woman; he *deflowers* her; he *performs;* he *scores;* he *takes away* her virginity. Although a woman can *seduce* a man, she cannot offer him her virginity. When talking about virginity, the only way to make the woman the actor in the sentence is to say that "she lost her virginity," but people lose things by accident rather than by purposeful actions, and so she's only the grammatical, not the real-life, actor.

The reason that women brought the term *Ms.* into the language to replace *Miss* and *Mrs.* relates to this point. Many married women resent being identified in the "Mrs. Husband" form. The dictionary cards showed what appeared to be an attitude on the part of the editors that it was almost indecent to let a respectable woman's name march unaccompanied across the pages of a dictionary. Women were listed with male names whether or not the male contributed to the woman's reason for being in the dictionary or whether or not in his own right he was as famous as the woman. For example:

Charlotte Brontë = Mrs. Arthur B. Nicholls
Amelia Earhart = Mrs. George Palmer Putnam
Helen Hayes = Mrs. Charles MacArthur
Jenny Lind = Mme. Otto Goldschmit
Cornelia Otis Skinner = daughter of Otis
Harriet Beecher Stowe = sister of Henry Ward Beecher
Dame Edith Sitwell = sister of Osbert and Sacheverell

Only a small number of rebels and crusaders got into the dictionary without the benefit of a masculine escort: temperance leaders Frances Elizabeth Caroline Willard and Carry Nation, women's rights leaders Carrie Chapman Catt and Elizabeth Cady Stanton, birth control educator Margaret Sanger, religious leader Mary Baker Eddy, and slaves Harriet Tubman and Phillis Wheatley.

Etiquette books used to teach that if a woman had Mrs. in front of her name, then the husband's name should follow because Mrs. is an abbreviated form of Mistress and a woman couldn't be a mistress of herself. As with many arguments about "correct" language usage, this isn't very logical because Miss is also an abbreviation of Mistress. Feminists hoped to simplify matters by introducing Ms. as an alternative to both Mrs. and Miss, but what happened is that Ms. largely replaced Miss to become a catch-all business title for women. Many married women still prefer the title Mrs., and some even resent

?? Difference b/ween Miss & Ms. ??

being addressed with the term Ms. As one frustrated newspaper reporter complained, "Before I can write about a woman I have to know not only her marital status but also her political philosophy." The result of such complications may contribute to the demise of titles, which are already being ignored by many writers who find it more efficient to simply use names; for example, in a business letter: "Dear Joan Garcia," instead of "Dear Mrs. Joan Garcia," "Dear Ms. Garcia," or "Dear Mrs. Louis Garcia."

25   Titles given to royalty show how males can be disadvantaged by the assumption that they always play the more powerful role. In British royalty when a male holds a title, his wife is automatically given the feminine equivalent. But the reverse is not true. For example, a count is a high political officer with a countess being his wife. The same pattern holds true for a duke and a duchess and a king and a queen. But when a female holds the royal title, the man she marries does not automatically acquire the matching title. For example, Queen Elizabeth's husband has the title of prince rather than king, but when Prince Charles married Diana, she became Princess Diana. If they had stayed married and he had ascended to the throne, then she would have become Queen Diana. The reasoning appears to be that since masculine words are stronger, they are reserved for true heirs and withheld from males coming into the royal family by marriage. If Prince Phillip were called "King Phillip," British subjects might forget who had inherited the right to rule.

The names that people give their children show the hopes and dreams they have for them, and when we look at the differences between male and female names in a culture, we can see the cumulative expectations of that culture. In our culture, girls often have names taken from small, aesthetically pleasing items; for example, Ruby, Jewel, and Pearl. Esther and Stella mean "star," and Ada means "ornament." One of the few women's names that refers to strength is Mildred, and it means "mild strength." Boys often have names with meanings of power and strength; for example, Neil means "champion"; Martin is from Mars, the God of war; Raymond means "wise protection"; Harold means "chief of the army"; Ira means "vigilant"; Rex means "king"; and Richard means "strong king."

We see similar differences in food metaphors. Food is a passive substance just sitting there waiting to be eaten. Many people have recognized this and so no longer feel comfortable describing

Just sitting waiting to be eaten

women as "delectable morsels." However, when I was a teenager, it was considered a compliment to refer to a girl (we didn't call anyone a "woman" until she was middle-aged) as a cute tomato, a peach, a dish, a cookie, honey, sugar, or sweetie-pie. When being affectionate, women will occasionally call a man honey or *Food* sweetie, but in general, food metaphors are used much less often with men than with women. If a man is called "a fruit," his masculinity is being questioned. But it's perfectly acceptable to use a food metaphor if the food is heavier and more substantive than that used for women. For example, pin-up pictures of women have long been known as "cheesecake," but when Burt Reynolds posed for a nude centerfold the picture was immediately dubbed "beefcake," that is, a hunk of meat. That such sexual references to men have come into the language is another reflection of how society is beginning to lessen the differences between their attitudes toward men and women.

Something similar to the fruit metaphor happens with references to plants. We insult a man by calling him a "pansy," but it wasn't considered particularly insulting to talk about a girl being a wallflower, a clinging vine, or a shrinking violet, or to give girls *Plants* such names as Ivy, Rose, Lily, Iris, Daisy, Camelia, Heather, and Flora. A positive plant metaphor can be used with a man only if the plant is big and strong; for example, Andrew Jackson's nickname of Old Hickory. Also, the phrases *blooming idiots* and *budding geniuses* can be used with either sex, but notice how they are based on the most active thing a plant can do, which is to bloom or bud.

Animal metaphors also illustrate the different expectations for males and females. Men are referred to as studs, bucks, and wolves, while women are referred to with such metaphors as kitten, bunny, beaver, bird, chick, and lamb. In the 1950s we said that boys went "tom catting," but today it's just "catting around," and both boys and girls do it. When the term foxy, meaning that someone was sexy, first became popular it was used only for fe- *Animals* males, but now someone of either sex can be described as a fox. Some animal metaphors that are used predominantly with men have negative connotations based on the size and/or strength of the animals; for example, beast, bullheaded, jackass, rat, loanshark, and vulture. Negative metaphors used with women are based on smaller animals; for example, social butterfly, mousey, catty, and vixen. The feminine terms connote action, but not the same kind of large scale action as with the masculine terms.

WOMEN ARE CONNECTED WITH NEGATIVE CONNOTATIONS; MEN WITH POSITIVE CONNOTATIONS

30 The final point that my note cards illustrated was how many positive connotations are associated with the concept of masculinity, while there are either trivial or negative connotations connected with the corresponding feminine concept. An example from the animal metaphors makes a good illustration. The word *shrew* taken from the name of a small but especially vicious animal was defined in my dictionary as "an ill-tempered scolding woman," but the word *shrewd* taken from the same root was defined as "marked by clever, discerning awareness" and was illustrated with the phrase "a shrewd businessman."

Early in life, children are conditioned to the superiority of the masculine role. As child psychologists point out, little girls have much more freedom to experiment with sex roles than do little boys. If a little girl acts like a tomboy, most parents have mixed feelings, being at least partially proud. But if their little boy acts like a sissy (derived from *sister*), they call a psychologist. It's perfectly acceptable for a little girl to sleep in the crib that was purchased for her brother, to wear his hand-me-down jeans and shirts, and to ride the bicycle that he has outgrown. But few parents would put a boy baby in a white-and-gold crib decorated with frills and lace, and virtually no parents would have their little boy wear his sister's hand-me-down dresses, nor would they have their son ride a girl's pink bicycle with a flower-bedecked basket. The proper names given to girls and boys show this same attitude. Girls can have "boy" names—Cris, Craig, Jo, Kelly, Shawn, Teri, Toni, and Sam—but it doesn't work the other way around. A couple of generations ago, Beverly, Frances, Hazel, Marion, and Shirley were common boys' names. As parents gave these names to more and more girls, they fell into disuse for males, and some older men who have these names prefer to go by their initials or by such abbreviated forms as Haze or Shirl.

When a little girl is told to be a lady, she is being told to sit with her knees together and to be quiet and dainty. But when a little boy is told to be a man, he is being told to be noble, strong, and virtuous—to have all the qualities that the speaker looks on as desirable. The concept of manliness has such positive connotations that it used to be a compliment to call someone a he-man, to say that he was doubly a man. Today many people are more ambivalent about this term and respond to it much as they do to the word *macho*. But calling someone a manly man or a virile man is nearly always meant as a compliment. Virile comes from the Indo-European *vir,* meaning "man," which is also the basis of *virtuous.* Consider the positive connotations of both virile and virtuous with the negative connotations of hysterical. The Greeks took this latter word from their name for uterus (as still seen in *hysterectomy*). They thought that women were the only ones who experienced uncontrolled emotional outbursts, and so the condition must have something to do with a part of the body that only women have. But how word meanings change is regularly shown at athletic events where thousands of *virtuous* women sit quietly beside their *hysterical* husbands.

Differences in the connotations between positive male and negative female connotations can be seen in several pairs of words that differ denotatively only in the matter of sex. Bachelor as compared to spinster or old maid has such positive connotations that women try to adopt it by using the term *bachelor-girl* or *bachelorette.* Old maid is so negative that it's the basis for metaphors: pretentious and fussy old men are called "old maids," as are the leftover kernels of unpopped popcorn and the last card in a popular children's card game.

Patron and matron (Middle English for "father" and "mother") have such different levels of prestige that women try to borrow the more positive masculine connotations with the word *patroness,* literally "female father." Such a peculiar term came about because of the high prestige attached to patron in such phrases as *a patron of the arts* or *a patron saint.* Matron is more apt to be used in talking about a woman in charge of a jail or a public restroom.

When men are doing jobs that women often do, we apparently   35
try to pay the men extra by giving them fancy titles. For example, a male cook is more likely to be called a "chef" while a male seamstress will get the title of "tailor." The armed forces have a special problem in that they recruit under such slogans as "The Marine Corps builds men!" and "Join the Army! Become a Man." Once the recruits are enlisted, they find themselves doing much of the work that has been traditionally thought of as "women's work." The solution to getting the work done and not insulting anyone's masculinity was to change the titles as shown below;

    waitress = orderly
    nurse = medic or corpsman
    secretary = clerk-typist

assistant = adjutant
dishwasher = KP (kitchen police) or kitchen helper

Compare *brave* and *squaw*. Early settlers in America truly admired Indian men and hence named them with a word that carried connotations of youth, vigor, and courage. But for Indian women they used an Algonquin slang term with negative sexual connotations that are almost opposite to those of brave. Wizard and witch contrast almost as much. The masculine *wizard* implies skill and wisdom combined with magic, while the feminine *witch* implies evil intentions combined with magic. When witch is used for men, as in witch-doctor, many mainstream speakers feel some carry-over of the negative connotations.

Part of the unattractiveness of both witch and squaw is that they have been used so often to refer to old women, something with which our culture is particularly uncomfortable, just as the Afghans were. Imagine my surprise when I ran across the phrases *grandfatherly advice* and *old wives' tales* and realized that the underlying implication is the same as the Afghan proverb about old men being worth listening to while old women talk only foolishness.

Other terms that show how negatively we view old women as compared to young women are *old nag* as compared to *filly, old crow* or *old bat* as compared to *bird,* and being *catty* as compared to being *kittenish*. There is no matching set of metaphors for men. The chicken metaphor tells the whole story of a woman's life. In her youth she is a chick. Then she marries and begins feathering her nest. Soon she begins feeling cooped up, so she goes to hen parties where she cackles with her friends. Then she has her brood, begins to henpeck her husband, and finally turns into an old biddy.

I embarked on my study of the dictionary not with the intentions of prescribing language change but simply to see what the language would tell me about sexism. Nevertheless, I have been both surprised and pleased as I've watched the changes that have occurred over the past three decades. I'm one of those linguists who believes that new language customs will cause a new generation of speakers to grow up with different expectations. This is why I'm happy about people's efforts to use inclusive languages, to say "he or she" or "they" when speaking about individuals whose names they do not know. I'm glad that leading publishers have developed guidelines to help writers use language that is fair to both sexes. I'm glad that most newspapers and magazines list women by their own names instead of only by their husbands' names. And I'm so glad that educated and thoughtful people no longer begin their business letters with "Dear Sir" or "Gentlemen," but instead use a memo form or begin with such salutations as "Dear Colleagues," "Dear Reader," or "Dear Committee Members." I'm also glad that such words as *poetess, authoress, conductress,* and *aviatrix* now sound quaint and old-fashioned and that *chairman* is giving way to *chair* or *head, mailman* to *mail carrier, clergyman* to *clergy,* and *stewardess* to *flight attendant.* I was also pleased when the National Oceanic and Atmospheric Administration bowed to feminist complaints and in the late 1970s began to alternate men's and women's names for hurricanes. However, I wasn't so pleased to discover that the change did not immediately erase sexist thoughts from everyone's mind, as shown by a headline about Hurricane David in a 1979 New York tabloid, "David Rapes Virgin Islands." More re- *they should be sued* cently a similar metaphor appeared in a headline in the *Arizona Republic* about Hurricane Charlie, "Charlie Quits Carolinas, Flirts with Virginia."

What these incidents show is that sexism is not something existing independently in American English or in the particular dictionary that I happened to read. Rather, it exists in people's minds. Language is like an X-ray in providing visible evidence of invisible thoughts. The best thing about people being interested in and discussing sexist language is that as they make conscious decisions about what pronouns they will use, what jokes they will tell or laugh at, how they will write their names, or how they will begin their letters, they are forced to think about the underlying issue of sexism. This is good because as a problem that begins in people's assumptions and expectations, it's a problem that will be solved only when a great many people have given it a great deal of thought. 40

Words on a Feminist Dictionary
CHERIS KRAMARAE AND PAULA A. TREICHLER

Linguist Cheris Kramarae, a visiting professor at the Center for the Study of Women in Society at the University of Oregon, and Paula A. Treichler, a professor of women's studies and medical communication at the University of Illinois, have authored several books and articles on language and gender. In an excerpt from the selection "Words on a Feminist Dictionary" from *A Feminist Dictionary,* Kramarae and Treichler discuss feminist lexicography, the study of women's words and definitions.

1. What do the authors mean when they state that "a dictionary not merely reflects sexist social attitudes but acts in a variety of ways to preserve and recreate stereotypes as well?" What do words say about women?
2. Consult *A Feminist Dictionary.* How does the approach of this dictionary differ from that of dictionaries with which you are familiar? Look up the words "herstory" and "womyn." Are there certain words in *A Feminist Dictionary* not found in a standard college dictionary? Do the definitions differ? Why?
3. The authors introduce a number of different dictionaries. Why is there a need for so many dictionaries?
4. Explain how male dictionary making is different from female dictionary making.

Writing Assignments

1. The 20-volume *Oxford English Dictionary* is one of the most complete works on the history of the English language. Examine the treatment of a pair of words such as "woman-man" or "girl-boy." Write up a full description on how the history of each word has changed in connotation.
2. Examine the treatment of a gendered word in a variety of dictionaries, usage handbooks, and thesauri. Compare these definitions and uses to those in *A Feminist Dictionary.* (Onelook dictionary site, www.onelook.com, searches 907 different dictionaries.) What are your conclusions?
3. Expressions such as *sexism, feminism,* and *sexual harassment* are fairly recent to the English language. Examine the treatment of one of these "new" words in a number of different dictionaries. Write an essay showing how the word has changed in meaning. Provide your own complete dictionary entry.
4. Many feminist scholars have made efforts to reclaim the dominant patriarchal language that has undervalued and muted women and their pasts. When writers use "herstory," "everywoman," "womyn," or other female-based innovations,

they are removing maleness and expanding the English language to include the female gender. Create your own words to express thoughts and ideas where no equivalent exists in the English language.

5. Discuss the following quotes on feminism. Write a paper on the various definitions of the term.

Feminists hate men, that's the problem.

JERRY FALWELL, FOUNDER OF THE MORAL MAJORITY

Feminism was established to allow unattractive women access to mainstream society.

RUSH LIMBAUGH, RADIO TALK SHOW HOST

I am not afraid to show my feminine side—it's part of what makes me a man.

GERARD DEPARDIEU, ACTOR

Self-esteem is the basis for feminism because self-esteem is based on defining yourself and believing in that definition. Self-esteem is regarding yourself as a grown-up.

SUSAN FALUDI, AUTHOR

I'm really sick of people apologizing for feminism as if it would leave nasty stains. Feminism is one of the greatest humanisms. It's about making the world more human.

JODIE FOSTER, ACTOR

My definition of the word "feminist" is a strong women who looks out for her sisters, who would go out of her way to see another woman make it and who wants to build our self-esteem up as a whole. If we don't have any strong women in this world to back us up, then, you know, we're lacking what we should be stacking.

YOLANDA SHITAKER, HIP-HOP SINGER YO YO

---- ✦ ----

This is a word-book with several purposes: to document words, definitions, and conceptualizations that illustrate women's linguistic contributions; to illuminate forms of expression through which women have sought to describe, reflect upon, and theorize about women, language, and the world; to identify issues of language theory, research, usage, and institutionalized practice that bear on the relationship between women and language; to demonstrate ways in which women are seizing the language; to broaden knowledge of the feminist lexicon; and to stimulate research on women and language. Like many other dictionaries, it is a compendium of words arranged in alphabetical order together with definitions, quoted citations and illustrations, and other forms of commentary. Yet in some respects, it is different from what many people expect a "dictionary" to be. In this introduction, we will briefly elaborate on our goals for this book in relation to those of other lexicographic projects by women and men and suggest what future dictionary-making might include. . . .

Lexicography (the writing or compiling of dictionaries), as we note below, may have a variety of aims and encompass many different sorts of projects. Though *A Feminist Dictionary* shares some of the aims and characteristics of other dictionaries, several important points should be noted:

(1) We recognize women as linguistically creative speakers—that is, as originators of spoken or written language forms. The identification, documentation, and celebration of *women's* words and definitions depart from traditional lexicographic practice. Though dictionary editors claim (often militantly) to collect words and definitions from diverse sources, their criteria and procedures (both explicit and implicit) for identification and preservation nearly always preclude the gathering of women's definitions. Definitions for many dictionaries, for example, are constructed from usages found in works of the "best authors"; though the equation has been challenged in recent years, this designation usually means "male authors." Similarly, one criterion for the inclusion in a dictionary of a "new word" is the number of times it is found cited in print; given current cultural practices, not only are men's words more likely to be cited in the mainstream press, but also few dictionary editors seek out print media where women's words would predominate (such as feminist periodicals). Thus despite whatever usage practices may actually exist in the world, multiple mechanisms act to exclude women's usages from dictionaries.

Sexism is also at work. H. Lee Gershuny (1973), examining sentences in the *Random House Dictionary* that illustrated word usage, argued that a dictionary not merely reflects sexist social attitudes but acts in a variety of ways to preserve and recreate stereotypes as well—thus perpetuating notions of women as particular kinds of speakers (to illustrate usage for the word *nerves,* the *RHD* used "Women with shrill voices get on his *nerves*".) As Meaghan Morris (1982) notes, a dictionary may also render women invisible; the Australian *Macquarie Dictionary* obliterates women's linguistic and political achievements through the way in which it constructs definitions and thus achieves what Morris calls "code control": *sexism* is defined as "the upholding or propagation of sexist attitudes," a *sexist attitude* as one which "stereotypes a person according to gender or sexual preference, etc.," and *feminism* as an "advocacy of equal rights and opportunities for women." As Morris points out, *sexism* was originally used by *women* attempting to construct a theory of patriarchy; the notion of stereotyping a "person" by virtue of holding certain "attitudes" obscures and almost makes nonsense of its original political meaning; by defining *feminism* in terms of its lowest common denominator, both current and historical distinctions among different feminist positions are eliminated. "While it is true," writes Morris, "that the usages accepted by the *Macquarie* are standard liberal currency today, the point is that the concepts developed by feminists are not even marginalised into second place, but rather omitted entirely" (89). For another example, one might point to the *Doublespeak Dictionary* (William Lambdin 1979) which cites a small number of feminist linguistic innovations—largely, it would appear, to ridicule them; though one of the dictionary's stated aims is to identify deceptive, distorted, or ambiguous language, the nonsexist usage *him/her* [or her/him], designed to reduce the ambiguity of the so-called generic *he*, is castigated as a "clumsy," "legal," and "neutered" style (109–10). Dictionaries are, in fact, a prime example of discourse in which the generic *he* has evidently seemed adequate to represent the whole of humankind.

In short, the systematic—even when inadvertent—exclusion 5 of one sex replicates and preserves the linguistic and cultural rule of the other. The traditional focus on "literary," "newsworthy," or "authoritative" sources obscures women's very existence as speaking subjects. Interestingly, women's documented reputation for speaking more "correctly" than men do does not help them here: for they are interpreted to be mere receivers and transmitters of the code and hence incapable of making original contributions to the language. While men's definitions have been preserved in hundreds of dictionaries, this view of women's speech has excluded their words; in producing this dictionary, it is this view that we most wish to challenge and subvert. Accordingly, *A Feminist Dictionary* insists upon the significance of women as speaking subjects and documents their linguistic contributions.

(2) We acknowledge the sociopolitical aspects of dictionary-making. While we see this dictionary as a balance to the weight of other dictionaries in men's favor, we have tried as well to be self-conscious and explicit about our decisions and procedures. A recurrent difficulty in creating a "feminist" dictionary concerns *whose* feminism an entry represents. Our 1980s feminism has inevitably pulled us toward the material that seems most useful and enriching to us. Though citations from earlier periods perform the valuable task of making women's names and words visible and attesting to the existence of women's rebellious words through the years, we are especially aware as we make selections from archival materials that we may be disturbing somewhat the links between the words of our foresisters and their times. Forms of domination and the texture of feminist discussions have changed over the years in ways our selection process and the structure of the dictionary may obscure. The dictionary format can only hint at the complexities involved in feminist discussions.

As feminist lexicographers, we do not claim objectivity nor believe that simply by offering a dictionary of "women's words" we can reverse the profound structural inequities of history and culture. The dictionary is also therefore a critique of current and past practices; collectively, the entries provide commentary on the institutionalized processes and politics through which some forms of language are privileged over others—how words get into print, why they go out of print, the politics of bibliography and archival storage, the politics of silence, of speech, of what can be said, of who can speak and who listen.

(3) We preserve women's *own* words. *A Feminist Dictionary* is subtitled *In Our Own Words*. Though *our* words—as scholars and writers—figure in many of the entries, the core of the book lies in the verbatim citation of other women's words. These citations are intended not only to illustrate word usage or illuminate a particular perspective but also to encourage a reading of the original source in its entirety. As we initially talked about this project, we thought it might be a book of key words—that is, a set of short essays about words or concepts that have had special significance for feminism. But such synthesizing articles would have hidden the diversity we found as well as obscured both the problematics and pleasures of feminist talk and writing. We have tried to provide narrative entries at certain key points to create a framework

for the book as a whole but these are not forced on the reader; rather they are offered as background, interpretation, and allusion. Accordingly, as we note below, entries take a variety of shapes including short aphorisms, longer citations, dialogues and trialogues, etymologies, and narrative text.

(4) We are not seeking to set forth a linguistic norm for a given community of speakers. In practical terms, the fact that we forsake this traditional theoretical grounding for lexicography means that with few exceptions we do not specify "part of speech" (noun, verb, etc.) nor label entries according to their linguistic status (obsolete, rare, visionary, neologism, etymologically incorrect, politically incorrect, etc.). The entry for HERSTORY, for example, labels it neither as a coinage (all words are coinages) nor as folk linguistics; such labels have meaning only in reference to a "real" body of "authorized" words, and as we have already noted there are many reasons why we should be dubious of this authorization process. At the same time, the dictionary draws words and definitions from such utopian works as Monique Wittig's and Sande Zeig's *Lesbian Peoples: Material for a Dictionary* (1976), Sally Miller Gearhart's *Wanderground,* and Suzette Haden Elgin's *Native Tongue* (1984), thereby suggesting not only what is or has been but what might be.

(5) Though *A Feminist Dictionary* is not intended to be a guide to women's intellectual thought, individual entries (see for example FARKSOO, GIRL, MARRIAGE, TRAFFIC IN WOMEN) are intended to stimulate research or theoretical development; collectively, the dictionary's entries should work to illuminate many lines of feminist thinking and debate. At the same time, by tracing a word or idea through a series of cross-references, the reader may begin to explore a particular line of theoretical thinking and see links between particular words and ideas. Our dictionary does not spell out all those links nor attempt to fashion contemporary feminisms into a seemingly codified and interpreted body of thought. We hope that *A Feminist Dictionary* will be used as women work to name and analyze specific structural oppressions and work for revolutionary change.

10

A NOTE ON MALE DICTIONARY-MAKING

We have suggested ways in which *A Feminist Dictionary* is different from many other dictionaries. But it is also important to note that our project addresses many of the same theoretical questions and practical problems that other dictionary-makers have had to address. Further, the term *dictionary* itself encompasses projects of striking diversity—many of which, like this one, depart from the practices characteristic of the "standard" American dictionary with its familiar claims to authority, comprehensiveness, legislative value, and scientific objectivity.

Under the rubric "dictionary" go the *Oxford English Dictionary, Webster's Third International,* the *Random House Dictionary,* the *American Heritage Dictionary,* and other standard contributions to lexicography. But the term also includes a range of individual, often quirky, projects. These include Gustave Flaubert's *Dictionary of Accepted Ideas,* published in 1881 (See ACTRESS) and Ambrose Bierce's 1911 *The Devil's Dictionary* (See MUSH); even Raymond Williams' *Keywords* (1976) can in some sense be called a dictionary. A number of influential dictionaries explicate and analyze subsets of the lexicon: J. Laplanche and J.-B. Pontalis' *Dictionary of Psychoanalysis* (1973), Thomas Bottomore's *Dictionary of Marxist Thought* (1983), and Oswald Ducrot and Tzvetan Todorov's *Encyclopedic Dictionary of the Science of Language* are examples. There have also been hundreds of man-made dictionaries produced to explicate even more specialized subsets of the lexicon, virtually all oriented toward traditionally masculine occupations, interests, or values. Dictionaries vary as to organizational arrangement (some, like *Roget's Thesaurus* or David Wallechinsky and Irving Wallace's *The People's Almanac* (1975), are arranged by semantic category as opposed to alphabetical format, for example), purpose (some dictionaries are essentially glossaries of "hard words"), accessibility, influence, and methodology (e.g., whether the data are primarily qualitative or quantitative—the latter an important feature of linguistic atlases and many dialect dictionaries). Finally, dictionaries vary enormously in terms of resources. Some are products of one person alone in a room with books. In contrast, the *Oxford English Dictionary* took 70 years to complete. *Webster's Third* was estimated to have required 757 "editor years" and to have cost more than $3,500,000 to produce.

The 1612 Italian *Vocabolario degli Accademici della Crusca* was the first big dictionary of a modern standard language; based almost exclusively on citations from classical Florentine writers like Dante, it did not claim to describe or prescribe general speech norms but did establish the tradition of drawing meanings from the "best authors." The disjunction between spoken and written language continually complicates the task of specifying what a given language consists of. Many countries established academies, language boards, or commissions to legislate upon this question; in France, most notoriously, the Académie Française officially determines what *the code* is to be. Despite attempts to establish similar bodies as keepers of the code in Britain and the United States, a generally anti-authoritarian tradition has prevailed, with dictionaries—beginning with Samuel Johnson's very influential *Dictionary* of 1755—taking on this codifying role. When the final volume of James Murray's *Oxford English Dictionary* was published in 1928 (seventy years after the British Philological Society initiated the project), the Oxford University Press expounded upon its "superiority to all other English dictionaries, in accuracy and completeness . . . [It] is the supreme authority, and without a rival" (K. M. Elisabeth Murray 1977, 312). Most other English and American dictionaries have been directed toward the documentation of existing language forms; a tradition of lexicographic positivism leads editors to claim "scientific objectivity." In contrast, dictionary editors in other languages have often inserted themselves much more forcefully into the codification process; one German lexicographer, for example, invented an elaborate system for labelling entries which among other things distinguished between obsolete words "recently introduced by good writers or deserving re-introduction" and those "incapable of re-introduction" (Ladislav Zgusta ed. 1980, 9).

In contemporary linguistics, attempts to define "the lexicon" are linked to various theoretical questions: How is our internal knowledge of a language—its "internalized norm"—to be externally and explicitly represented? What is the source of our knowledge of these norms (e.g., introspection, experience, empirical research)? How do dictionary entries relate to each other and to objects in the world? What is the status of cultural knowledge in our understanding of the meaning of a word? What is the relation of word usage to conditions for speaking? How is it possible to represent anything in language when in representing or interpreting one text, we inevitably create another? These questions are relevant as we explore the relationship between women and language: How is a concept like *woman* to be explicitly specified in a definition? (See BLACK WOMEN, DICTIONARY, ETYMOLOGY, WHITE WOMEN, WOMAN, WOMEN OF COLOR) Whose data will be used to formulate such a definition? (See OBJECTIVITY) What kind of "research" is deemed necessary (and by whom) for the construction of dictionary definitions? (See WOMEN AND LANGUAGE RESEARCH) Whose purposes will particular definitions serve? (See LANGUAGE) What consequences (e.g. legal) might a given definition have for women in the "real world"? (See RAPE, PROSTITUTION, WOMAN) From what stance or perspective does one present "new" definitions of women without inscribing authority and universality upon the definition by its very construction and publication? (See AUTHOR, AUTHORITY, DICTIONARY)

15   There is no doubt that the "male" dictionaries, constructed almost entirely by men with male readers and users in mind, offer useful information about words and about the world. Yet their exclusion of women, together with their pervasive claims to authority, is profoundly disturbing. The authority inherent in dictionary-making, and the strange arrogance toward language it may generate, is explicitly articulated by some lexicographers:

> To me, making a dictionary has seemed much like building a sizable house singlehanded; and, having built it, wiring, plumbing, painting and furnishing it. Moreover, it takes about as long. But there can be no question that there is great satisfaction in the labor. When at last you survey the bundles of manuscript ready for the press you have the pardonable but, alas, fleeting illusion that now you know everything; that at last you are in the position to justify the ways of man to God. (J. A. Cuddon 1977)

Thus despite the immense achievements that some of these dictionaries represent and their unique contributions to scholarship, they have been created within the context of social arrangements where hostility toward and exclusion of women have thrived.

As H. Lee Gershuny (1977) has pointed out, the dictionary's significant role as the cultural authority for meaning and usage makes it an important site for feminist analysis. As the review above suggests, lexicography is a complex enterprise that encompasses many kinds of projects. It is all the more striking then that for women, no matter what the project, the ultimate outcome is the same: whether descriptive or prescriptive, authoritarian or democratic, massive or minimal, systematic or quixotic, these dictionaries have systematically excluded any notion of women as speakers, as linguistic innovators, or as definers of words. Women in their pages have been rendered invisible, reduced to stereotypes, ridiculed, trivialized, or demeaned. Whatever their intentions, then, dictionaries have functioned as linguistic legislators which perpetuate the stereotypes and prejudices of their writers and editors, who are almost exclusively male.

WOMEN'S DICTIONARIES, FEMINIST DICTIONARIES

But there is another tradition. In 1892, Anna Julia Cooper in her essay "The Higher Education of Women" wrote:

> In the very first year of our century, the year 1801, there appeared in Paris a book by Silvain Marechal, entitled 'Shall Woman Learn the Alphabet.' The book proposes a law prohibiting the alphabet to women, and quotes authorities weighty and various, to prove that the woman who knows the alphabet has already lost part of her womanliness. The author declares that woman can use the alphabet only as Moliere predicted they would, in spelling out the verb *amo;* that they have no occasion to peruse Ovid's *Ars Amoris,* since that is already the ground and limit of their intuitive furnishing; that Madame Guion would have been far more adorable had she remained a beautiful ignoramus as nature made her; that Ruth, Naomi, the Spartan woman, the Amazons, Penelope, Andromache, Lucretia, Joan of Arc, Petrarch's Laura, the daughters of Charlemagne, could not spell their names; while Sappho, Aspasia, Madame de Maintenon, and Madame de Staël could read altogether too well for their good; finally, that if women were once permitted to read Sophocles and work with logarithms, or to nibble at any side of the apple of knowledge, there would be an end forever to their sewing on buttons and embroidering slippers. (Anna Julia Cooper 1892; in Bert James Loewenberg and Ruth Bogin, eds 1976, 318)

But women were not to be kept from the alphabet. While N. H.'s *The Ladies Dictionary* (1694), was not a sisterly effort but a male effort which offered ladies some definitions of women's names and essays on topics such as love and religion, several eighteenth-century dictionaries suggested the growth of more genuine interest in women as readers; they were dedicated not only to "scholars" but also to "the Female sex" (Shirley Morahan 1981, 55).

Women became writers as well. Elizabeth Elstob produced the first grammar of Anglo-Saxon in 1715; her dedication to the Princess of Wales noted that her royal highness had probably never before received a book written by a member of the female sex.

20   With the feminist movement, certainly by the time of Mary Wollstonecraft's *Vindication of the Rights of Women* in 1789, came increasing self-conscious attention to the meaning of words. Not only have feminists been concerned with women's access to words—through reading, education, writing, and publication—but also they write about how words like WOMAN, RIGHTS, JUSTICE, MARRIAGE, and EQUALITY are to be defined (see the dictionary entries under these words). They critique existing definitions (see WILL) and propose new ones (see HOME, CHIVALRY, WOMEN). They point to words and concepts in the cultural mainstream that undermine our ability even to articulate women's condition (see ANGEL); the so-called "generic" use of *he* and *man* was challenged (e.g., by Charlotte Carmichael Stopes 1908; and see entries under HE and MAN). They challenge existing language and originate new language (see-ESS, BIBLE, OBEY, PRAYER). With the organization of the suffrage movement, this engagement with language grew even more intense, with women beginning the process of reclaiming male-defined negative words about women (see RECLAMATION, SUFFRAGETTE). Suffragists and suffragettes published their own ABCs ("N is for NOW, Mr. Putoff, M. P., The day after no-time Will not do for me"). In 1941 Mary Ritter Beard undertook a feminist critique of the *Encyclopaedia Britannica;* though the editors who had commissioned the 42-page report did not act on her suggestions, she recommended redefining many entries and adding material on the contributions and concerns of women (Ann J. Lane 1977).

In the modern feminist movement, beginning in the late 1960s, feminists have addressed language issues in relation to feminist theory, scholarship, action, and policy. A central problem is the relationship of women to a male-oriented symbolic system: what the writer Varda One called "Manglish" in her language columns in the early 1970s and what Dale Spender identifies as "man-made language" (1980). Examination of the processes of cultural authorization has led feminists to the institution where language and authority most dramatically intersect: the dictionary. Gershuny, mentioned above, undertook a systematic study of the dictionary in the early 1970s. At the same time, Varda One's columns inspired the *New Feminist English Dictionary,* subtitled

"An Intelligent Woman's Guide to Dirty Words" (1974). Ruth To-dasco and her colleagues began their project as they "sat around with an unabridged dictionary and started shouting out dirty words," a process that yielded six types of "patriarchal epithets: Woman as Whore, as Whorish, as Body, as Animal, as -ess, and as -ette" (Ruth Todasco 1974). This demonstration of men's myths about women and their sexuality was drawn primarily from the established dictionaries of the English language which, Todasco wrote, "are museum pieces of an archaic culture," but also a "powerful reinforcing expression of men's prejudice against women." Julia Penelope Stanley (1977b) also used standard dictionaries and grammars to identify words designating males and females, pointing out both structural and political exclusions of females; Muriel Schulz (1975), examining pairs of words like dog and bitch, proposed a process that she called the SEMANTIC DEROGATION OF WOMEN to account for the repeated "sliding" of the female term toward negative meanings, usually associated with sexuality or prostitution. Many other projects during the last fifteen years have sought to illuminate the implications for women of the received male standard and of the semantic and so-cial space in which words and their meanings come to life. (E.g., Alice Molloy c. 1973, Alleen Pace Nilsen, Jenny R. Snider 1975, Una Stannard 1977; and see references in Casey Miller and Kate Swift 1976, Dale Spender 1980, Barrie Thorne and Nancy Henley eds 1975, Barrie Thorne, Cheris Kramarae, and Nancy Henley eds 1983, and the journal *Women and Language*).

A different approach is taken in the "Woman's New Word Dictionary," an issue of a feminist journal edited by Midge Lennert and Norma Willson (1973). Feminist definitions replace man-made ones; *construction,* for example, is defined as "a well-paying field of human endeavor not open to women" and *tipping* as "a fantasy that allows our society to justify less than minimum wages for waitresses." In the 1976 *Lesbian Peoples: Material for a Dictionary,* published first in French, Monique Wittig and Sande Zeig offer their work as a corrective to what they call the "lacunary"—the empty spaces of our history as represented by most dictionaries and fables. More recently Suzette Haden Elgin, a linguist, has cre-ated a women's language to incorporate women's concerns; the Láadan lexicon includes many words about, for example, the com-plexities of and feelings toward pregnancy, menstruation, the fail-ure of published histories to record accomplishments of women, the varieties of love—concepts which exist at present only through lengthy explanations. (Begun in 1982, the Láadan language project is the subject of Elgin's 1984 science fiction novel *Native Tongue*.) Other projects, similarly, seek not merely to challenge the male lexicon but to offer radical new interpretations of it (Barbara G. Walker 1983), to change what the lexicon of the English language is to consist of (Bina Goldfield 1983, Judy Grahn 1984) and how it is organized (Joan Marshall 1977), and in doing so to challenge the processes and institutions which create and codify language use. Thus Liz Mackie's "Socialist Feminist Dictionary (59th edition)" defines CAREER WOMAN as

> an archaic term which correlates strongly with the meritocratic phase of British monopoly capitalism. It became obsolete in the twenty-first century when the entry of large numbers of women into the workforce reduced the working day, improved conditions at the workplace and eventually brought about universal 'part-time' working and shared childrearing. (Liz Mackie 1984, 8)

Thus a "dictionary" is created not to authorize but to challenge and envision.

While different in scope and format, all these projects are companions to *A Feminist Dictionary* and signal the continuing and intense interest women have had in finding, creating, and using alternatives to male lexicographic traditions.

A FEMINIST DICTIONARY

25   We have called this book "a feminist dictionary" to capture the multiple meanings that those words convey. It is at once a dictionary of feminist thinking and word-making; a conceptual guide to that subset of the lexicon concerned with feminism; a documentation of feminist perspectives, interpretations of words, and contributions to linguistic creativity and scholarship; and a dictionary itself made by feminists (See DICTIONARY). Though this book is concerned with *women*, we have called it a feminist dictionary rather than a women's dictionary because we are particularly interested in the words of writers and speakers who have taken a self-conscious stand in opposition to male definition, defamation, and ignorance of women and their lives. All women are subject to masculine laws and linguistic forms, but not all women have the same resources, opportunities, or desires to

challenge words and meanings and to explore the theoretical and transformative powers of language. Thus while we are interested in commentary that illuminates all women's lives and experiences, we find that "feminist" commentary does this in the most linguistically conscious and challenging ways.

Marked Women

Deborah Tannen

Sociolinguist Deborah Tannen is a professor of linguistics at Georgetown University. Having published 18 books, Tannen is most noted for her work on the different conversational styles of women and men, most notably *You Just Don't Understand, That's Not What I Meant!, Talking Voices,* and *Talking from 9 to 5.* In her work, she suggests that "women speak and hear a language of connection and intimacy, while men speak and hear a language of status and independence." In "Marked Women," Tannen shows that women are marked by the ways they talk, dress, and act. The world assumes that everyone is male unless otherwise designated.

1. What does Tannen mean when she says that men's styles are unmarked, women's styles are marked?
2. Do you agree with Tannen that there is "no unmarked woman"?
3. How does sociolinguist Ralph Fasold support the view that biologically, the female sex is the unmarked sex?
4. How is a child marked for gender?
5. Explain how the gendered terms in the following quotations are marked:

The term "working mother" is redundant.

Erma Bombeck, humor columnist

I'm tough, ambitious, and I know exactly what I want. If that makes me a bitch, okay.

Madonna, singer

I told him I wanted to be recognized as a good driver, not a girl driver.

Shawna Robinson, race car driver, when presented with a pink racing suit

I am an actor, *I don't understand* actress. *You don't call doctors "doctoresses" or "doctorettes," you call them doctors.*

WHOOPI GOLDBERG, ACTOR

I don't ordinarily allow anyone to use that "Ms." in this courtroom. What if I call you sweetie?

HUBERT TEITELBAUM, FEDERAL JUDGE, TO FEMALE PITTSBURGH ATTORNEY

I didn't like either one of my husbands. Why carry their names around? I don't want to be identified as Mrs. anybody.

CHER, ACTOR

Writing Assignments

1. Look at the students in your class. Select a couple of men and a couple of women. Make note of their clothing, their hair styles, their makeup and jewelry, and their behaviors. What are your attitudes and assumptions about these persons? Write an essay explaining how an individual's appearance marks her or him.

2. How does the use of swear words mark the user? Gather evidence and explore how women and men swear.

3. Popular, best-selling author John Gray has produced a series of books and tapes entitled, *Men Are from Mars, and Women Are from Venus.* Read some of his work or listen to the tapes. How does Gray explain the miscommunication that exists between women and men?

4. Role-play the following gender-related situations. Observe how women and men "do" gender differently when they ask for directions, give advice, divulge a secret, order or fire an employee, or flatter a friend.

✦

Some years ago I was at a small working conference of four women and eight men. Instead of concentrating on the discussion I found myself looking at the three other women at the table, thinking how each had a different style and how each style was coherent.

One woman had dark brown hair in a classic style, a cross between Cleopatra and Plain Jane. The severity of her straight hair was softened by wavy bangs and ends that turned under. Because she was beautiful, the effect was more Cleopatra than plain.

The second woman was older, full of dignity and composure. Her hair was cut in a fashionable style that left her with only one eye, thanks to a side part that let a curtain of hair fall across half her face. As she looked down to read her prepared paper, the hair robbed her of bifocal vision and created a barrier between her and the listeners.

The third woman's hair was wild, a frosted blond avalanche falling over and beyond her shoulders. When she spoke she frequently tossed her head, calling attention to her hair and away from her lecture.

Then there was makeup. The first woman wore facial cover   5 that made her skin smooth and pale, a black line under each eye and mascara that darkened already dark lashes. The second wore only a light gloss on her lips and a hint of shadow on her eyes. The third had blue bands under her eyes, dark blue shadow, mascara, bright red lipstick and rouge; her fingernails flashed red.

I considered the clothes each woman had worn during the three days of the conference: In the first case, man-tailored suits in primary colors with solid-color blouses. In the second, casual but stylish black T-shirts, a floppy collarless jacket and baggy slacks or a skirt in neutral colors. The third wore a sexy jump suit; tight sleeveless jersey and tight yellow slacks; a dress with gaping armholes and an indulged tendency to fall off one shoulder.

Shoes? No. 1 wore string sandals with medium heels; No. 2, sensible, comfortable walking shoes; No. 3, pumps with spike heels. You can fill in the jewelry, scarves, shawls, sweaters—or lack of them.

As I amused myself finding coherence in these styles, I suddenly wondered why I was scrutinizing only the women. I scanned the eight men at the table. And then I knew why I wasn't studying them. The men's styles were unmarked.

The term "marked" is a staple of linguistic theory. It refers to the way language alters the base meaning of a word by adding a linguistic particle that has no meaning on its own. The unmarked form of a word carries the meaning that goes without saying— what you think of when you're not thinking anything special.

The unmarked tense of verbs in English is the present—for   10 example, *visit.* To indicate past, you mark the verb by adding *ed* to yield *visited.* For future, you add a word: *will visit.* Nouns are presumed to be singular until marked for plural, typically by adding *s* or *es,* so *visit* becomes *visits* and *dish* becomes *dishes.*

The unmarked forms of most English words also convey "male." Being male is the unmarked case. Endings like *ess* and *ette* mark words as "female." Unfortunately, they also tend to mark them for frivolousness. Would you feel safe entrusting your life to a doctorette? Alfre Woodard, who was an Oscar nominee for best supporting actress, says she identifies herself as an actor because "actresses worry about eyelashes and cellulite, and women who are actors worry about the characters we are playing." Gender markers pick up extra meanings that reflect common associations with the female gender: not quite serious, often sexual.

Each of the women at the conference had to make decisions about hair, clothing, makeup and accessories, and each decision carried meaning. Every style available to us was marked. The men in our group had made decisions, too, but the range from which they chose was incomparably narrower. Men can choose styles that are marked, but they don't have to, and in this group none did. Unlike the women, they had the option of being unmarked.

Take the men's hair styles. There was no marine crew cut or oily longish hair falling into eyes, no asymmetrical, two-tiered construction to swirl over a bald top. One man was unabashedly bald; the others had hair of standard length, parted on one side, in natural shades of brown or gray or graying. Their hair obstructed no views, left little to toss or push back or run fingers through and, consequently, needed and attracted no attention. A few men had beards. In a business setting, beards might be marked. In this academic gathering, they weren't.

There could have been a cowboy shirt with string tie or a three-piece suit or a necklaced hippie in jeans. But there wasn't. All eight men wore brown or blue slacks and nondescript shirts of light colors. No man wore sandals or boots; their shoes were

15   dark, closed, comfortable and flat. In short, unmarked.

Although no man wore makeup, you couldn't say the men didn't wear makeup in the sense that you could say a woman didn't wear makeup. For men, no makeup is unmarked.

I asked myself what style we women could have adopted that would have been unmarked, like the men's. The answer was none. There is no unmarked woman.

There is no woman's hair style that can be called standard, that says nothing about her. The range of women's hair styles is staggering, but a woman whose hair has no particular style is perceived as not caring about how she looks, which can disqualify her for many positions, and will subtly diminish her as a person in the eyes of some.

Women must choose between attractive shoes and comfortable shoes. When our group made an unexpected trek, the woman who wore flat, laced shoes arrived first. Last to arrive was the woman in spike heels, shoes in hand and a handful of men around her.   *DAMSEL IN DISTRESS*

If a woman's clothing is tight or revealing (in other words, sexy), it sends a message—an intended one of wanting to be attractive, but also a possibly unintended one of availability. If her clothes are not sexy, that too sends a message, lent meaning by the knowledge that they could have been. There are thousands of cosmetic products from which women can choose and myriad ways of applying them. Yet no makeup at all is anything but unmarked. Some men see it as a hostile refusal to please them.

Women can't even fill out a form without telling stories about themselves. Most forms give four titles to choose from. "Mr." carries no meaning other than that the respondent is male. But a woman who checks "Mrs." or "Miss" communicates not only whether she has been married but also whether she has conservative tastes in forms of address—and probably other conservative values as well. Checking "Ms." declines to let on about marriage (checking "Mr." declines nothing since nothing was asked), but it also marks her as either liberated or rebellious, depending on the observer's attitudes and assumptions.   20

I sometimes try to duck these variously marked choices by giving my title as "Dr."—and in so doing risk marking myself as either uppity (hence sarcastic responses like *Excuse me!*) or an overachiever (hence reactions or congratulatory surprise like "Good for you!").

All married women's surnames are marked. If a woman takes her husband's name, she announces to the world that she is married and has traditional values. To some it will indicate that she is less herself, more identified by her husband's identity. If she does not take her husband's name, this too is marked, seen as worthy of comment: she has done something; she has "kept her own name." A man is never said to have "kept his own name" because it never occurs to anyone that he might have given it up. For him using his own name is unmarked.

A married woman who wants to have her cake and eat it too may use her surname plus his, with or without a hyphen. But this too announces her marital status and often results in a tongue-tying string. In a list (Harvey O'Donovan, Jonathan Feldman, Stephanie Woodbury McGillicutty), the woman's multiple name stands out. It is marked.

I have never been inclined toward biological explanations of gender differences in language, but I was intrigued to see Ralph Fasold bring biological phenomena to bear on the question of linguistic marking in his book "The Sociolinguistics of Language." Fasold stresses that language and culture are particularly unfair in treating women as the marked case because biologically it is the male that is marked. While two X chromosomes make a female, two Y chromosomes make nothing. Like the linguistic markers s, es or ess, the Y chromosome doesn't "mean" anything unless it is attached to a root form—an X chromosome.

Developing this idea elsewhere, Fasold points out that girls are born with fully female bodies, while boys are born with modified female bodies. He invites men who doubt this to lift up their shirts and contemplate why they have nipples.

In this book, Fasold notes "a wide range of facts which demonstrates that female is the unmarked sex." For example, he observes that there are a few species that produce only females, like the whiptail lizard. Thanks to parthenogenesis, they have no trouble having as many daughters as they like. There are no species, however, that produce only males. This is no surprise, since any such species would become extinct in its first generation.

Fasold is also intrigued by species that produce individuals not involved in reproduction, like honeybees and leaf-cutter ants. Reproduction is handled by the queen and a relatively few males; the workers are sterile females. "Since they do not reproduce," Fasold says, "there is no reason for them to be one sex or the other, so they default, so to speak, to female."

Fasold ends his discussion of these matters by pointing out that if language reflected biology, grammar books would direct us to use "she" to include males and females and "he" only for specifically male referents. But they don't. They tell us that "he" means "he or she," and that "she" is used only if the referent is specifically female. This use of "he" as the sex-indefinite pronoun is an innovation introduced into English by grammarians in the 18th and 19th centuries, according to Peter Mühlhäusler and Rom Harré in "Pronouns and People." From at least about 1500, the correct sex-indefinite pronoun was "they," as it still is in casual spoken English. In other words, the female was declared by grammarians to be the marked case.

Writing this article may mark me not as a writer, not as a linguist, not as an analyst of human behavior, but as a feminist—which will have positive or negative, but in any case powerful, connotations for readers. Yet I doubt that anyone reading Ralph Fasold's book would put that label on him.

I discovered the markedness inherent in the very topic of gen- 30 der after writing a book on differences in conversational style based on geographical region, ethnicity, class, age and gender. When I was interviewed, the vast majority of journalists wanted to talk about the differences between women and men. While I thought I was simply describing what I observed—something I had learned to do as a researcher—merely mentioning women and men marked me as a feminist for some.

When I wrote a book devoted to gender differences in ways of speaking, I sent the manuscript to five male colleagues, asking them to alert me to any interpretation, phrasing or wording that might seem unfairly negative toward men. Even so, when the book came out, I encountered responses like that of the television talk show host who, after interviewing me, turned to the audience and asked if they thought I was male-bashing.

Leaping upon a poor fellow who affably nodded in agreement, she made him stand and asked, "Did what she said accurately describe you?" "Oh, yes," he answered. "That's me exactly." "And what she said about women—does that sound like your wife?" "Oh yes," he responded. "That's her exactly." "Then why do you think she's male-bashing?" He answered, with disarming honesty, "Because she's a woman and she's saying things about men."

To say anything about women and men without marking oneself as either feminist or anti-feminist, male-basher or apologist for men seems as impossible for a woman as trying to get dressed in the morning without inviting interpretations of her character.

Sitting at the conference table musing on these matters, I felt sad to think that we women didn't have the freedom to be unmarked that the men sitting next to us had. Some days you just want to get dressed and go about your business. But if you're a woman, you can't, because there is no unmarked woman.

Small Ads: Matrimonials

ASHWINI DHONGDE

Translated from the South Asian Indian language Marathi, "Small Ads: Matrimonials" describes a marriage advertisement between a potential Indian bride and an Indian groom. Written by Ashwini Dhongde, a novelist, poet, and short story writer, this poem illustrates how marital matches are arranged in India. Two families solicit profiles of brides and grooms whose families share similar values or belief systems. In matrimonials, for the most part, only positive qualities are identified; the Indian bride offers more information on her attractiveness, physical characteristics, and personal traits than the groom.

1. What is the function of an Indian matrimonial advertisement in India? How is it similar to personal ads in U.S. newspapers?
2. What are the basic elements of a matrimonial advertisement? What are the basic elements of a personal ad in the United States?
3. Describe the ideal Indian bride. Describe the ideal Indian groom.
4. How do you know that "Small Ads" is a matrimonial from India? What cultural and religious values are emphasized?

Writing Assignments

1. Bring to class some personal ads and matrimonials that appear in newspapers around the world. How do women and men describe themselves? How is gender displayed?
2. Compare the function of Indian matrimonial advertisements to that of personal ads in the United States. Write an essay showing the differences between the two cultures.
3. It seems that males and females all over the world are eager to find romance or meet future marriage partners. Through personal columns, video-mate tapes, highway billboards, computer matches, online chats, and horoscopes, we advertise ourselves. Write a matrimonial ad and a personal ad for yourself, or interview a classmate and write the ads for him or her.
4. Have you ever submitted a personal ad or answered a personal ad? Describe the experience.
5. It is said that Western cultures "love then marry," whereas non-Western cultures "marry then love." Support this view by conducting research on matchmaking in two cultures.

◆

Wanted A Bride—Height 5 ft 3½"

Age—21½ years
Very fair, delicate
Good-looking, slim
Highly educated graduate, working woman
(handing over all money to the husband)
Gentle and submissive
(able to live under her mother-in-law's thumb)
Highborn, from a well-to-do family,
(able to provide an excellent dowry and suitable gifts)
Hard-working and modest
Able to adjust to a joint family, no foolish ideas
(the wind of 'women's lib' not having gone to her head)
Advertising only for a better choice.

Wanted A Groom—No conditions.
(must be male)
Adult, either
Marrying for the first time or
A widower with children, anyone will do.

In Japan, Women Fight for the Last Word on Last Names

Mark Magnier

Although under the civil law in Japan, a husband or a wife must share a single surname, choosing either the husband's or wife's birth name at the time of marriage, in practice, women have little freedom to choose. Ninety-seven percent of wives give up their surnames in favor of their husbands'. In this selection, Mark Magnier describes how conservative male lawmakers in Japan resist changing the civil code to allow couples to have different last names.

1. How is the issue of surnaming after marriage an issue of inequality between husbands and wives and between men and women?
2. What are the arguments against the proposal of allowing dual surnames after marriage in Japan? Do you agree with these arguments?

3. Do you agree that the controversy surrounding surnaming is an issue of male control and dominance in Japanese society?
4. So often, people are resistant to change in the name of tradition. Can you think of other instances where tradition wins over social change?
5. In what other ways does society control the way we name and address each other?

Writing Assignments

1. Gender roles and attitudes are changing. An increase in the number of women in the labor force, a rise in women's levels of education, women's postponement of marriage, shrinking households, and increased divorce rates have changed the way that women look at themselves in Japan. Examine one facet of the changing roles of women and men in Japan. Write an essay.
2. Research the laws of name changing in the United States. Report on what you find.
3. Interview a couple of friends and family members about their names. Ask them how they feel about their names, under what circumstances they would change their name, and how they would react if someone close to them changed his or her name.
4. Ask some friends, family members, and classmates about their opinions on using the different titles Mr., Mrs., Miss, and Ms. What form do they prefer to be called? Why?

———————— ✦ ————————

Like many people, Mizuho Fukushima is quite attached to her name—and wants to remain so. When she met her prospective husband, Yuichi Kaido, more than 20 years ago, giving up her surname seemed like killing an old friend.

"It just didn't seem natural," she said.

In another country, she could have kept her maiden name. Or both partners could have used a hyphenated name. But in Japan, law dictates that married partners share a single surname, and culture and tradition ensure that it's the man's name 97% of the time.

In the end, the couple registered their protest at the bureaucratic inflexibility by not getting married. Over the ensuing two decades, which included the birth of their daughter, Fukushima ratcheted up her fight, writing several books on women's rights.

Since becoming a lawmaker in 1998, she has fought for legislation to allow couples to have different last names.

Although Japanese increasingly side with Fukushima and 5
other supporters of dual names, conservative male lawmakers within the ruling Liberal Democratic Party continue to resist changing the Civil Code. Japan is alone among major developed nations and even among such Confucian neighbors as China and South Korea in prohibiting dual surnames.

A poll last fall by the government Cabinet Office found that 65% of respondents favored letting married couples keep separate last names, a 10-percentage-point jump from 1996 and the first time supporters outweighed critics. Late last year, reformers even became hopeful for a short time when the LDP agreed after years of opposition to consider the issue.

But traditionalists have roared back, arguing that allowing two-name families will promote excessive individuality, encourage the complete dissolution of the family and even create misunderstandings at mailboxes and gravestones.

"I understand it's inconvenient for working women to change their surnames mid-career, but we should continue the existing system to avoid confusion and to give a good example to children," said Sanae Takaichi, an LDP lawmaker. "Dual surnames are not part of Japanese culture."

OLD SYSTEM AT ISSUE

Just look at the Scandinavian countries, where marriages break up about 20% more frequently than in Japan, said Eiko Araki, director general of the conservative Japan Women's Society. "It's obvious from their high divorce rates that separate surnames loosen family ties."

At the heart of the debate is the several-centuries-old ie sys- 10
tem, a tradition that is getting weaker, particularly in cities, but still holds a grip on parts of Japanese society. Under ie, a bride became part of the man's house, took his name, cared for his mother and expected that her ashes would be buried in his family tomb. So complete was the loss of identity that even in cases in which wives were beaten or abused, their own families frequently dared not intervene.

"It's as though women were property owned by the husband's family," said Moriho Hirooka, a law professor at Chuo University in Tokyo. "Wrapped up in this naming issue are some very old patriarchal conventions."

As more women have entered the work force, married later and attained more prestigious jobs, the logic of this hidebound system has come under greater scrutiny, even as the mismatch between real life and tradition has produced an awkward patchwork of exceptions.

Wives are required to use their registered—that is, married—name on driver's licenses, health insurance cards and residence permits. Ditto for passports, although maiden names can be annotated if the wife can prove she had a preexisting career that requires overseas travel.

Architects, teachers, doctors, chemists, nurses and a host of other licensed professionals must use their married name, even if their professional reputation was built using a maiden name. Lawyers, court clerks and accountants can use maiden names, as long as they also list their registered names.

15 Some companies allow married women to keep their maiden names; others don't. And last year, bureaucrats were given the right to keep their names, pending action by parliament.

Although Fukushima may be among the most vocal critics of the single-surname system, many other women have fought quiet battles in the shadows.

Noriko Higuchi, a 42-year-old municipal worker in the northeastern city of Sendai, has faced social stigma and marital tension over her decision to use Higuchi, her maiden name, in all but the most official situations during her 17 years of marriage.

In fact, she says, her husband worried early on that she was on the verge of divorcing him, even as his colleagues chided him for not being able to control his wife.

"If the separate-surname law passes, I'll rush down to the municipal counter at 8:30 a.m. on the very first day to get my maiden name back," she said. "I miss it!"

20 With 97% of married couples choosing the man's name, pressure on the 3% who defy tradition can be intense.

Makoto Yamada, a 31-year-old dentist, took his wife's name when he married Yuko Kuji several years ago. He says it seemed like a far more interesting name than Yamada, which in Japan is akin to Jones or Smith.

People quickly registered their disapproval—including his parents, who had lived overseas and otherwise seemed quite liberal.

"With their own son, however, they were very opposed to my taking her name," he said. "And the arguments I heard were quite irrational: You should keep your name because it's expected of you. You should do it because your father will be embarrassed to tell your grandfather."

Ultimately the pressure became so great, linked implicitly to his taking over the family dental practice, that the couple divorced—the only way he could legally recover the Yamada name. They remain married in all but name, he says, and the lack of legal ties has made them work harder to secure the emotional ties.

OLD GUARD BLOCKS PLAN

The fight to change the law is not a new one. The idea was first 25 floated officially in 1991, draft legislation was introduced in 1996, and the issue has been raised repeatedly by lawmakers since then.

Late last year, the favorable polls, a doubling during the last decade in the number of female lawmakers to 74, including the justice minister, and the political exit of a powerful LDP opponent over a payoff scandal seemed to suggest change was possible.

But resistance by the old guard was too great, and analysts now don't expect a change before next year. The latest compromise under discussion would allow dual surnames but label them "exceptions." Dual-name couples would be allowed later to switch back to a single name, but those married under a single name could not switch.

Supporters of change say opponents are mistaking cause and effect. In the last decade, Japan's official divorce rate has doubled and its child-abuse rate is 17 times what it once was. Supporters point out that this is because of a range of economic, social and technological issues seen around the world, not the result of the policy on names.

"Decisions in Japan have long been made by old men" intent on seeing women stay at home, Fukushima said. "To me, there's no single, stereotypical family. It's a network of individuals who care for each other."

For Fukushima and Kaido, it took some courage to spurn tra- 30 dition. Their parents were aghast when they heard about the couple's decision not to marry. Their daughter, now 15, was born out of wedlock, a status that can subject parents and children to often-cruel social pressures.

On the positive side, society gradually has become more accepting and they have faced very little overt discrimination.

"Fortunately, we haven't run into too much direct prejudice," Fukushima said. "Maybe because both my partner and I are lawyers, no one would dare."

Guidelines for Gender-Neutral Language or Nonsexist Language

Linguistic sexism is the use of words that arbitrarily assigns roles or characteristics to people on the basis of sex or gender. Sexist language applies to both females and males, but research into the history of language shows that English has not treated both genders equally. Therefore, most of the discussion on gender-neutral language seeks to make the English language more inclusive of and less offensive to females.

Gender-neutral language is the use of names, words, and expressions that are unmarked for gender; it is language inclusive of both sexes, terms that are equally distributed to encompass both sexes, and expressions that do not stereotype. If an expression cannot be applied to both females and males, then the term should be avoided. The rule of thumb is, "Would I want to be called or referred to in such a way?" Male-biased language can be eliminated in a number of ways.

Androcentric Generics "Man" and "He"

Rule 1. Eliminate androcentric generics "man" and "he" and any compound forms with overt masculine gender marking.

The masculine generic noun "man" and the generic pronoun "he" and its forms of "him," "himself," and "his" carry two meanings: (1) sex-specific "adult male human being" and (2) universal "human being." Convincing research and solid arguments demonstrate that these masculine generics do not function to include all persons equally but are confusing, exclusive, and ambiguous. Females find the usage irrelevant and male-inclusive; the prescriptive usage influences the motivation, perseverance, level of aspiration, emotional state, cognitive ability, and behavior of female and male children.

Alternatives to Masculine Generics for References to People in General

1. Replace the masculine generics with plural nouns and pronouns.

    Example: By immersing *himself* in another way of life, the anthropologist comes to view *himself, his* own way of life, and *man* in a new perspective.

Revised: By immersing *themselves* in another way of life, anthropologists come to view *themselves, their* own ways of life, and *other cultures* in a new perspective.

2. Replace the masculine generics with a specific genderless noun.

Example: *Man* not only talks, *he* talks about how people talk, and such talk reflects *his* attitudes about language.

Revised: *Speakers/linguists/human beings* not only talk, *they* talk about how people talk, and such talk reflects *their* attitudes about language.

3. Replace "he" and masculine pronouns with "he" or "she," "he/she," "him" or "her," or "his/her" instead of "he."

Example: Everyone should have *his* teeth cleaned twice a year.

Revised: Everyone should have *his/her* teeth cleaned twice a year.

4. Eliminate the masculine pronoun or replace it with the articles "a" and "the."

Example: Everyone has a right to *his* opinions.

Revised: Everyone has a right to opinions.

Example: The judge must give *his* ruling on the case by noon tomorrow.

Revised: The judge must give *a* ruling on the case by noon tomorrow.

5. Replace the masculine pronoun with a gender-neutral pronoun: "we," "us," "I," "me," "you," or "one."

Example: Hardly a moment of *man's* life goes by without *his* thinking about *himself.*

Revised: Hardly a moment of *my/our/your* life goes by without *my/our/your* thinking about *myself/ourselves/yourself.*

6. Replace the masculine pronoun by repeating the noun or substituting the noun for another word.

Example: No one teaches *a child* the rules of *his* language; *he* acquires them in stages.

Revised: No one teaches *a child* the rules of language; *the child* acquires them in stages.

Example: *A child* learns to distinguish between the sounds of *his* language and the sounds that are not part of *his* language.

Revised: *A child* learns to distinguish between the sounds of the *child's* language and the sounds that are not part of *the* language.

7. Recast the sentence into passive voice or restructure the sentence to eliminate masculine forms.

   Example: The judge must give *his* ruling on the case by noon tomorrow.

   Revised: A ruling on the case must be given (by the judge) by noon tomorrow.

8. Replace "man" in the beginning, middle, and end of words.

Alternatives to using expressions with "man"

Masculine term	Gender-neutral term
man-hours	hours, work hours, work time
mankind	humanity, humankind, people, human beings
man-made	artificial, handmade, synthetic, manufactured
manpower	work force, personnel, employees
workman's compensation	worker's compensation
congressman	representative, legislator, member of Congress
man the table	work/run/staff the table

9. Replace masculine pronouns with singular "they." Not endorsed by all language authorities, this alternative is quickly becoming the natural and acceptable choice for the lack of a singular gender-neutral pronoun in English.

   Example: Everyone has a right to *his* opinion.

   Revised: Everyone has a right to *their* opinion.

   Example: I don't want to give anybody the impression that *he* is always right.

   Revised: I don't want to give anybody the impression that *they* are always right.

Overt Gender Marking of Nouns

Rule 2. Eliminate unnecessary, irrelevant overt sex markings.

Unless gender must be specified, the use of overt gender markers such as "woman," "lady," and "girl" and other gender-marked compound forms or suffixes is irrelevant and should be avoided.

Alternatives to using expressions with sex marking

Male term	Female term	Gender-neutral term
chairman	chairwoman	chair, moderator, head, presiding officer, group leader

Male term	Female term	Gender-neutral term
family man		family-oriented person
fireman	woman fireman	firefighter
fisherman		fisher, angler
janitor	cleaning lady	housekeeper, custodian
male nurse	nurse	nurse
policeman	police woman/ lady cop	police officer
	stewardess	flight attendant
	welfare mother	welfare recipient

Rule 3. Eliminate gender-marked modifiers.

Female-marked items convey a meaning of triviality and lightheartedness.

Alternatives to using gender-marked modifiers

Gender-marked term	Gender-neutral term
brotherly love	love, goodwill, compassion, neighborly love
female intuition	intuition
feminine wiles	wiles
forefather	ancestor, predecessor, forebear
lady luck	luck
male chauvinist	chauvinist, sex chauvinist
mama's boy	spoiled, immature child
maternal instinct	instinct
old wives' tale	superstition, folktale, myth, family tales

Rule 4. Avoid sex stereotyping.

The characteristics we generally identify as *feminine* are passive, immature, unimportant, beautiful, tender, and nurturing, and those characteristics we generally identify as *masculine* are strong, eminent, breadwinning, sexually potent, and powerful. Avoid falling into the trap of sex stereotyping.

Male stereotype	Female stereotype
discuss	chatter
remind	nag
network	gossip

Male stereotype	Female stereotype
complain	bitch
was upset	was hysterical
was friendly	was flirting
bull, stud, wolf	promiscuous, prostitute
bachelor	old maid, spinster, maiden

Rule 5. Avoid personification.

Refrain from referring to nature, nations, boats, cars, disasters, church, and guns in female terms.

> "Fill her up!" (gas tank)
> "There she blows!" (ship)
> mother earth, mother nature, Mother India
> "She's a goner"!

Rule 6. Avoid lexical asymmetries and gaps.

Use parallel treatment whether describing jobs, appearances, marital status, or activities to portray both sexes equally.

Non-parallel term	Parallel term
man and wife	husband and wife
college man, college girl, coed	college student
men's team, girl's team	college team

Rule 7. Reword proverbs, adages, and other set expressions that contain sexist usage.

Rather than alter a direct quote, paraphrase or reword it, use "[sic]" to call attention to the error, or avoid the quote altogether.

Sexist usage	Gender-neutral alternative
all men are created equal	men and women/people are created equal
dead men tell no lies	the dead tell no lies
he who hesitates is lost	anyone who hesitates is lost

Rule 8. Avoid gender-biased titles, salutations, professional names, occupational terms, and forms of address.

> Avoid marital status: Mr., Miss, Ms., Mrs.

Don't assume your audience is male: Dear Sir or Gentlemen
Avoid endearments: honey, my girl, dear, sweetie, babe
Avoid the nonreciprocal use of names: woman's first name or marital status, but man's last name or title; "babe" versus "sir"

Use gender-neutral salutations when addressing a letter:

Dear Board Member, Director, Homeowner, Friends of (name of organization), Volunteer, or specific name of addressee
Greetings! Hello! (no name or address)
TO: Board Members, Parents, Students, Taxpayers

Rule 9. Use "girl," "lady," and "woman" appropriately.

"Girl" is used to refer to a preteen female. It has the connotation of young, immature, and childish. "Lady" refers to a nonsexual, proper, polite, and well-mannered female. Its use is condescending and reinforces keeping "women in their place." "Woman" is the preferred term to refer to an adult female. Its usage conveys respect and importance. Avoid the use of "gal" or "guy" when referring to a female and avoid "guys" when referring to a group of females (and males). "Boy," on the other hand, refers strictly to young boys, and "man" refers to adult males.

Language
and Sexuality

I have come to believe over and over again that what is most important to me must be spoken, made verbal and shared, even at the risk of having it bruised or misunderstood.

AUDRE LOURDES

Although homosexuality has an ancient history, the social oppression of people with homosexual or bisexual orientations is fairly recent. The study of homosexuality has been wrought with fear, ignorance, and intolerance as noted in the past use of such stigmatized terms as "sexual deviate" or "sexual pervert" to describe persons of same-sex orientation. Only recently, have we grown to accept alternative sexualities and lifestyles. Although the groundwork for a cultural revolution was laid in the 1950s and 1960s in the United States, June 27, 1969, marked a major turning point in the sexual revolution when outraged gay men and lesbian patrons of the Stonewall Inn in Greenwich Village responded to a New York City police raid with a weekend-long riot. Soon afterward, the Gay Liberation Front was founded and "gay power" and "gay pride" were born.

Although the 1970s are identified as the advent of what became known as the gay rights movement, as a result of unrelenting pressures from religious groups, traditional fundamentalists, right-wing politicians, and the U.S. military, homosexuality continues to be condemned as immoral, criminal, and sick in U.S. society. This irrational fear of homosexuals, coined *homophobia*, has led to laws and social practices forbidding sexual liaisons between members of the same sex. Recent legislation to protect the institution of traditional marriage, the prohibition of same-sex

149

unions, and the establishment of "don't ask, don't tell" policies in various settings demonstrates society's reluctance to support gay rights, extend insurance benefits and legal rights to partners, and overturn discriminating policies such as sodomy laws that have perpetuated and sanctioned discrimination, prejudice, and hostility against gay men and lesbians. Research shows that the most negative attitudes and resistance to social tolerance may be attributed to less well-educated, older men who endorse orthodox religious beliefs and reside in politically conservative regions of the United States.

When psychologist George Weinberg coined homophobia in 1969, he defined it as an "aversion to gay or homosexual people or their lifestyle or culture" and as "behavior or an act based on this aversion." At about the same time, the term *heterosexism* was introduced to describe an ideological system that denies, denigrates, and stigmatizes any nonheterosexual form of behavior, identity, relationship, or community. Heterosexism parallels antigay and antilesbian sentiment and the other *isms*, such as racism, anti-Semitism, and sexism. To refer to all negative attitudes based on sexual orientation, whether the target is homosexual, bisexual, or heterosexual, the general term *sexual prejudice* is commonly used. However, such prejudice is almost always directed at people who engage in same-sex behavior or label themselves as gay, lesbian, or bisexual. Like other forms of discrimination, sexual prejudice is an attitude of judgment, often negative, if not hostile or hateful, directed at a particular social group and its members. The increase in *hate crimes*—criminal actions intended to harm or intimidate people because of their race, ethnicity, sexual orientation, religion, or other minority group status—only underscores the need for a greater acceptance of alternative lifestyles, civil rights legislation to prevent discrimination and hate crimes, and an end to the social control of minority freedoms.

Same-sex orientation is replete with negative descriptions, labels, and stereotypes of lesbians, gay men, and bisexual persons. Often perpetuated in the form of heterosexual-bias or homophobic language is the imposed view that heterosexism is the societal norm. Homophobic language is so commonplace that teenagers today call each other "fag" or "queer" and use "gay" to mean "stupid," as in "that's so gay." The use of such speech constructs a certain gender identity, confirming the speaker's identity as a heterosexual as well as serving to remove any association with being homosexual. Language shapes perception and sends a clear message of belonging or not belonging to a particular social group.

In the following selections, several different authors address the use of terms associated with same-sex and bisexual orientations. Because there is a lack of universal agreement on terminology, it is crucial that we as users of a language be sensitive to social change and the role language plays in that change. To introduce you to this chapter, the "Homophobia Questionnaire" is provided to measure your personal feelings, thoughts, and behaviors toward sexual orientation, sexual identity, and homophobic behavior. The higher the score, the greater the negative attitudes and beliefs about homosexuality. In the next selection "Language: A Pernicious and Powerful Tool," high-school teacher Jessica Parker confirms her sexual orientation by "coming out" to her students and addressing their use of homophobic language. She challenges students to become sensitive to their use of prejudicial language. "Respect my Right to Be Responsible: Homophobia's Last Day in School," the next reading, is a letter written by a young gay male student to his senator sincerely pleading for the day when he and other gay men and lesbian students will not have to face daily verbal prejudice and harassment. Writer and professor Lillian Faderman then traces the history of the word "queer" and shows how the term has lost its negative connotations and been redefined by the gay male and lesbian populations. And in the final selection "Ironic Genius?" Tom Pearson asks whether hip-hop artist Eminem is a homophobe, a product of his environment, or a "genius with a talent for irony." "Guidelines for Avoiding Heterosexist and Homophobic Language" are additionally offered in an effort to eliminate linguistic bias toward the gay, lesbian, bisexual, and transgendered communities.

Discussion Questions

1. Can you describe an event in your life that made you realize the power of language and the power of words.

2. Language is a strong and powerful instrument for raising consciousness. How can we raise consciousness and challenge prevailing assumptions about lesbians, gay males, bisexuals, and transgenders in society?

3. Make a list of homophobic language use that you have heard. Who uses these terms? When? Where? What does this language reflect about attitudes toward sexual orientation in U.S. society?

4. How can parents and educators respond to the homophobic attitudes and language of children?

5. What are the arguments that sexual orientation is biologically determined or socially constructed?

6. Traditional explanations of sexual orientation have described heterosexuality as the normative and prescriptive model. Why is the approach to heterosexism biased and parallels other forms of prejudice such as racism, sexism, and ageism?

7. What role should the government play in directing the personal and sexual lives of its citizens?

Projects and Other Writing Activities

1. Interview a gay man, lesbian, bisexual, or transgendered person about the different forms of discrimination that he or she has experienced in his or her daily life. Write about one of these experiences.

2. Write an essay about hate speech, the criminal action intended to verbally harm or intimidate people because of their race, ethnicity, sexual orientation, religion, or belonging to another minority group.

3. Think back to your childhood and how you learned about "the birds and the bees." What do you remember? Do you think your learning experience was different from that of children today?

4. A decade or so ago, any open discussion on homosexuality was considered taboo. Gay men and lesbians refrained from coming out and identifying their sexual orientation. Recently, because of the gay rights movement and the spread of acquired immunodeficiency syndrome (AIDS), we have developed a greater understanding of and respect for diverse sexual orientations. What major social and political events in society provided the impetus for this change in thinking?

5. In 2003, the U.S. Supreme Court struck down state laws banning sodomy between same-sex partners, offering the "right to privacy" argument for gay men and lesbians. Research the history of gay rights from as early as 1895, when writer Oscar Wilde was convicted of "gross indecency between males," to the present laws of "civil unions," adoptions and births by same-sex couples, and equal protection and rights of gay men and lesbians in the workplace, the military, schools, and religion. Or, write about the backlash to rulings that grant gay males and lesbians their full legal rights.

6. Consult one of the following gay, lesbian, bisexual, and transgender (GLBT) organizations and write a report reviewing its approach toward issues related to sexual orientation, gender identity, and homophobia.

Gay-Straight Alliance Network (GSA), www.gsanetwork.org

Gay and Lesbian Alliance Against Defamation (GLAAD), www.glaad.org

Gay, Lesbian and Straight Education Network (GLSEN), www.glsen.org

OutProud! The National Coalition for Gay, Lesbian, Bisexual, and Transgender Youth, www.outproud.org

Parents, Families, and Friends of Lesbians and Gays, (PFLAG) www.pflag.org

---

Homophobia Questionnaire

As part of a study on homophobia, Dr. Henry Adams and his colleagues at the University of Georgia developed a 25-item questionnaire designed to measure your thoughts, feelings, and behaviors with regard to heterosexuality and homosexuality. Take the following "Homophobia Questionnaire" to identify your personal attitudes about homosexuality and homophobic behavior.

For much of this century, homosexuality was defined by the medical and scientific community as a psychiatric disorder. In the last several decades, however, "homosexuality" has been removed from the diagnostic manual of disorders, and research emphasis has shifted to the other side of the problem: the study of the negative, sometimes pathological, reactions to homosexuals by heterosexuals.

The term "homophobia" has gained currency as a one-word summary of this widespread problem. Since the early 1980's, scientists attempting to measure homophobia have developed a number of different homophobia scales and questionnaires.

As part of his 1996 study on homophobia, Dr. Henry Adams and his colleagues developed their own "Homophobia Scale" by modifying scales used by other researchers in earlier studies. Their 25-item questionnaire is "designed to measure your thoughts, feelings and behaviors with regards to homosexuality." The instructions stressed: "It is not a test, so there are no right or wrong answers."

Below, *Frontline* has reproduced this "Wright, Adams, and Bernat Homophobia Scale." It is not a perfect measure of anti-gay feelings or ideas, and is not a predictor of potential for anti-gay violence. (Though this scale was used in a research project designed to test the theory that homophobia is a manifestation of repressed homosexual desire, the scale is not a measure of homosexuality.)

Answer each question by using the numbers that follow:

1 = Strongly agree
2 = Agree
3 = Neither agree nor disagree
4 = Disagree
5 = Strongly disagree

After taking the quiz, in a group discuss each question and answer. In general, the higher the score, the greater the negative attitudes and beliefs about homosexuality. You can compare your score to the participants in the study on-line: www.pbs.org/wgbh/pages/frontline/shows/assault/etc/quiz.html.

1. Gay people make me nervous.
2. Gay people deserve what they get.
3. Homosexuality is acceptable to me.
4. If I discovered a friend was gay I would end the friendship.
5. I think homosexual people should not work with children.
6. I make derogatory remarks about gay people.
7. I enjoy the company of gay people.
8. Marriage between homosexual individuals is acceptable.
9. I make derogatory remarks like "faggot" or "queer" to people I suspect are gay.
10. It does not matter to me whether my friends are gay or straight.
11. It would upset me if I learned that a close friend was homosexual.
12. Homosexuality is immoral.
13. I tease and make jokes about gay people.
14. I feel that you cannot trust a person who is homosexual.
15. I fear homosexual persons will make sexual advances towards me.
16. Organizations which promote gay rights are not necessary.
17. I have damaged property of a gay person, such as "keying" their car.
18. I would feel uncomfortable having a gay roommate.
19. I would hit a homosexual for coming on to me.
20. Homosexual behavior should not be against the law.
21. I avoid gay individuals.
22. It bothers me to see two homosexual people together in public.
23. When I see a gay person I think, "What a waste."
24. When I meet someone I try to find out if he/she is gay.
25. I have rocky relationships with people that I suspect are gay.

Language: A Pernicious and Powerful Tool

JESSICA PARKER

Jessica Parker, a teacher at Berkeley High School in California, describes the difficult process of her "coming out" to students in her classes. Understanding the importance of language's use in human lives, Parker initiates discussions about the marginalization of homosexuals in a heterosexist society and the impact of homophobic language. She learns that having the courage to promote "an inclusive and appreciative community that respects all people and all differences" amidst the wave of socially conservative values is the most important step in young people's gaining an understanding of the lifestyles of gay males and lesbians.

1. What does "pernicious" mean? How is language a pernicious tool?
2. What does Parker mean when she writes, "I was making a conscious decision to become a target of oppression"?
3. The readings in this book emphasize the notion that the privilege of naming and labeling belongs to people in power. In this selection, how does Parker show that heterosexuals have the power to name nonheterosexuals and that the homophobic use of language marginalizes gay men and lesbians?
4. Many argue that *isms* have a hierarchy of offensiveness. We would never want to exhibit racism, but we find humor in blatant displays of sexism (e.g., "MCP" for "male chauvinist pig"), ageism (e.g., "senior moment"), or homophobism ("don't be queer"). Why are we unable to draw comparisons among the *isms?*
5. Why do people remain silent when a social injustice occurs? What do you think of the student who says, "If I stand up for gay people, then my friends will assume that I am"?
6. Why is the process of coming out so challenging for lesbians and gay men?

Writing Activities

1. Consult the *Oxford English Dictionary* for the etymology of the word "gay." Trace its history. Write a full description of how the meaning of the word has changed throughout

history. Examine another homophobic expression of your choice and trace its semantic shifts.

2. Parker states that "a backlash has currently produced more antigay laws than ever before." Research this issue in the library.

3. Associated in the past with deviance, sin, mental illness, and criminal behavior, same-sex orientation is clearly aligned with negative stereotypes. Go to the library and examine how history has treated homosexuality.

4. View the Indian film *Fire* by Deepa Mehta about two sisters-in-law who fall in love, read the works of Black lesbian poet Audre Lourde, or examine *Dennis Shepard's Statements to the Court* of November 4, 1999 (www.matthewsplace.com), describing the loss of his gay son Matthew. Write a review of one of these works and present your reaction to the class.

———————————— ✦ ————————————

I will overcome the tradition of silence.

Anzaldua 59

I was washing the dishes in our small, shingled home in Sonoma, California, when my mother, who was eyeing me from the dining room, said, "You know, honey, your father and I will still love you if you are gay." My hands immediately froze. I snapped back in an irritated tone, "Mother, I am not gay. How could you think something like that?" and continued with the nightly routine of scrubbing and rinsing.

Throughout my high school years, most of my best friends were gay. Despite this fact, I did not question my own sexuality. I felt emotionally immature compared to my peers who had long-lasting relationships, and since my romances barely lasted two months, I did not try to untangle my feelings for the girls on whom I had crushes or the boys I thought were cute. Even if my parents had already assumed my sexual orientation as a result of my affiliation with gay friends or my lack of boyfriends, I needed to develop my own understanding of sexuality and become comfortable with my sexual identity.

A year after my mother's vote of confidence in our kitchen, I was a freshman at the University of California at Berkeley. I became intimately involved with a female friend and began to negotiate a gay identity; ultimately, it would take another two years before I would come out to my parents, not to their surprise. Ironically, it was not an easy task. My coming out was a political statement. Although I was ecstatic that my parents accepted me with warm smiles and embraced me with hugs when I came out to them, I was making a conscious decision to become a target of oppression. Society's heterosexual majority, I knew, would not embrace me with those same smiles and hugs. Yet, when I began to witness a handful of my gay and lesbian friends become ostracized by their loved ones after they came out to their families, it became apparent that I should not fear rejection from a homophobic society, when the people I most loved had accepted my sexual orientation unconditionally.

After witnessing the alienation of my friends, I promised myself never to be in the closet—"the identity prison"—regarding my homosexuality. I vowed to overcome the tradition of silence. Unfortunately, my profession as a teacher lends itself to just this dilemma. Coming out to my students differed greatly from confirming my sexual orientation with my supportive loved ones. With 120 new students every fall (I had fewer students than most English teachers because I taught ELL students), I pondered my motivation and the value of revealing my sexual orientation. Why should I expose such a personal issue?

WILL STUDENTS STOP USING LANGUAGE SUCH AS "FAG" AND "GAY" TO BELITTLE THEIR PEERS?

I taught the 1999–2000 school year at Berkeley High School, in   5
Berkeley, California. My world literature classes discussed and analyzed thematic units: the powerful and the powerless, difference and diversity, social and political injustice, and prejudice. We read historical fiction concerning the Japanese-Canadian and Japanese-American internment camps and apartheid in South Africa. We created PowerPoint presentations highlighting the systems in our lives that controlled our actions and related our findings to a Latin American novel by Isabelle Allende. We analyzed gender by reading short stories—written by two female authors from Mexico and Brazil—about women, their families, and coming to terms with illness and boredom. Throughout the school year, we assessed how to bring change to our school and community and make it a more inclusive and appreciative place for people and difference. In this context, which incorporated issues like

gender, race, ethnicity, privilege and power, and powerlessness, I felt obligated to overcome the tradition of silence around homosexuality in schools. But, I wondered, how do I weave "coming out" into the curriculum? The answer presented itself during a group project. A student confided in me that two boys could not refrain from claiming "that's so gay" to anything they found displeasing. I decided to come out to my classes the very next day.

From a teacher's perspective, it is essential to have students analyze the language of Shakespeare, the symbolism of Alice Walker, or the metaphors of Sandra Cisneros. From a personal perspective, it is also essential to have students analyze the language of everyday use. So, for my fifth period class, primarily composed of tenth graders, I drew a line on the board and asked a simple question, "What does the word *gay* mean?" One student responded, "It means a homosexual." "As opposed to heterosexual," I replied, "*so gay* has to do with one's sexual orientation?" The student nodded. I wrote "sexual orientation" under the line. The students' responses looked like this:

Gay

happy	sexual orientation	abnormal
		sick
		different
		lame
		stupid
		femmie male
		put down
		weird

I wanted the students to dissect and assess the language they were using (from the right column) to belittle their peers, but lecturing them was futile. I needed to create dialogue and have them reflect upon their own actions and usage.

I asked the class, "Do you think it is wrong for people to use the word *gay* or *fag* in a derogatory manner, even though it refers to a group of people and their sexual orientation?" Christine responded, "I don't think it is wrong. I have gay friends. They just need to get used to it." Despite the fact that Christine has gay friends, she still perceives homosexuals as the "other," who have to change to fit the needs of the people in power—heterosexuals. In addition, she marginalizes her gay friends with her homophobic use of language, since she has the ability to define the term "gay" for them.

Sitting directly behind Christine, a student named John added, "You know, you will always insult someone no matter what you say." The nihilistic philosophy the student offered was an impetus for a new teaching strategy. Although we had previously discussed privilege and power in class, Christine and John did not realize they were agents of oppression. I needed to illustrate the connection between our previous discussions and their current use of language. By drawing a comparison with another word, I thought it would clarify how their language was dehumanizing and discriminating against gay and lesbian people. I was going to take a chance.

I then replied to the class: 10

> The term *gay* has multiple meanings. The formal definition has to do with sexual orientation, but the term has also taken on negative connotations. What if I took another term that has multiple meanings and started using it in a negative way, like the word *black*? *Black* has multiple meanings. What if I went around and instead of saying "That's so gay" said "That's so black"?

With uncertain eyes, the students looked at me and said in harmony, "You would be racist." I replied, "Damn right I would be racist." I was using the fact that most of the students at Berkeley High School were intensely aware of racial issues and could easily recognize racism to follow up with a question regarding homophobia, "So why is it different when people use the word *gay?*" Hands shot in the air. I noticed that Nora was shaking her head. "Why are you shaking your head?" I asked. She replied, "But I don't mean it that way."

I needed to develop strategies to ensure that my curriculum and classroom, my school, and the atmosphere of both environments do not promote homosexuals as the "other." These three students viewed homosexuals as people who had to alter themselves to fit dominant society's view of what is acceptable rather than have people alter their use of pernicious terms like *gay* and *fag*. Unfortunately, we were short on time. I still needed to explain why I initiated this discussion. I did not have time to direct the conversation into the area of heterosexism and hegemony and begin to deconstruct the prevailing belief that heterosexuality is "the norm" rather than a segment on the continuum of sexuality.

I continued the discussion by stating. "The reason I wanted to talk about this is because I am gay. I have a partner of two and a half years, and you have actually met her mother. She was the guest speaker during our unit on the Japanese concentration camps in North America, who was interned as a young child." I could tell that most of the students were trying to jog their memory and recall that day. "But, more importantly, the next time someone says, 'Oh, that's so gay,' I want you to say, 'No, Ms. Parker is gay and what you said offends me.'" Although I wanted, initially, to create a dialogue and have students reflect upon their own use of language, I found myself putting words in their mouths. I wanted the students to use me as an example and stand up for me when homophobic labels and terms were used. I felt I was presenting them with a feasible opportunity to make change in their communities. Then Dan replied, "I can't do that Ms. Parker. If I stand up for gay people, then my friends will assume that I am." I nodded in understanding.

Months later, a student e-mailed me about our class discussion, saying, "The conversation made everyone stop and think. We, as individuals, are the only ones who can control how we choose to perceive things in life."

WHY SHOULD I EXPOSE SUCH A PERSONAL ISSUE?

15   One of my goals as a teacher is to create a curriculum in which the students' education connects with their lives. When I teach literature—for instance, *Romeo and Juliet*—the themes of teen suicide, gang violence, and parent-child relationships usually resonate with students. This connection is essential. The students can relate to the experiences of the characters and see themselves within the text. If one of my goals as a teacher is to connect literature and history to my students' lives, why can't my history, my personal experiences connect with their lives? Yet, I hear the critiques from the religious right: "Don't bring your personal life into the public schools." "Don't talk about sexual orientation because the parents and/or the church have the right to discuss the subject at home or during mass," and "Don't manipulate the students with your talk about homosexuality." Their rhetoric reminds me that, although it is no longer a crime to be openly gay in the United States, my silence would perpetuate their political agenda rather than assist in dismantling the laws and prejudice

that continue to promote and justify discrimination towards homosexuals. Because more and more people are coming out and breaking the silence, a backlash has currently produced more antigay laws than ever before (Eskridge 205), and most gay teachers in the United States do not work in districts that protect their employment rights. The decision to come out to my students, to share and teach my personal history, was something I could not afford to dismiss.

During my eighth period world literature class, which was comprised of tenth through twelfth graders, I opened the discussion with a different question, "Do you hear students using the word *gay* or *fag?*" I assumed that my students already knew the formal and colloquial definitions because most of the students had been in the United States for three or more years. Some of the students replied that their friends used the words to belittle other students. One girl raised her hand and asked, "What does the word *gay* mean anyway?" I was surprised and eager to answer her question. I responded, "It means that a man or a woman loves a person of the same sex." Sushila's hand shot up in the air, "We don't have people like that in my country." She was from India. Alex added, "Maybe in China they did have gay people, but now we don't anymore." I was disappointed by the pride in the students' statements: their home countries supposedly did not have any (more) of "those" people. That these students were not fully aware of American cultural references regarding homosexuality but were enculturated to believe that homosexuality was an abnormal deviation reinforced my desire to come out as a gay teacher. Again, it was important for me to be one of "those" people, since I was already an authority figure, and they trusted my guidance as a teacher; I could now give voice to an ignored and/or hidden minority of gays and lesbians that these students did not hear about in their home countries. I told the class, looking at Alex and Sushila, that their countries probably *did* have gay and lesbian people, and asked if homosexual people would be accepted in their countries. The students agreed that they would not.

The conversation changed when a student named Chen asked, "Is there something physically wrong with gay people?" Anneaka, who had just finished her injustice essay on AIDS in South Africa, replied, "It's not biological. There is nothing wrong with gay people. They should be allowed to love whoever they want to." The student made a direct connection between homosexuality and biological defects; hence, a scientific justification for their social abnormality. Historically, homosexuality was viewed as a mental illness. Scientists claimed there was a pathological condition affecting gays and lesbians and have tried even in the late 1990s to find biological reasons for homosexuality. Yet, Anneaka automatically guided the discussion away from scientific claims to focus on the love between two people.

I came out to this class by stating, "The reason I wanted to discuss this issue is because I am gay." There was a moment of silence and shock. A student responded, "Really?" Amilca then added, "We don't care Ms. Parker, we love you for who you are." Although Amilca's stamp of approval was welcoming, I knew it was just a step in the long process toward visibility and equality. After the school day had ended, a student said to me privately:

> I commend you for having such courage and love of education. I think that parts of our class discussion were very ignorant, and I am definitely reminded that homophobia and prejudice run rampant in the world and age in which I live. Even in Berkeley, my classmates have a very closed-minded outlook on life.

WHAT REAL DIFFERENCE WILL I MAKE BY COMING OUT TO MY STUDENTS?

I need to continue coming out to my classes and initiating discussions about homosexuality and homophobia in the hope that one day soon all educators will work for an inclusive and appreciative community that respects all people and all differences and, simultaneously, emphasizes our similarities. Our classroom curriculum is a nexus for this hope. Yet, throughout each semester, I am under pressure to read a number of novels and plays, produce top scores on standardized tests, and align curriculum with the district and state standards. Under these pressures, it is extremely difficult to devote two weeks to a unit on gays and lesbians and adequately discuss the issues presented above. After coming out to my classes, I realized that I needed to integrate gay and lesbian fiction, nonfiction, and history into my curriculum by placing it side-by-side with canonical literature. By implementing thematic units, I am able to weave *Like Water for Chocolate* with the lesbian-themed movie *Fire* (an edited version) and the poetry of Jamaica Kincaid; Audre Lorde with *Obasan;* and *The Crucible* with Dennis Shepard's appeal to the killers of his son, Matthew (*New*

York Times). Below is a table of the literature and themes I have used and plan to use within the classroom to provide a context of inclusion, where gays and lesbians are not viewed as the "other."

	Theme	Making the Connection	Final Assignment
LWFC/*Fire*/ Kincaid	Tradition	Women/ obligation/ gender roles	Tradition essay (Teacher assigned topic)
The Crucible/ Shepard	Hegemony and difference	The powerful/ influence/ appreciating difference	A response to *The Crucible* (short story, editorial, spoken word, etc.)
Lorde/*Obasan*	Fighting against oppression	Using your voice to take a stand	Injustice essay (student topic)

When students read *Obasan* and empathize with the main   20
character, Aunt Emily, and her desire to find justice, and when they read Lorde's appeal to use one's voice to attain this justice, gays and lesbians can be viewed as people who overcome obstacles in life rather than as mere abstractions. When students recognize how women overcome obligation in order to pursue their own desires and needs, the lesbian characters in the movie *Fire* can be viewed as people who follow their hearts instead of prescribed gender roles. This type of combination allows gays and lesbians to move from the position of "other" to an inclusive setting, where themes are discussed and analyzed, and gays and lesbians are a part of everyday life.

Language is both a pernicious and powerful tool. With 97 percent of students in public high schools regularly hearing homophobic remarks from their peers and 53 percent of students hearing homophobic comments made by school staff, teachers have an obligation to analyze the language of everyday use with their students. With 77 percent of prospective teachers stating that they would not encourage a class discussion on homosexuality and 85 percent opposing gay/lesbian themes in their curriculum, teachers have an obligation to educate other teachers on the impact of homophobia and homophobic language (GLSEN).

After the school year had ended, one of my former students e-mailed me about my coming out and the discussion the class had. The young woman stated:

> You touched upon something we needed to hear and needed to discuss. I remember leaving your class feeling enlightened, not in any spiritual way, yet I left feeling hopeful. School could be a place of higher learning. School could be a loving, outreaching, empowering, educating community. Everyone respected you for that, no matter their personal experience or views of the truth you shared.

Works Cited

Anzaldua, Gloria. *Borderlands/La Frontera: The New Mestiza*. San Francisco, CA: Aunt Lute, 1987.

Eskridge, William. *Gaylaw: Challenging the Apartheid of the Closet*. Cambridge, MA: Harvard UP, 1999.

Esquivel, Laura. *Like Water for Chocolate*. Trans. Carol Christensen and Thomas Christensen, New York: Doubleday, 1992.

Fire. Dir. Deepa Mehta. Zeitgeist, 1998.

GLSEN. *Just the Facts*. 24 September 1999. <http://www.glsen.org/binary-data/GLSEN_ARTICLES/pdf_file/424.pdf>

Janofsky, Michael. "Parents of Gay Obtain Mercy for His Killer." *New York Times* 4 Nov. 2000: A1+.

Kincaid, Jamaica. *At the Bottom of the River*: New York: Farrar, Straus & Giroux, 1983.

Kogawa, Joy. *Obasan*. Boston, MA: David R. Godine, 1982.

Lorde, Audre. *Sister Outsider*. Freedom, CA: The Crossing Press, 1984.

Miller, Arthur. *The Crucible: The Text and Criticism*. New York: Penguin, 1996.

Shakespeare, William. *Romeo and Juliet*. New York: Penguin, 1992.

Respect My Right to Be Responsible: Homophobia's Last Day in School
CHRISTOPHER M.

Advocates for Youth is an organization that "champions efforts to help young people make informed and responsible decisions about their reproductive and sexual health." It encourages teens to voice their concerns and make efforts to change the way societies all over the world deal with adolescent reproductive and sexual health. This letter appeared on the teen Web page of Advocates for Youth. Addressed to a senator, it was written by Christopher M., a gay male student who had experienced five years of constant harassment and homophobic taunts.

1. Why does Christopher M. write this letter to his senator?
2. Christopher M. states that the number one form of harassment in school is teasing gay male and lesbian students with homophobic language. How is the use of offensive language a form of harassment?
3. According to the letter, in what ways have schools been successful in combating homophobic harassment? What have proven to be unsuccessful methods?
4. How do teachers help perpetuate the marginalization of gay and lesbian students? Why do you think that teachers and school administrators ignore the harassment of gay and lesbian students?
5. Do you think that the subject of minority sexual orientations should be included in school curriculum so that teachers and students can gain a better understanding of the lifestyles of gay men and lesbians?

Writing Assignments

1. What can be done about homophobic harassment in schools? Design an antihomophobia project that could be implemented in your former high school to create a comfortable environment where all students of differing sexual orientations are accepted and respected.
2. Write a convincing letter to your legislator regarding an issue related to sexuality education, sexual health, and health care for young adults.
3. Write a letter in response to Christopher M.'s.
4. Homophobic taunts are commonly used in the playground among young children and adolescents as a means of bullying: "You're gay," "Your shoes look gay," "Don't be queer." Many schools establish policies related to homophobic language and behavior. Research a school policy related to sexual harassment. What has its success rate been?

◆

Dear Senator:

This probably isn't the first time you heard about this or the last time you will, but I hope what I have to say makes great enough an impact that we can see a change occur in this lifetime. A change that will affect the lives of all students today and tomorrow. A change that will make students think twice before using a homophobic language, action, or joke in school. A change that will make schools safer. A change that will make students feel comfortable in school once again. And most importantly a change that will let us all see the "demon," homophobia, plunge into the eternal wrath of Hell where it belongs.

I speak for all students when I say that homophobia can only be tackled by the teachers and administrators themselves. I have experienced all forms of tackling homophobia in schools and only one solution has brought an end to it. That solution was something I was not willing to bring to the attention of administrators until my senior year of high school after I had endured the verbal abuse of other students for five straight years. In this case I had something to teach the teachers. Something they were completely oblivious to until I brought it to their attention. That or they ignored the situation completely in fear of reprisals without explicit support. I told my administrators that teachers were ignoring students' use of homophobic language, actions, and jokes in classrooms. Some teachers went as far as to laugh at the jokes, or tell the jokes themselves. Very few teachers recognized the growing problem, and even those who did were not tackling it correctly. I think it's because many teachers don't see it as wrong. That disappoints me tremendously. How can schools turn a blind eye towards this growing problem? Many can and will until someone speaks up about the issue. Sadly enough, most students are afraid to say anything at all in fear they will be targeted for discrimination, outed if they are gay, or other students will somehow find out they said something.

Homophobic language is no better than racist language. It is just as hurtful and just as damaging. So why do we allow the words "Faggot," "Dyke," "Homo," etc., to be used in school? It confuses and upsets me greatly. And believe me I am not the only one who is upset by this. Recent statistics prove that. According to a national survey, youth (gay AND straight) described being called "lesbian" or "gay" as the most deeply upsetting form of sexual harassment they experienced in school. This is also the number one form of harassment in schools. It is also believed to have been partially to blame for FIVE of the recent school shootings. These students were teased and taunted right in school with homophobic words and actions. What is this saying about the lack of education on the subject of homophobia in schools? A LOT! That is why my organization (GYAD—Gay Youth Against Discrimination) is here to educate teachers and administrators how to tackle the subject correctly. We have been successful in two schools so we feel there is no reason we can't be successful in EVERY school. We are currently seeking the support of students around the country in order to aid us in this mission of fighting homophobia one on one in schools. There are other organizations also in this fight, but I am afraid to say they are not effective enough in schools. Students coming to schools to talk to other students has proven to be ineffective. Gay advocates talking to students has been ineffective as well. It is upsetting to know that when these speakers leave, the students that were using these words before continued to use them even more frequently after the speakers left. The message has not struck a chord with students because you cannot change a person's mind on something they believe. If a student believes that gay people are bad and disgusting, they will continue to think that. It also has a lot to do with the mob mentality of a lot of students in schools. Being a student I know that many students long to be a part of a group and will do and say anything that the group does in order to become a part of them. These groups grow and grow and the outsiders get teased and taunted. If anyone is different from them, they get teased and taunted. I was called anti-gay slurs for five years right in front of teachers and the most the teachers ever said to the students was "please stop." That is not enough. Discipline is the most effective means of fighting homophobia. After I had brought it to the attention of administrators in my school, they carried the message to every teacher in the school and the teachers then finally took action against it. The teachers began disciplining the students right when they used anti-gay slurs, and homophobic language was BANNED. Students were shut down immediately after they used the word, and by the end of the year guess what happened? NONE of the students used those words in class again. I was no longer teased and I felt a lot more comfortable at school. I actually looked forward to going to school everyday and I no longer felt like an outsider. It was a change that affected me and A LOT of other students greatly. We now believe today that 1 in every 10 students may be gay, lesbian, or bisexual. That knowledge should really show us how important this mission is. This is not something that is affecting a few students, it is affecting a lot of students. Another survey shows that gay students hear anti-gay slurs as often as 26 times each day and faculty intervention occurs in only about 3% of those cases. A survey administered by SIECUS showed that few administrators discipline students for name-calling and harassment of gay and lesbian students. You cannot dispute the facts folks, they are right in front of your face, it is time you learn them and do something about them. No school wants to be another statistic in these staggering reports.

Do something. Students spend thousands of hours in school, shouldn't they be free of this harm and these worries they have to harbor each and everyday? Of course! Many students have written to me and going to school is a day in hell for them. Let us move on into a brighter future where we can all live in a world free of homophobia and where we can see homophobia's last day in school. I urge you to please help us in the enforcement of sexual orientation discrimination laws in school. If this is not done we are leaving a very dangerous environment for gay and straight kids alike. I thank you very much for taking the time to read this letter.

Sincerely,
Christopher M.
New Jersey

Queer
LILLIAN FADERMAN

Lillian Faderman, feminist author and professor of English at California State University, Fresno, is noted for her work on the lesbian subculture. Among her many publications are *Surpassing the Love of Men: Romantic Friendship and Love between Women from the Renaissance to the Present* (1981), *Odd Girls and Twilight Lovers: A History of Lesbian Life in Twentieth-Century America* (1991), and *Chloe plus Olivia: An Anthology of Lesbian Literature from the Seventeenth Century to the Present* (1994). In "Queer," Faderman explains how the term "queer" is an empowering term when used among the gay and lesbian populations.

1. Trace the history of the word "queer" as described by Faderman. At what point in time did "queer" become associated with homosexuality?
2. What does Faderman mean when she says that in the 1970s African Americans coined slogans such as "Black is beautiful" to defuse the word "Black"? Can you think of other words that have been adopted by a minority group in order to defuse a term?
3. Why don't some conservative gay men and lesbians accept the positive connotation of "queer"?
4. What is the message in the author's last line: ". . .We're exceptional. We're fabulous—we're queer"?

Writing Assignments

1. Consult the *Oxford English Dictionary* for the etymology of the word "queer." Trace its history. Write a full description of how the meaning of the word has changed throughout history.
2. Interview friends and classmates about their use of words such as "gay," "faggot," "queer", and "dyke." How do they define these terms? Write a paper comparing your peers' definitions to those in standard dictionaries and slang dictionaries.
3. Throughout history, many famous people have hidden their homosexuality from the public. Write about an important figure in history and why he or she resisted "coming out."
4. Only recently have television and film portrayed gay men and lesbians in a positive, more realistic light. Videotape a television program or view a film where gay men and lesbians are central characters. Write a critique of how accurately or inaccurately the mass media portrays gay men and lesbians.

———————————— ✦ ————————————

When I was in elementary school in East Los Angeles during the late 1940s, playground lore had it that Thursday was queer day. I had no idea what "queer" meant, but I knew it was something you did not want to be. I was 16 when I had my first relationship with another female, who told me that in the Midwestern elementary school she had attended, Friday was queer day, and that what we had just done together made me a queer. I think that was the only time, until a couple of years ago, that I had heard that word used by a lesbian, though I did hear drag queens use it when they were camping it up in the gay bars of the 1950s and 1960s: "Hello, Miss Thing, Hello, Duchess Ding-a-Ling, Hello, all you queers."

However, most of us guys and lesbians hated that word, not only because "queer" was the term straight people were most likely to hurl at us as an insult for our sexuality, but also because it had nonsexual connotations—weird, eccentric, suspicious—that were disturbing to us in our desire to fit in and to be just like heterosexuals in all ways but what we did in bed. In fact, long before the word "queer" became a pejorative for "homosexual," it meant bad things. In Old German (whence it eventually evolved into English) *queer* denoted "oblique," "perverse," "odd." Its meanings deteriorated in English. In the 1600s, for example, a "queer mort" was a syphilitic harlot. A 1796 "Dictionary of the Vulgar Tongue" lists 23 uses of the word "queer," all of them negative, but none of them denoting a person who loves the same sex. In the 19th century, "queer bub" was bad liquor, a "queer chant" was a false name or address. To "shove the queer" meant to pass counterfeit money.

According to Eric Partridge, the slang lexicographer, it was not until 1910 in the United States and 1915 in the British Empire that the term queer was first used to refer to "sexually degenerate men or boys." Hugh Rawson in "Wicked Words" traces the word back a bit earlier. He cites an ad placed in a 1902 issue of "The Blue Book," a directory of the red-light district of New Orleans, that seems to suggest (though ambiguously) a homosexual definition of the word: The ad copy says of Diana and Norma, "Their names have become known on both continents, because everything goes as it will, and those that cannot be satisfied there must surely be of a queer nature."

It's possible, also, that the term had some early, less hostile, usage among homosexuals themselves, perhaps as a code word (like "gay") that few heterosexuals would have understood. For example, in Gertrude Stein's 1903 manuscript about lesbian relationships, "QED." Helen invites Adele to meet Jane Fairfield by saying, "She is queer and will interest you and you are queer and will interest her. Oh! I don't want to listen to your protests, you are queer and interesting even if you don't know it and you like queer and interesting people even if you think you don't." Yet such uses of the term were apparently rare. In Farmer and Henley's 1909 "Dictionary of Slang . . . Past and Present," "queer" continued to have many negative definitions, but not one of them referred to homosexuality. As late as 1927, a novel by Fredrick Niven was entitled "Queer Fellows," but the eponymous characters were hoboes, not gay men.

By the time I came on the gay and lesbian scene in the 1950s, the term was interchangeable with other homophobic words such as "fairy" and "bulldyke." It even had a variety of forms, all expressing hostility: "eerquay" in Pig Latin, "queervert" in place of "invert," "Timesqueer" to mean a "queer of Times Square," etc. The word was certainly "queered" for us homosexuals. Linguistics researcher Julia Penelope, in a 1970 article for American Speech, said that the gays and lesbians she interviewed all knew the term but felt it was only used by heterosexuals to express their disdain for homosexuals. However, pejoratives were beginning by then to be put to interesting use. African-Americans had already adopted the term "black," perhaps because it had once been the worst thing that could be said about a person of color in America to insult him or her. They knew that to coin slogans such as "Black is Beautiful" would defuse that word, take all its power to hurt and turn it around to make it heal.

Lesbians understood the same thing to be true about the word "dyke" by the early 1970s, when young lesbians began to prefer calling themselves "dyke" to any other label. "Dyke" became synonymous for them with a brave, beautiful, powerful modern "Amazon." Harry Hay, the founder in the 1950s of the first national gay organization in America, the Mattachine Society, began using the term "fairy" publicly in 1970 to say that he and his friends were not only different from heterosexuals but more spiritual, more artistic and much nicer. He formed another organization, which he called Radical Faeries in 1978. But "queer" remained a politically incorrect term in the gay and lesbian subculture.

For some gays and lesbians, it remains politically incorrect today. When the rather conservative national gay and lesbian news magazine, *The Advocate*, first used the term in a positive manner in late 1990, the Letters to the Editor section was filled with protests and many threatened to cancel their subscriptions. My middle-aged lesbian friends tell me, "It will always be an insult to me," and "It's a put-down. Queer as a three-dollar bill. False currency. Like you don't ring true." But many younger gays

[handwritten margin note: But that's letting them dictate]

and lesbians have embraced the term "queer" in self-description *that not only valorizes it but also says to straights who might still want to use that word derogatorily,* "In your face!"

Young gay and lesbian culture has become suffused with it in the last year or two. The crossover lesbian rock group 2 NICE GIRLS flash the term in many of their lyrics. . . .

In April 1990, a New York group of young gays and lesbians who felt that homosexual rights were not advancing quickly enough *designed some radical militant tactics that hark back to the 1960s and 1970s and began to call themselves Queer Nation.* The idea caught on quickly. There are now enclaves of Queer Nation all over the country. Yoav Shernock of Los Angeles Queer Nation explains that *"queer" is an ideal term because it includes "faggots," "fairies," "lezzies," "dykes."* It's an umbrella term for both men and women (as the term "gay" once was but ceased to be in the 1970s when many lesbian-feminists wanted to break away from all men, including homosexual men, and form their own women's culture). But it does more than bring gay men and lesbians together, Shernock observes. *"Gay" used to be an empowering term 20 years ago. But now it means middle-class white men who want to assimilate.* It hasn't included blacks or poor people or women. The word "queer" helps set up a new community that "gay" has excluded.

10   It is a fighting word, a rallying cry to battle and a warning to heterosexuals of the new homosexual militancy. Shernock, explains of the term "queer": "It's a word of pride. *It tells people that we're opposed to assimilating. Those who believe that they're just like anyone else except for who they sleep with aren't queer. They're gay. Being queer is more than who you sleep with.* We don't want to fit into the straight world like gays do. We just want to make our own safe space. Sure, the dictionary says that 'queer' means deviating from the normal. We do—we're exceptional. We're fabulous—we're queer." *[handwritten: Why should it have to be a bad thing.]*

Ironic Genius?

TOM PEARSON

White rapper Eminem is identified as a misogynist, homophobe, and bigot, but his lyrics "have all the depth and texture of the greatest examples of English verse." A musical genius, Eminem has won rave reviews and Grammy awards, and performed concerts throughout the world. As a human being, however, he seems to lack sensitivity to the impact of biased language. In "Ironic Genius?" Tom Pearson questions whether popular hip-hop artist Eminem is a homophobe, a product of his environment, or a "genius with a talent for irony."

1. Bring to class some recordings of Eminem's music. Read the lyrics to his songs. What is your reaction to his music?
2. Can you identify other artists who exploit the use of words for fame and fortune?
3. Do you think that Eminem is a "disturbed homophobe" or an "ironic genius"? Support your answer.
4. Do you believe that because Eminem is a young white American male, he can get away with such homophobic, racist, and sexist lyrics?
5. Do you think that music containing offensive lyrics should be banned? Do such lyrics encourage violence?

Writing Assignments

1. According to Gay and Lesbian Alliance Against Defamation (GLAAD), "While hate crimes against gay people are on the rise, these epithets create even more bias and intolerance toward an entire community. The real danger comes from the artist's fan base of easily influenced adolescents, who emulate Eminem's dress, mannerisms, words and beliefs." Write a paper supporting this statement or rebutting it.
2. Retail stores such as Wal-Mart and Kmart sell "clean" versions of certain albums, with any profane, drug-related, and violent lyrics eliminated. They do not, however, delete antigay, antilesbian, and misogynist content. What is your reaction to this selective ban of music?
3. Write an essay about how hate language incites violence.

───────────── ◆ ─────────────

Eminem is an artist who has garnered massive mainstream success. His last album, the *Marshall Mathers LP,* has sold eight million records, mainly due to his lyrics, which deal with controversial subjects such as underage sex, drug use, rape and violence.

The liberal press is split: is Eminem a disturbed homophobe or a troubled ironic genius? One side argues that Eminem is a violent homophobic misogynist who perpetuates and legitimises these views in society and actually promotes them to 'our children.' Take these lyrics from the song 'Criminal' from the *Marshall Mathers LP*:

> My words are like a dagger with a jagged edge/
> That'll stab you in the head/
> Whether you're a fag or lez/
> Or the homosex, hermaph or a trans-a-vest/
> Pants or dress—hate fags? The answer's 'yes'/
> Homophobic?/ Nah, you're just heterophobic/

The opposing argument is that Eminem is a voice for the disillusioned young, white male of America. A genius with a level of wit and irony to rival the likes of Oscar Wilde.

Both of these arguments are overly simplistic. However, no middle ground is to be found in the mass media. Bourgeois liberals do not know what to think. Though his gay-bashing lyrics spit in the face of their views, they feel they ought to be on the side of free speech and against censorship. This is why Eminem has become such an issue—it is not all hype. He offends and confuses the politically correct.

5   It has to be recognised that though Eminem is perceived to be an overnight sensation, who exploded into public consciousness after his number one hit single 'My name is,' this is simply not true. Eminem had been slogging around the underground hip-hop scene for years before gaining fame.

It was only after he started rapping as his 'evil' *alter ego*, 'Slim Shady', with the release of his *Slim Shady EP*, that he started to receive attention and got signed by Dr Dre, a veteran of the hip-hop scene. This is important because, although Eminem had the musical integrity and a good reputation from the underground rap community, there is no way that he would have achieved the success he has if his lyrical content had not changed.

It also has to be acknowledged that Eminem's lyrics are nothing exceptional in comparison to many of his contemporaries. A fellow white rapper, Cage, has made a career of talking about subjects even more depraved than Eminem. (Cage spent a number of his teenage years in mental institutions—compared to Cage, Eminem is normal.) It is in fact widely acknowledged that Eminem simply copied Cage's 'style' from a few years previously.

Homophobic language is nearly as widespread as misogynistic language in the hip-hop scene. Two examples of this are the lines, "Homos won't fit in", to be found on the track 'Dangerous' off OC's second album *Jewelz*, released in 1997; and "That's unnatural/like love between faggots", from 'The deer hunter', a song off the Jedi Mind Tricks album *Violent by design*, released last year.

This sort of language is endemic in the underground hip-hop movement that spawned Eminem. His lyrics are only an issue in that the mainstream bourgeois press pays little attention to the underground hip-hop scene. It is hard to be outraged at something if you are not aware it exists.

There are other questions to be asked. Would Eminem have received such bad publicity if he were not a hip-hop artist? The likes of Steely Dan have recorded songs in which the narrator has an affair with an underage girl, and Johnny Cash and Nick Cave have both recorded songs in which they kill their girlfriends. Why haven't *they* been attacked in the press?

Also, if Eminem had been black, would he have gained such massive success? And would he have had so much support from the 'ironic genius' side of the equation? Hip-hop artists have been attacked in the past for being homophobic. Until Eminem, the 'ironic' argument had never surfaced. Was it because previous offenders had been black, and a black person could never be that clever (note the sarcasm here)?

The answers to these questions reveal the hypocritical, racist nature of the media. It is all right for a white person or a country artist to say these things, but not a black person or a hip-hop artist. These 'liberals' are in fact not very liberal at all.

What of my personal views on Eminem? Personally I do not buy into the 'ironic' theory. On the subject of gays, I do believe Eminem is homophobic. There is a culture of homophobia in both the hip-hop scene and the inner-city areas where Eminem grew up. As attitudes are shaped through social conditioning, it is not surprising that he shares the views of his peers. When some liberals came to his defence in the press to say that he was some kind of genius with a talent for irony, I believe he simply took this notion on board as a weapon to attack his detractors.

On the other hand, I do accept that Eminem simply does say some things to 'piss people off' and spark controversy: i.e., sell more records. Though not a genius, he is no idiot. Knowing sex and violence sells, he is taking this as his mantra to make money.

Eminem's talent is unquestionable. However, some of his lyrics should be condemned, but not to the extent of calling for his songs to be banned, etc. That is simply political correctness gone mad.

15   We may not like the content, but it has to be acknowledged that a large proportion of our class shares his views. This should be addressed, but his right to free speech should not be compromised.

This debate has further shown the hypocritical nature of the British press. They should be attacked as much as Eminem.

Guidelines for Avoiding Heterosexist and Homophobic Language

Heterosexual bias or *heterosexism* is the assumption that the norm and ideal for sexual orientation, sexual attraction, and sexual behavior is a male-female union, that is, girlfriend-boyfriend, wife-husband, and mother-father.

Heterosexual bias in language is the use of terms and expressions that assume heterosexual orientation is the norm for social/sexual attraction and social/sexual behavior. *Homophobic language* is the use of language that describes, labels, and stereotypes gay men, lesbians, and bisexual persons as inferior and deviant.

Rule 1. Do not refer to a person's sexual orientation unless it is relevant.

Avoid terms that refer to marital status. Describing people as either married or single ignores other forms of social and sexual relationships.

Rule 2. Use the preferred term "sexual orientation" instead of "sexual preference"

Sexual orientation applies to a heterosexual homosexual, or bisexual person. *Sexual preference* suggests voluntary choice; most people do not consider their sexuality a matter of choice. "Lesbian sexual orientation," "heterosexual sexual orientation," "gay male sexual orientation," and "bisexual sexual orientation" are favored expressions over "lesbianism," "heterosexuality," "homosexuality," and "bisexuality." Emphasize the individual. Whereas the former terms focus on people, the latter terms are associated with pathology.

Rule 3. Use the preferred term "gay male" for male same-sex orientation. Use "lesbian" for female same-sex orientation.

Avoid using the term "gay" or "gay persons" to refer to both male and female same-sex orientation; such usage is vague, ambiguous, and sexist. In some contexts, the use of gay, lesbian, and bisexual as an adjective is preferred over those terms used as nouns. Rather than reducing a group under one umbrella term such as "the gays" or "the lesbians," use the preferred alternatives "gay males," "bisexual persons," or "lesbians."

Rule 4. Avoid referring to gay men, lesbians, and bisexual persons as "homosexual."

Because of the heavy social emphasis on sexuality and sexual activity, terms such as "gay male" and "lesbian" are preferable to "homosexual," "male homosexuality," "female homosexuality," and "lesbianism." Overemphasizing sexual behavior rather than social identity has perpetuated the negative stereotypes associated with past biased beliefs about pathology and criminal behavior. Avoid the commonly heard improper usage "they are homosexual" when referring to someone who is gay or lesbian.

Rule 5. As an outsider, avoid derogatory terms such as "homo," "butch," "fairy," "fag," "queer," "dyke," and "limp-wrist."

Many of these terms considered offensive by outsiders, however, have recently been embraced by the communities of gay men, lesbians, and bisexual persons. Insiders can describe themselves in terms that outsiders cannot. For example, "queer," "dyke," "fag," "faggot," and "queer" are positive terms acceptable among communities of gay men, lesbians, and bisexual persons.

Rule 6. Avoid offensive expressions that discriminate against gay men, lesbians, and bisexual persons.

Avoid expressions such as "queer as a three dollar bill" and "the idea is so gay."

Rule 7. Be sensitive to preferred terms when referring to social alliances.

"Partner," "domestic partner," "life partner," and "significant other" are terms used to refer to both same-sex and heterosexual unions. Gaining in popularity are the terms "companion," "domestic companion," and "lifetime companion."

Language
and Age

Old age is like flying through a storm. Once you're aboard, there's nothing you can do.　　　　　　　　　　　　　　　　　　　　GOLDA MEIR

The world population is getting older. One out of every ten persons is now 60 years old or above; by 2050 one out of five people will be 60 or older; and by 2150 one out of three people will be 60 or older. We are healthier and living longer than ever before. Early in our nation's history, the average U.S. citizen lived to the age of 35; at the turn of the millennium, average life expectancy in the United States was 76.5 years: A male's life expectancy is 78 years, a woman's 83 years. More significantly, the older population itself is aging; persons 65 years and older are the fastest-growing age group. The oldest old (85 years or older) may be a mere 1 percent of the U.S. population, but that number equals 3.5 million persons, the fastest-growing segment of the older population. The number of centenarians (aged 100 years or older) is projected to increase 15 times from approximately 145,000 in 1999, to 2.2 million by 2050. Among the oldest old, 65 percent are women. Exceeding all odds, the life expectancy for women in Japan is currently 84.11 years, for men 78 years. The world life expectancy, however, drops to 66 years. These trends will certainly continue into the next century as the baby boomer generation grows older.

Even though all individuals go through the developmental stages of childhood, adolescence, adulthood, and advanced age, making the transition from young to old is not always easy, especially in the United States where the cultural values of youth, vibrancy, independence, and physical beauty reign supreme.

179

Although there is no magical antiaging pill, we continue to search for eternal youth with antiaging products and therapies to reverse the effects of aging. No one escapes graying hair, deteriorating eyesight, wrinkles, and middle-aged spread. Whereas in most Asian and African cultures, old age is life's pinnacle and elders are valued for their wisdom and for maintaining old traditions and customs, we in the United States fear the process of growing old and the imminent loneliness, senility, dependency, inactivity, ill health, and sagging bodies associated with advanced aging.

As with other minority groups, the elderly population faces discrimination, prejudice, and exclusion in society in general, and in language in particular. The term used to describe the practice of the negative stereotyping of older adults is *ageism:* "any attitude, action, or institutional structure which subordinates a person on the basis of age." Ageism is an ism that reflects a prejudice in modern societies where at the "ripe" age of 50 an adult is "over the hill" and sent "out to pasture." Our use of language reflects the prejudices we hold toward this particular age group. *Ageist language* is the use of terms and expressions that oppress a particular age group, most notably older adults. Understandably, ageism impacts women differently than men. Even though women make up the majority of the older population and both sexes experience ageism, older women are more harshly judged as inactive, physically and mentally unhealthy, sexless, and dependent. Ageist language reflects this gender bias, describing an older woman as a "hag," "old maid," "granny," "blue hair," and "widow lady"; an older man is labeled a "coot," "geezer," "codger," and "old fuddy-duddy."

The selections in this chapter address the issues facing the world's elderly populations. In Western societies, advanced aging suggests the devaluation of a human being. Older people are generally not appreciated for their years of experience and knowledge, and this bias is reflected in language. In the first selection, "What is Your Aging IQ?", a quiz helps you identify your personal attitude toward aging. In the second reading, "Ageism," Barrie Robinson introduces the basic notion of prejudice toward older adults, the myths and stereotypes about old age entrenched in U.S. society, and the medical, government, and professional institutions that perpetuate ageist attitudes. In the next selection "Gender and Ageism," psychologist Linda M. Woolf examines the double discrimination older women experience. Although both men and women are victims of prejudice, women experience a double dose of ageism and sexism. The fourth reading "The

Language of Ageism" by linguist Frank H. Nuessel examines ageist language and stereotypes. He suggests that "ageist vocabulary for women is more derisive because it represents them as thoroughly repugnant and disgusting." He raises awareness of the negative connotations of common terms such as "aging," "old," and "elderly," and encourages the use of neutral or positive terms.

At the end of the chapter "Guidelines for Age-neutral or Nonageist Language" are provided to heighten your awareness of the central role language plays in society and how language perpetuates ageism and other prejudices. As you read the following articles, keep in mind what Groucho Marx once exclaimed: "Anyone can get old. All you have to do is live long enough."

Discussion Questions

1. When is a person "old?" Describe an "old" person. What does he or she wear? Where does he or she live? What does he or she eat? What activities is he or she involved in?

2. What are some common stereotypes about "old" people and "young" people?

3. What are ways that we refer to older people? Are these positive images?

4. Describe what happens to us as we age. What happens to us physically, mentally, socially? What are the outward signs of aging?

5. If you could stop the aging process, at what age would you choose to remain forever? Why?

6. In what ways can you as a young person get involved and become an advocate for the older population?

7. Founded in 1970 by social activist Maggie Kuhn, the Gray Panthers is a national organization of intergenerational activists dedicated to making the United States a better place to live for citizens of all ages by working on issues related to health care, peace, rights for the disabled, housing, anti-discrimination legislation, and the environment. Maggie Kuhn once said, "The best age is the age you are." Do you agree?

Projects and Other Writing Activities

1. As we age, we undergo a number of physiological changes that affect not only how we look, but also how we function and respond to daily living. Overall, the changes in the later life span involve a general slow-

ing down of all organs. Look through some old photos of your parents or grandparents. Choose a series of photos that show an individual going through various stages in his or her life. In examining these images, what do you discover about getting older? Write an essay describing the process of aging.

2. The United States is said to be a culture obsessed with youth and physical beauty. Do you agree? Write a convincing essay to support your answer.

3. Draw a timeline that highlights the major events of your life from birth to the present. Select one "flash of time" and write a narrative chronicling that event.

4. Interview an older person such as your grandparent. Record the oral history of this person.

5. View a film (e.g., *Cocoon* or *Grumpy Old Men*) or a television series (e.g., *Golden Girls, Matlock,* or *Diagnosis Murder*) that deals directly with age, for example, the coming of age, getting older, or the search for eternal youth. Write an essay arguing that the media fairly or unfairly represents different age groups.

6. How do the media, popular culture, and institutions such as business, government, and human service systems perpetuate ageist attitudes and behaviors? Write an essay showing the ways that we as a society or as individuals can counteract ageism.

7. Many television commercials employ older adults as actors, uttering such lines as, "Help! I've fallen and I can't get up" or "Clap on! Clap off!" Write a paper describing how the older population is used as part of a marketing strategy.

8. Consult one of the following national organizations and write a report reviewing its approach toward aging adults. What social and economic issues related to aging do these groups address? How do they go about addressing the needs and interests of older persons?

   Gray Panthers, www.graypanthers.org

   AARP (formerly known as American Association of Retired Persons), www.aarp.org

   National Council on the Aging (NCOA), www.ncoa.org

   American Geriatrics Society (AGS), www.americangeriatrics.org

   The Gerontological Society of America (GSA), www.geron.org/geron

   National Council of Senior Citizens (NCSC), www.ncseine.org

What Is Your Aging I.Q.?

To help identify your personal attitudes and biases about aging, take the following quiz: What is your aging I.Q.? Answer true or false to the following popular beliefs held in the United States. In a group compare and discuss your answers. Then as a class, discuss the correct answers provided after the quiz.

TRUE OR FALSE?

1. Most people will become "senile" sooner or later if they live long enough.
2. Intelligence declines with age.
3. Most elderly have little interest in or capacity for sexual relations.
4. American families, by and large, have abandoned their elderly members.
5. At least 25% of all elderly live in nursing homes.
6. Aged drivers have more accidents than younger drivers.
7. Depression is one of the most common problems of the elderly population.
8. Only children need to be concerned about consuming enough calcium.
9. More men than women survive to old age.
10. Older people tend to become more religious with age.
11. The majority of the aged are socially isolated and lonely.
12. The life expectancy for African Americans is about the same as for whites.
13. The life expectancy of women is four years higher than that of men.
14. Personality changes with age, just like hair color and skin texture.
15. All five senses decline with age.
16. The elderly have the highest poverty rate of all adult groups.
17. Older adults represent the group at most risk for suicide.
18. Older adults have more acute, short-term illnesses than younger persons.

19. The elderly naturally withdraw from participation in commu-
    nity life in advanced old age.
20. Hearing loss is the third most common chronic condition for
    the elderly.

ANSWERS

1. **FALSE:** Even among those who live to be 80 or older, only
   20–25% develop Alzheimer's disease or some other incurable
   form of brain disease. Among the overall elderly population,
   it is estimated that less than 10% are disoriented or de-
   mented; of these, some have conditions which are reversible
   through treatment. In either case, dementia or memory loss
   is not a normal part of aging, but typically indicates some organic condition. Further, the word "senility" is a meaningless
   term which should be discarded in favor of a specific description of the cognitive impairment.
2. **FALSE:** Intelligence per se does not decline with age. Most
   people maintain their intellect or improve as they grow older.
   While studies have shown that the elderly typically take
   somewhat longer to learn something new and have somewhat
   slower reaction times than younger people, this does not impair their ability to reason and function well.
3. **FALSE:** The majority of older adults continue to have both
   the interest and capacity for satisfying sexual relations well
   into their 70's, 80's, and even 90's.
4. **FALSE:** The American family is still the number one care-
   taker of older Americans. Most older persons live close to
   their children with their spouses; 8 out of 10 older men and 6
   out of 10 older women live in family settings.
5. **FALSE:** Only 5% of persons over 65 are living in nursing
   homes at any given time. Even among those 75+, only 10%
   are residents in nursing homes.
6. **FALSE:** Drivers over the age of 65 have fewer accidents per
   person than drivers under age 65.
7. **TRUE:** Depression is one of the most serious mental health
   problems among older adults. As many as 10% of adults of all
   ages experience serious depression, but the occurrence is
   even more frequent among the elderly. An estimated 30–60%
   experience an episode of depression severe enough to impair

their ability to function. Despite the high prevalence rates, few elderly are seen in mental health settings when compared with the young. This is partly attributable to the fact that depression in the elderly often goes undetected or is misdiagnosed as dementia.

8. **FALSE:** Older people require fewer calories, but adequate intake of calcium for strong bones is important as we age. This is particularly true for women whose risk of osteoporosis increases after menopause; men also develop osteoporosis, but in fewer numbers than women.

9. **FALSE:** Women tend to outlive men by an average of 8 years. There are 150 women for every 100 men over age 65, and nearly 250 women for every 100 men over age 85.

10. **FALSE:** Older people do not tend to become more religious as they age. While it is true that the present generation of older persons tend to be more religious than younger generations, this appears to be a generational difference rather than a characteristic of aging. In other words, the present older generation has been more religious all of their lives rather than becoming more so in older age.

11. **FALSE:** The majority of the elderly are not socially isolated and lonely. According to one study, about two-thirds of the aged reported that they are never or hardly ever lonely or identify loneliness as a serious problem. Most elderly have close relatives within easy visiting distance and have frequent contact. They also reported fairly high rates of socializing with friends and participation in church activities and/or voluntary organizations. This level of activity does tend to decline somewhat with advanced age and/or disability, but contact with relatives remained fairly constant or increased.

12. **TRUE** and **FALSE:** In general, the life expectancy for whites is 72 for men and 79 for women; the life expectancy for African Americans is 65 for men and 73 for women. However, the average life expectancy for African Americans begins to exceed that for whites after age 80 for reasons that are not well understood.

13. **FALSE:** The overall life expectancy for women of all races (78 years) exceeds that for men (71.5 years) by seven years.

14. **FALSE:** Personality doesn't change with age. Therefore, all old people cannot be described as rigid or opinionated, only those who were always rigid or opinionated.

15. **TRUE:** All five senses do tend to decline with age, although the extent of these changes varies greatly among individuals.
16. **TRUE:** In 1989, the elderly as a group had a poverty rate of approximately 11.4% as compared with those age 18 to 64 whose poverty rate was 10.2%. However, the near poverty rates are more instructive ("near poverty" means 125% of the poverty level): in 1990, 19% of the elderly were poor/near poor as compared to 14.4% of the 18–64 group. Poverty rates for children exceed those for both the elderly and other adults at 26% poor/near poor in 1990. Poor/near poor rates for certain elderly subgroups far exceed the average 19% poor/near poor figure for all elderly: elderly minorities are two and three times more likely as non-minority elders to be poor/near poor; 23.4% of elderly women were poor/near poor in 1990; 25% of the elderly aged 75+ were poor/near poor in 1990.
17. **TRUE:** Suicide is a more frequent cause of death among the elderly than among any other age group, primarily due to the high suicide rate among older men, especially older white men age 85+. People age 65 and older have a 50% higher suicide rate than the rest of the population.
18. **FALSE:** Older persons have less acute illnesses than younger persons. Older adults have more chronic illnesses than younger age groups, however.
19. **FALSE:** Although the "disengagement" theory was once accepted to explain the relative decrease in activity for some older adults, it has generally been discredited as a valid explanation. More current research has explored the vast diversity among the elderly and many new theories have been developed which better explain the variety of aging observed in this heterogeneous population.
20. **TRUE:** After arthritis and heart disease, hearing loss is the most common chronic disorder reported in the elderly population.

Ageism

BARRIE ROBINSON

Barrie Robinson, a field work consultant and lecturer in gerontology at the University of California at Berkeley, has had extensive experience in a wide variety of agencies serving older adults. Addressing the stereotypes associated with aging, Robinson introduces the intellectual and societal challenges facing an aging society. She suggests that negatively stereotyping the older person as sick, sexually inactive, ugly, mentally declining, forgetful, unproductive, lonely, and poor dehumanizes older adults and promotes age discrimination in the forms of unfair employment practices, physical abuse, and isolation/segregation.

1. According to the reading, what is ageism? What are the basic characteristics of age stereotyping? Can you think of other forms of stereotyping besides ageism?
2. With an understanding of age stereotyping, what are some positive and negative age stereotypes affecting the elderly?
3. We all age and die, yet we continually discriminate against the older adult population. What are some factors that account for discrimination against older adults?
4. Do you agree that when you are told "you are stupid," "you are ugly," or "you are old," you will believe that image and conform to it? Explain the harmful effects of internalizing a negative image of yourself.
5. Do you think that the United States is obsessed with youth? In what ways do Americans in the United States try to stop the aging process?
6. What does "to grow old gracefully" mean?

Writing Assignments

1. In what ways does society perpetuate ageist stereotypes and attitudes? Write an essay on how the media, government policies, and social practices foster an ageist society.
2. What are the most common myths about aging? Choose one of these myths and write an essay refuting it. Conduct research to support your answer.
3. Have you ever been treated unfairly because of your age? What was the incident? How did you feel? Write about this experience.
4. Collect cartoons or jokes related to age. Analyze the way we view and treat persons of different ages. Write an essay on your conclusions.

✦

I. WHAT IS "AGEISM"?

The term "ageism" was coined in 1969 by Robert Butler, the first director of the National Institute on Aging. He likened it to other forms of bigotry such as racism and sexism, defining it as a process of systematic stereotyping and discrimination against people because they are old. Today, it is more broadly defined as any prejudice or discrimination against or in favor of an age group (Palmore, 1990).

Erdman Palmore, who has written extensively about ageism, lists the basic characteristics of stereotyping which forms the basis of ageism in his 1990 book *Ageism* (pp. 151–152):

1. The stereotype gives a highly exaggerated picture of the importance of a few characteristics.
2. Some stereotypes are invented with no basis in fact, and are made to seem reasonable by association with other tendencies that have a kernel of truth.
3. In a negative stereotype, favorable characteristics are either omitted entirely or insufficiently stressed.
4. The stereotype fails to show how the majority share the same tendencies or have other desirable characteristics.
5. Stereotypes fail to give any attention to the cause of the tendencies of the minority group—particularly to the role of the majority itself and its stereotypes in creating the very characteristics being condemned.
6. Stereotypes leave little room for change; there is a lag in keeping up with the tendencies that actually typify many members of a group.
7. Stereotypes leave little room for individual variation, which is particularly wide among elders.

Ageism is manifested in many ways, some explicit, some implicit. The following piece by Edith Stein illustrates some graphic examples of negative ageism (Palmore, 1990, pp. 3–4):

> Older persons falter for a moment because they are unsure of themselves and are immediately charged with being "infirm."
> Older persons are constantly "protected" and their thoughts interpreted.
> Older persons forget someone's name and are charged with senility and patronized.
> Older persons are expected to "accept" the "facts of aging."

Older persons miss a word or fail to hear a sentence and they are charged with "getting old," not with a hearing difficulty.

Older persons are called "dirty" because they show sexual feelings or affection to one of either sex.

Older persons are called "cranky" when they are expressing a legitimate distaste with life as so many young do.

Older persons are charged with being "like a child" even after society has ensured that they are as dependent, helpless, and powerless as children.

II. HOW IS AGEISM PERPETUATED?

Ageist attitudes are perpetuated in many ways. Examples are abundant in the popular culture such as birthday cards which decry the advance of age, the lack of positive images of the elderly in advertisements and on TV programs, and the widespread use of demeaning language about old age. Some illustrative examples of such language include such colloquialisms as "geezer," "old fogey," "old maid," "dirty old man," and "old goat."

In addition, institutions perpetuate ageism. Businesses frequently reinforce ageist stereotypes by not hiring or promoting older workers. The American health care system focuses on acute care and cure rather than chronic care which most older adults need. Also, the federal laws which prohibit mandatory retirement exclude elected officials and their staff, and highly paid executives with annual retirement benefits of at least $44,000. Other government policies which reinforce ageism include use of a higher federal poverty standard for the elderly and job training targeted for younger age groups. Another example is the use of state welfare funds which are often targeted at children and adolescents, excluding equivalent services for older adults such as adult protective services and geriatric mental health services.

Human service professionals also perpetuate ageism. This is done more covertly by denying or limiting services, by not including aging issues in training material or educational offerings, and by not requiring geriatrics training for medical students even though older adults will comprise a significant proportion of their patients. The same criticism can be made about training of professional social workers who receive little information about the aging process although many of their clients will be elderly.

Underlying these attitudes are myths and stereotypes about old age which are deeply entrenched in American society. Even those who would not say that they are ageist probably have some ageist attitudes based on distorted or inaccurate information.

Palmore discusses the most common of these negative myths and stereotypes about aging in his book *Ageism: Negative and Positive* (1990, pp. 18–25). A summary of his main points follows:

1. **Illness.** Perhaps the most common prejudice against elders is that most are sick or disabled. About half of Americans think that poor health is a "very serious problem" for most people over 65 (Harris, 1981) and that older people spend much time in bed because of illness; have many accidents in the home; have poor coordination; feel tired most of the time; develop infection easily (Tuckman & Lorge, 1958); are confined to long-stay institutions; have more acute illness than younger people; and that the majority of elders are not healthy enough to carry out their normal activities.

   FACTS: Most elders (about 78% of those 65+) are healthy enough to engage in their normal activities (National Center for Health Statistics, 1981). Only 5 percent of those 65 and over are institutionalized and about 81 percent of the noninstitutionalized have no limitation in their activities of daily living, i.e., eating, bathing, dressing, toileting, and so on (Soldo & Manton, 1983).

   While more persons over 65 have chronic illnesses that limit their activity (43%) than do younger persons (10%), elders actually have fewer acute illnesses than do younger persons, have fewer injuries in the home, and fewer accidents on the highway than younger persons. Thus, the higher rate of chronic illness among elders is offset by the lower rates of acute illness, injury, and accidents. In addition there is evidence that rates of disability are decreasing among elders (Palmore, 1986; Crimmins, Saito, & Ingegneri, 1989).

2. **Impotency.** A related stereotype is the belief that most elders no longer engage in any sexual activity or even have sexual desire, and that those few who do are morally perverse or at least abnormal (Golde & Kogan, 1959; Cameron, 1970). Even physicians, who should know better, often assume that sexuality is unimportant in late life (Butler, 1975).

FACTS: The majority of persons past 65 continue to have both interest in and capacity for sexual relations. Masters and Johnson (1966) found that the capacity for satisfying sexual relations usually continues into the seventies and eighties for healthy couples. The Duke Longitudinal Studies (Palmore, 1981) found that sex continues to play an important role in the lives of the majority of men and women through the seventh decade of life. A large-scale survey (Starr & Weiner, 1981) found that most elders said that sex after 60 was as satisfying or more satisfying than when younger.

3. **Ugliness.** Another stereotype is that old people are ugly. Beauty is associated with youth, and many people, especially women, fear the loss of their beauty as they age. The following terms reflect this stereotype of ugliness: crone, fossil, goat, hag, witch, withered, wizened, wrinkled.

> **FACTS:** While our culture tends to associate old age with ugliness, and youth with beauty, some other cultures tend to admire the characteristics of old age. For example in Japan, silver hair and wrinkles are often admired as signs of wisdom, maturity, and long years of service (Palmore, 1985).
>
> Thus, there is nothing inherently ugly or repelling about the characteristics of old age. Ugliness is a subjective value judgment, or, in other words, "ugliness is in the eye of the beholder." These value judgments usually conform to cultural standards of beauty and ugliness.

4. **Mental Decline.** Another common stereotype is that mental abilities begin to decline from middle age onward, especially the abilities to learn and remember, and that cognitive impairment (e.g., memory less, disorientation, or confusion) is an inevitable part of the aging process (Palmore, 1988).

> **FACTS:** Most elders retain their normal mental abilities, including the ability to learn and remember. It is true that reaction time tends to slow down in old age and it may take somewhat longer to learn something. However, much of the difference between older and younger persons can be explained by variables other than age including illness, motivation, learning style, lack of practice, or amount of education. When these

other variables are taken into account, chronological age does not provide a significant amount of influence on learning ability (Poon, 1987).

Most studies of short-term memory agree that there is little or no decline in everyday short-term memory among normal elders (Kausler, 1987). As for long-term memory, various community surveys have found that less than 20 percent of elders cannot remember such things as the past President of the United States, their correct age, birth date, telephone number, mother's maiden name, or address; or the meaning of ordinary words (Botwinick, 1967; Pfeiffer, 1975). Thus, it is clear that while there may be some increase in long-term memory problems, the majority do not have serious memory defects. In summary, significant learning and memory problems are due to illness, not to age per se.

5. **Mental Illness.** A similar stereotype is that mental illness is common, inevitable, and untreatable among most aged. Both elders themselves and many health professionals think that most mental illness in old age is untreatable, which partially explains why few mental health professionals choose to specialize in geriatric mental health and also why elders use mental health facilities at one-half the rate of the general population (Lebowitz, 1987).

   FACTS: Mental illness is neither common, inevitable, nor untreatable in the elderly population. Only about 2 percent of persons 65 and over are institutionalized with a primary diagnosis of psychiatric illness (George, 1984). All community studies of psychopathology among elders agree that less than 10 percent have significant or severe mental illness, and another 10 to 32 percent have mild to moderate mental impairment; but that the majority are without impairment (Balzer, 1980). In fact, according to the most comprehensive and careful community surveys, the incidence of mental illness among the elderly is less than that of younger persons (Myers, Weissman, Tischler, Hozer, & Leaf, 1984).

6. **Uselessness.** Because of the beliefs that the majority of old people are disabled by physical or mental illness, many people conclude that the elderly are unable to continue working and that those few who do continue to work are unproductive.

This belief is the main basis for compulsory retirement policies and discrimination in hiring, retraining, and promotion.

FACTS: The majority of older workers can work as effectively as younger workers. Studies of employed older people under actual working conditions generally show that they perform as well as, if not better than, younger workers on most measures (Krauss, 1987; Riley & Foner, 1968). Consistency of output tends to increase with age, and older workers have less job turnover, fewer accidents, and less absenteeism than younger workers (Riley & Foner, 1968).

7. **Isolation.** From a third to half of respondents to Palmore's Facts on Aging Quiz think "The majority of old people are socially isolated and lonely" and "The majority of old people live alone" (Palmore, 1988). Two-thirds of persons under 65 think that loneliness is a "very serious problem" for most people over 65 (Harris, 1981).

> **FACTS:** The majority of elders are not socially isolated. About two-thirds live with their spouse or family (U.S. Senate Special Committee on Aging, 1988). Only about 4 percent of elders are extremely isolated, and most of these have had lifelong histories of withdrawal (B. Kahana, 1987). Most elders have close relatives within easy visiting distance, and contacts between them are relatively frequent.
>
> Most studies agree that there tends to be a decline in total social activity with age, but the total number of persons in the social network tends to remain steady (Palmore, 1981). The types of persons in the social network tend to shift from older to younger persons, and from friends and neighbors to children and other relatives.

8. **Poverty.** Views about the economic status of elders range from those who think most elders are poor, to those who think the majority are rich. At present those thinking elders are poor tend to outnumber those thinking elders are rich.

> **FACTS:** Most elders have incomes well above the federal poverty level (U.S. Senate Special Committee on Aging, 1988). A higher proportion of elders than the total population have a net worth of over $50,000 and a slightly higher per capita family income than non-elderly headed households.

However, in 1989, 11.4 percent of the elderly had incomes below the poverty level and 27 percent were "near poor", i.e. those with incomes up to 150 percent of the poverty level. It is also important to note that certain groups of elderly experience very high rates of poverty. These include widowed elderly women (21%), Afro-American elders (31%), and Afro-American elderly women living alone aged 72 or older (64%).

9. **Depression.** Since many believe that the typical older person is sick, impotent, senile, useless, lonely, and in poverty, they naturally conclude that the typical older person must also be depressed.

   FACTS: Major depression is less prevalent among the elderly than among younger persons. However, of the various mental illnesses, depression is one of the most common among the elderly. Experts are not in agreement about the extent of its occurrence, but it has been estimated that between 30 percent to 60 percent of the elderly population experience at least one episode of depression severe enough to interfere with daily functioning (Solomon, 1981). This, along with the fact that the rate of elderly suicide is the highest of all age groups, makes depression a significant issue for this population.

10. **Political Power.** Another stereotype is that the elderly are a "potent, self-interested political force" (Binstock, 1983). The assumption is that the political power of the elderly hamstrings our politicians from undertaking needed reforms.

    FACTS: The aged do constitute a large portion of participating voters constituting about 16 percent of those who vote in national elections while comprising 12 percent of the national population (Binstock, 1983). While aging-based interest groups can exert some influence, elders usually do not vote as a block and, consequently, have less political power than presumed.

Although much less prevalent, *positive stereotypes* about aging are also held by some people. Although they are usually far less damaging than negative stereotypes, they are based on inaccurate information that reinforces a distorted view of the elderly. An example of positive age stereotyping is that wisdom, dependability, kindness and compassion invariably accompany old age.

III. WHAT ARE THE CONSEQUENCES OF AGEISM?

In general, the consequences of ageism are similar to those associated with all attempts to discriminate against other groups: persons subjected to prejudice and discrimination tend to adopt the dominant group's negative image and to behave in ways that conform to that negative image (Palmore, 1990, p. 91). Furthermore, the dominant group's negative image typically includes a set of behavioral expectations or prescriptions which define what a person is to do and not to do. For example, the elderly are expected to be asexual, intellectually rigid, unproductive, forgetful, happy, enjoy their retirement, and also be invisible, passive, and uncomplaining.

Palmore identifies four common responses of elders to these   10 prescriptions and expectations: acceptance, denial, avoidance, or reform (Palmore, 1990, pp. 96–102). All of these responses can have harmful effects on the individuals. For example, an elderly person who accepts the negative image may "act old" even though this may be out of keeping with their personality or previous habits. This may mean that they stop or reduce social activities, do not seek appropriate medical treatment, or accept poverty. In essence, this internalization of a negative image can result in the elderly person becoming prejudiced against him/herself, resulting in loss of self-esteem, self-hatred, shame, depression, and/or suicide in extreme cases.

Denial of one's status as an elderly person can also have negative consequences. One example, lying about one's age may not seem significant, but it can further erode morale. Another example is the attempt to "pass" for a member of the dominant, younger group by undergoing cosmetic surgery, having hair transplants, or using widely advertised anti-aging products such as hair dyes, skin creams, cosmetics, etc. While these practices are widespread, the quest for eternal youth can become inappropriate and, ultimately, self-defeating for those who attempt to stop the natural aging process entirely.

Avoidance of ageist attitudes may also take many forms. Examples include moving into age-segregated housing, self-imposed isolation, alcoholism, drug addiction, or suicide. The reform response, Palmore's last response pattern, is the antithesis of the avoidance response in that the person recognizes the discrimination and attempts to eliminate it. This attempt may be an individual one or a collective one through membership in an advocacy group such as the powerful American Association of Retired Persons.

, stereotypes are dehumanizing and promote one-
inking about others. Elders are not seen as human
objects who, therefore, can be more easily denied
ind rights. For example, elders are frequently misdiagnosed or denied medical treatment because they are seen as
"old" and, therefore, incurable. Elders are also frequently denied
employment or promotion opportunities because they are "old"
and less productive. Such discrimination is also evident on the
social policy level where the elderly are blamed for having medical problems and consuming public resources rather than seeing
them as having human needs requiring appropriate social responses. Seeing people as objects also increases the likelihood
that they may be subjected to abuse and other cruel treatment.

A final consequence of ageism is that by devaluing this segment of the population, a vital human resource is lost. This is
contrary to many American values which entail respect for human worth and dignity. Cumulatively, the elderly represent a vast
amount of experience, skill, and knowledge which this country
needs to remain strong and true to its ideals.

Gender and Ageism
Linda M. Woolf

Linda M. Woolf is an associate professor of psychology at Webster
University in St. Louis, Missouri. Her areas of interest include holocaust and genocide studies, women and global human rights, and
gerontology. According to "Gender and Ageism," older women experience greater discrimination than older men because of both their
age and their gender. Older adult women are viewed as sexless,
lonely, physically unhealthy, hypochondriacal, and dependent, a
viewpoint unsupported by empirical research. Moreover, there are
many more negative expressions for older women than for older
men, depriving older women of dignity, self-worth, and personhood.

1. What does the statement that "older women are subjects of
   both ageism and sexism" mean? Provide examples to support
   this viewpoint.
2. Make a list of stereotypes of older men and of older women.
   How do we stereotype older women and older men in language.

3. Here are a number of expressions related to age: "you are as young as you feel," "age is a state of mind," "grow up," "today is the first day of the rest of your life," "act your age." Try to explain what each of these phrases means. Can you think of other expressions that reflect cultural biases, such as "act like a man" or "act like a lady"?

4. Discuss the following celebrity quotes on getting older. Argue that "looks matter" in U.S. society, and that the standards of beauty created and perpetuated by the media, the fashion industry, and the cosmetics business are unrealistic.

I look forward to being older, when what you look like becomes less and less the issue and what you are is the point.

SUSAN SARANDON, ACTOR

Remember, age is not important unless you are a cheese.

HELEN HAYES, ACTOR

I really feel terrific about my wrinkles. I'm comfortable with them and I believe I would look most peculiar if I didn't have them. If I had my face pulled tight, I'd lose my identity.

ANGELA LANSBURY, ACTOR

They say getting thin is the best revenge. Success is much better.

OPRAH WINFREY, TALK SHOW HOST

Youth is in the mind, not in the condition of your flesh.

GINGER ROGERS, DANCER

I enjoy getting dressed as a Barbie doll.

VANNA WHITE, CO-HOST OF THE TELEVISION SHOW *WHEEL OF FORTUNE*

I don't like to be labeled as lonely just because I'm alone.

DELTA BURKE, ACTOR

Writing Assignments

1. Collect a number of examples of ageist and sexist language. How does language treat men and women differently? Write an essay showing how language unfairly treats the sexes.

2. Look through magazines, advertisements, cartoons, and other print materials for images of older women and older men. Are older adults represented fairly and proportionately? Write an essay based on your conclusions.

3. Do you think that television advertisers and programmers have an obligation to represent all minorities fairly and in true proportions? Write a paper supporting your answer.

———————— ✦ ————————

Ageism has an impact on both men and women. Studies have been conducted concerning the negative stereotyping of older women and older men. However, most of the ageism research has studied "the older adult". Thus, the differential effect of ageism on men and women has not been well examined. The research that has been conducted concerning ageism as it relates specifically to older women and men will be discussed below.

Even though women make up the majority of the older population, they have largely been ignored (Block, Davidson, & Grambs, 1981). References to older women usually take the form of generalizations despite the fact that the older population is characterized by its heterogeneity. These generalizations often take the form of stereotypes with the older women traditionally stereotyped as inactive, unhealthy, asexual, and ineffective (Block et al., 1981).

The sexless older woman is a common theme particularly in humor and greeting cards. Jokes concerning older women usually ascribe to the older woman the following characteristics: she is viewed as lonely, frustrated, and shriveled (Palmore, 1971). Palmore (1971) asserts that these attempts at humor merely reflect real societal attitudes. Hultsch and Deutsch (1981) state, however, that the factor having the greatest impact on sexual activity in old age is the availability of a socially approved and sexually capable partner. Sexual interest and ability generally do not decrease with age for women.

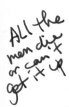
All the men die or can't get it up

Older women are often viewed as unhealthy. Interestingly, older men are perceived as being healthier than older women (Riley & Foner, 1968), even though, on the average, women live seven years longer than men. Women are also perceived to be hypochondriacal. However, on measures of perceived physical health, no differences have been found between old men and women or between an older and a younger population (Ross, Tait, Brandeberry, Grossberg, & Nakra, 1986). In addition, Ross et al. found that older women rated themselves as having greater body competency than either older men or young adults, both male

and female. Therefore, the image of the older woman as unhealthy or hypochondriacal is a myth.

In addition to the view that older women are physically un-   5
healthy, older women have been found to be diagnosed with psychological problems 3 to 4 times more often than men (Beeson,
1975). This may represent an ageist bias within psychology and
psychiatry. It has been hypothesized that the large number of
women seeking psychological support may be a consequence of
increased social stress on the older woman. Larson (1978) indicates that subjective well-being is most influenced by environmental factors. The factors having the greatest influence on
well-being are hypothesized to be health and socioeconomic status. In 1990, 50 percent of White women had incomes below 646
per month, African-American women had incomes below 419
per month, and Hispanic women had incomes below 426 per
month. With a poverty line for seniors of 437.91 per month, in
1990, it is clear that many women live near or below the poverty
line. Therefore, they are at risk for psychological difficulties.

Older women are also often viewed as ineffective, dependent,
and passive. This represents an extension of the view of all
women being ineffective, passive, and dependent, i.e., sexism
(Block et al., 1981). Often times, women will find this role difficult to shake. This is particularly true for an older women whose
sole identification has been with her husband (Payne & Whitting-
ton, 1976). This image of the older woman can also be a self-
fulfilling prophecy, particularly for new widows who are finding
it difficult to deal with independence (Block et al., 1981). In addition, as female, women continue to experience sexism during old
age and are placed, thus, in double jeopardy.

Interestingly, women's self image shows greater improvement
with age as compared to men (Clark & Anderson, 1967). It is hypothesized to result from increased social contacts that are characteristic of older women. Lowenthal, Thurnher, and Chiribaga
(1975) propose that older women's self image improves as they
become more assertive, less fearful, and less dependent.

Older men, however, are perceived as becoming more "feminine" with age; femininity being equated with psychological dependency and timidity (Silverman, 1977; Woolf, 1988). Silverman
(1977) conducted a study examining age differences in sex-role
stereotypes for men. College students were asked to complete the
Sex-Role Stereotype Questionnaire (Rosenkrantz et al., 1968).
Subjects were asked to rate either an average 25, 35, 45, 55, and
65-year-old man. Two control conditions were included: women

in general and men in general. The results indicated that women in general and men aged 65 were rated significantly higher in femininity (particularly on those items rated feminine but socially undesirable). Therefore, the perception of men undergoes a shift; older men are perceived as experiencing greater timidity and dependency during later life. It should be noted that the study does not look at how the older woman is perceived, nor does it include older adults as subjects. Woolf (1988) corrected for both of these problems. See *The Effects of Age and Gender on Perceptions of Younger and Older Adults.*

Nuessel (1982) has examined the language of ageism. Ageism is readily apparent in language against both men and women. The terms with which older women are described are representative of some of the more common stereotypes of older men and women. For example, the term "little old lady" suggests incompetency and impotency based upon age and gender. "Old hag" or "old witch" commonly refer to a woman who is physically unpleasant to look at and who has a disagreeable personality. Old men are commonly described by such terms as "old coot" and "codger." These terms suggest that old men are slightly odd or quaint. The commonly used term, "dirty old man," suggests some sort of unnatural sexual perversion in older men. Therefore, much of society's negative attitudes are reflected in its language.

10   Language may be more negatively ageist with respect to women than to men. Nuessel (1982) states, "ageist vocabulary for women is more derisive because it represents them as thoroughly repugnant and disgusting" (p. 274). This may represent the double jeopardy for older women as they are subject to both ageism and sexism.

In summary, both men and women experience ageism in the form of stereotyping. In addition, women experience not only ageism but sexism. Men are stereotyped as increasingly feminine, and women as asexual, unhealthy, and dependent. However, these stereotypes are not supported by empirical data regarding older men and women.

The Language of Ageism
Frank H. Nuessel, Jr.

Frank H. Nuessel, professor of classical and modern languages at the University of Louisville (Kentucky), examines negative cultural attitudes toward aging through language. Ageist terms are derogatory and demeaning because they depict the elderly as possessing largely undesirable traits and characteristics. Nuessel warns us that the way we treat older adults when we are young will be the way we are treated as older adults.

1. According to Nuessel, there are relatively few favorable expressions for the elderly. Can you think of positive images of older adults?
2. As in other articles, Nuessel, too, finds that there are many more negative terms for older women than for older men. List as many ageist terms for women and for men as possible. Can you come to any conclusions?
3. Nuessel provides a selected list of ageist terms. Have you heard these terms used? Are some no longer used? How and why does ageist language change?
4. "To ignore the awesome power of labeling is to contribute to the continued inhumane treatment of some of the elderly." Explain this quote from the article.

Writing Assignments

1. Conduct a survey like the one suggested by Nuessel. Ask people who are 65 years or older whether the following terms are acceptable when used to describe people 65 years and older: "senior citizen," "retired person," "mature American," "elderly person," "middle-aged person," "older American," "golden ager," "old timer," "aged person," "old man/old woman." Write an essay on your results.
2. The media and popular culture are criticized for *excluding* and *subordinating* older adults on screen and on television. Write an essay supporting the treatment of older adults in the media.
3. One interesting observation is that the patronizing way we talk to young children is similar to the way we address older people. Often, we use simpler vocabulary, less complex grammar, a singsong intonation, and other forms of baby talk. Write an essay on how we treat older adults as young children.

◆

The practice of ageism has existed for a much longer period of time than the term that refers to it. Dickman (1979, p. 1) states that the neologism was first coined by Robert N. Butler, director of the National Institute on Aging in 1967 (cf. Butler, 1969, 1975). Recognition of its lexicalization derives from the fact that it is now an entry in *The American Heritage Dictionary on the English Language* which defined ageism as "discrimination based on age; especially discrimination against middle-aged and elderly people" (Morris, 1979, p. 24).

The lexical items and phrases that allude to the potential victims of ageist bias are numerous, but finding an acceptable designation for this group has proven difficult. In a study conducted by Louis Harris and Associates for the National Council on Aging (Ward, 1979, p. 165), the following 10 terms were tested for acceptability on people 65 years and older. They include: *senior citizen, retired person, mature American, elderly person, middle-aged person, older American, golden ager, old timer, aged person,* and *old man/old woman.* One-third of those polled preferred the phrase *senior citizen,* whereas 55% liked the term *mature American.* Nevertheless, disagreement over the correct or proper expression continues. In fact, *senior citizen,* preferred by one-third and liked by exactly one-half of the respondents in the Harris poll, was declared a euphemism and was acceptable to only 47% of the Usage Panel of *The American Heritage Dictionary.* Clearly, an acceptable term must be neutral and omit any suggestion of stereotypes. The term *elderly* appears to accomplish this goal and will be used in the remainder of the text. Moreover, the favored item in journalism is *elderly* which avoids most negative implications.

In addition to the phrases already mentioned, others exist to name this group. The Gray Panthers, a political organization founded in 1970 by Margaret ("Maggie") Kuhn, has become the generic term for elderly activists. However, *geriatric generation, geritol generation,* and *Lawrence Welk generation,* which originated in the language of humor, are patently offensive.

Ageism is distinct from all other forms of discrimination because it cuts across all of society's traditional classifications: gender, race, religion, and national origin. Matthews (1979), for example, observes that "old age is not a social category with simple definition or an obvious membership. It is a social category with negative connotations but, because of the ambiguity surrounding membership, to whom negative attributes may be imputed is unclear" (p. 68). Moreover, in conjunction with other discriminatory practices, it can compound an individual's burden significantly in a coalescence of bigotry. Thus, an elderly, black, handicapped

woman suffers greater oppression than the individual without all
of these factors.

At this point it is necessary to point out that the language of   5
ageism is different from the lexicon of aging. Ageist terms are
derogatory and demeaning because they depict the elderly as
possessing largely undesirable traits and characteristics. The
language of aging is technical or erudite (Greco-Latin derivatives), with much of the terminology belonging to the clinical
domain (e.g., *geriatrics, geriatrist, geriatrician, gerontology*, and
gerontologist). Other related words are *gerontocracy, geron-
tophile, gerontophilia, gerontophobe*, and *gerontophobia*. Lexical
items of Latin stock include the following: *quinquagenarian,
sexagenarian, septuagenerian, octogenarian, nonagenarian*, and
centenarian.

It is interesting, if not disconcerting, to note that relatively
few favorable expressions exist to allude to the elderly. Positive,
age-specific attributions are scarce (e.g., *mature, mellow, sage,
venerable*, and *veteran*). It has been pointed out that certain adjectives relating to age convey favorable connotations if they refer to
alcoholic beverages, food, and certain handicrafts. *Old*, for example, when applied to wine or lace is a good trait. Likewise, *aged* attributed to brandy, cheese, and wood (for cabinetmakers) is a
choice characteristic. Consequently, context must be considered
when evaluating language use and abuse. This dearth of agreeable vocabulary is symptomatic of the deep-rooted nature of individual and institutional ageism in our society.

Ageist language falls into two distinct categories. One division includes words whose denotation specifically refers to the
elderly. The other component contains lexical items whose connotation or intensional meaning is associated only with the elderly.

Many ageist words are insidious in their deprecatory impact
because they demean people on the basis of age *and* gender (cf.
Matthews, 1979; Sontag, 1972: *passim* for a popular treatment).
Beldam(e), biddy, crone, granny, grimalkin, hag, and *witch* all refer
to women who possess unpleasant physical characteristics or disagreeable patterns of behavior. *Bag, bat*, and *battle ax(e)* denote
unattractive women with personality defects. As such, they are
not age specific. Normally, however, they are preceded by the descriptive adjective *old* and form a hybrid syntagm that is disparaging of elderly females. *Maid*, a semantically neutral term, in
conjunction with *old* and the term *spinster* also has unflattering
sexist and ageist connotations. Likewise, the phrase *little old lady*

suggests impotency based on age and gender. This subtle perpetu-
ation of the myth of sexism magnifies the outrage.

Denigrating lexical items that are marked for age and sex exist for males too. *Codger, coot, gaffer, geezer,* and *graybeard* all portray elderly males unfairly by attributing unconventional de-
meanor to them. The term *goat* prefixed by *old* and the phrase
dirty old man conjure up visions of an elderly man with misdi-
rected sexual desires. Nevertheless, ageist vocabulary for women
is more derisive because it represents them as thoroughly repugnant and disgusting.

10   One particularly unflattering term, *dotard,* is unspecified for
gender yet marked for age. Finally, a large group of words including
crank, fart, fogy, fool, fossil, fuddy-duddy, grump, and *miser* are terms
of general scorn and ridicule that describe males and females who
demonstrate a variety of disagreeable traits. However, when preceded by *old,* as they often are, they have a singularly ageist significance that reinforces the negative stereotypes of the elderly.

Decrepit, doddering, infirm, rickety, and *superannuated* are
specific ageist attributes for physical decline; *obsolete, old-
fashioned,* and *outmoded* are qualities that normally refer to objects or ideas. Recent usage, however, has applied them to people.
They have a denotation that means an item is no longer of general
or current use or value. Their new association with the elderly is
logical given society's disdain for this group of people. An additional adjective, *anile,* also has a sexist denotation. Many other
qualifying adjectives are not age specific but are frequently associated with the elderly: *cantankerous, constipated, cranky, crotch-
ety, eccentric, feebleminded, frumpy, garrulous, grumpy, over-age* (a
relative term), *peevish, rambling, toothless, withered, wizened,* and
wrinkled. Again, all of these qualities are objectionable or unattractive physical, mental, or behavioral characteristics.

Terminology for the state of being aged is abundant. Many of
these phrases—*anecdotage* (a blend of *anecdote* and *dotage*),
declining years, second childhood, over the hill, twilight years—insinuate decadence, decline, or foolish behavior. Nouns of Latin
origin, such as *longevity* and *senectitude,* appear to be neutral.
Other Latin derivatives to describe this status are *anility, caducity,
debility, decrepitude, dotage, infirmity,* and *senility.* Most of these
are nominalized adjectives that contain the same negative allu-
sions as their derivational sources. *Generation gap,* a 1960's
coinage, focuses on the polarization of the elderly and the young
as a by-product of our youth-centered culture. Finally, the exhor-

tation to *act one's age* when directed to the elderly demands that they behave in a passive, dependent, and sexless manner.

A Selected List of Ageist Terms

Act one's age	Dotard	Little old lady
Anecdotage	Eccentric	Maid
Anile	Fart	Miser
Anility	Feebleminded	Obsolete
Bag	Fogy	Old
Bat	Fool	Old-fashioned
Battle ax(e)	Fossil	Outmoded
Beldam(e)	Fuddy-duddy	Over-age
Biddy	Gaffer	Over the hill
Caducity	Garrulous	Peevish
Cantankerous	Geezer	Rambling
Codger	Generation gap	Rickety
Constipated	Geriatric generation	Second childhood
Convalescent center	Geritol generation	Senile dementia
Coot	Goat	Senility
Crank	Golden age	Senior citizen
Cranky	Granny	Spinster
Crone	Graybeard	Superannuated
Crotchety	Grimalkin	Toothless
Debility	Grump	Twilight years
Declining years	Grumpy	Witch
Decrepit	Hag	Withered
Decrepitude	Infirm	Wizened
Dirty old man	Infirmity	Wrinkled
Doddering	Lawrence Welk	
Dotage	generation	

The cumulative effects of individual and institutional ageism are devastating. Butler (1975, p. 11) states that ageist practices allow us to dehumanize the elderly, thereby making it easier for us to oppress this group. This subjugation is achieved through the use of labels that devalue the elderly. After all, if members of this group are perceived as deviating from accepted societal norms, we may find it easier to disenfranchise them. This misuse and abuse of language facilitates the segregation of the elderly into urban ghettos, nursing homes, and other modern concentration camps where their isolation from our daily existence occurs without guilt or remorse by employing euphemistic phrases for the places in which they are confined. One local telephone directory includes the following names: *Friendship Manor, Pine Tree Villa,* and *Tendercare*. Moreover, the categorical designation of *convalescent center* suggests that the patients of such institutions will gradually recuperate, whereas, in reality, they are penulti-mate repositories for the elderly. To ignore the awesome power of labeling is to contribute to the continued inhumane treatment of some of the elderly.

The consciousness of ageist language practice is only the first step in its correction. The pervasive nature of this phenomenon is found in a wide variety of forms in mass communication. In the mass media language may be oral or written or both. In newspa-pers, magazines, books, and other publications, it is always writ-ten or visual. In radio broadcasting language is strictly auditory. In telecommunication it is oral and occasionally visible. All of these communication sources are highly efficient and effective ways of disseminating fact and fiction through language. Thus, they may have a profound influence on the maintenance or the avoidance of stereotypes. Ageist language, together with other discriminatory verbiage such as racism, sexism, Indian derision, and antisemitism (cf. Bosmajian, 1974), promotes acceptance of the myths that such language creates. Monitoring (not censoring) of ageist language in the various media is one means of prevent-ing its unwitting continuance. Several organizations, including the American Association of Retired Persons (AARP), the Consul-tation of Older and Younger Adults (Gray Panthers), and the Na-tional Council on Aging (NCOA), have already established some form of media review to check for negative portrayals of the eld-erly in the television industry (cf. Dickman, 1979, pp. 22–23). In fact, the Gray Panthers circulate a Media Watch Observer's Re-port Form that facilitates the accurate documentation of televised ageist "incidents." Such scrutiny, however, is reactionary in that it responds to an offense after the fact. Moreover, this type of moni-toring tends to concentrate largely on oral as opposed to written language. It is noteworthy that the 1970s saw a proliferation of published guidelines on procedures for avoiding sexist and occa-sionally racist stereotypes (cf. Nuessel, 1977). However, only one such publication dealt even marginally with the question of ageism (*Avoiding Stereotypes: Principles and Applications,* 1975).

15   Thus far, this paper has merely focused on the existence and description of the phenomenon of ageist language. A plan of ac-tion for educating people outside the fields of gerontology and so-

ciolinguistics concerning the insidious nature of linguistic ageism may be useful. First, a task force should be formed that would consist of responsible members of various professional organizations (e.g., the American Geriatrics Society, the Gerontological Society of America, the National Council of Senior Citizens (NCSC), and other associations already mentioned). Next, this group should be charged with the responsibility of producing a set of guidelines to be published in booklet or pamphlet form for massive distribution to the various media. In fact, once produced, the media themselves could be utilized to publicize the existence of such a document. Third, a clear-cut distinction must be drawn between spontaneous or unrehearsed language versus scripted or written speech. The latter refers to both print (books, cartoons, commercials, greeting cards; cf. Kantrowitz & Deasy, 1980, pp. 42–48; magazines, newspapers, professional journals, textbooks, and so forth) and nonprint (movie, radio and television scripts, plays, prepared commercial copy) media that require deliberate and intentional composition. Likewise, it is important to realize that parenthetical portions of scripted materials for the visual and auditory media, such as stage directions, personal descriptions, as well as paralinguistic traits (prosody, intonation, stress, and so forth) and kinesics (gestures, emblems, and others) frequently indicated by certain adverbs and verbs, often reinforce ageist stereotypes in an especially malicious fashion. Moreover, an unfortunate choice of graphics (art, drawings, sketches, photographs) can intensify verbal images. Fourth, documentation of offensive language practices should be a priority of such a commission. The public and especially those in a position of power (authors, editors, and publishers) need to have concrete examples of specific abuses gleaned from the various media. Such illustrations are instructive in themselves because they offer a "case study" approach to problem solving. Finally, linked to such exemplification must be explicit suggestions for corrective action in the form of a set of guidelines that focus on the following areas of linguistic ageism:

1. Distortion: This refers to the attribution of negative physical, behavioral, and mental characteristics to the elderly (e.g., *toothless, grumpy, senile*).
2. Degradation: This alludes to the depiction of the elderly as inferior or obnoxious either intellectually or physically (e.g., *rambling, decrepit*).

Far more pernicious than the aforementioned verbal reflexes of ageism are two other practices whose net effect is to demean the elderly in a much more subtle fashion:

1. Exclusion: This is the total elimination or significant reduction of the presence of the elderly in scripted copy. Ignoring them is tantamount to saying that they are, in effect, worthless.
2. Subordination: The roles in which the elderly are portrayed are demeaning or subservient. Their contributions are viewed as insignificant or even worthless.

Any set of guidelines must be voluntary. Care should be exercised to avoid tyrannical prescriptivism. The ultimate purpose of such a project is public education.

In conclusion, this proposal for action seeks to inform the public, in particular those professionals capable of effecting change through their written work, by establishing a task force charged with the duty of documenting exemplary print and nonprint media instances of ageist language practices. Creation of a set of voluntary guidelines that address the major issues of distortion, degradation, exclusion, and sub-ordination will help to demythologize many popular misconceptions of this heterogenous group.

References

Avoiding Stereotypes: Principles and Applications. Houghton-Mifflin, Boston, MA, 1975.

Bosmajian, H. *The Language of Oppression.* Public Affairs Press, Washington, DC, 1974.

Butler, R. Age-ism; Another Form of Bigotry. *The Gerontologist,* 1969, 9, 243–246.

Butler, R. *Why Survive? Being Old in America.* Harper and Row, New York, 1975.

Dickman, I. *Ageism—Discrimination Against Older People.* Public Affairs Pamphlet No. 575. Public Affairs Committee, Inc., New York, 1979.

Kantrowitz, B., & Deasy, B. *Is Seeing Believing? Mass Media and the Negative Portrayal of the Elderly.* Unpublished master's essay. University of Louisville, Louisville, KY, 1980.

Matthews, S. *The Social World of Old Women: Management of Self-Identity.* Sage Library of Social Research (Vol. 78). Sage Publications, Beverly Hills, CA 1979.

Morris, W. (Ed.). *The American Heritage Dictionary of the English Language.* Houghton-Mifflin Company, Boston, MA, 1979.

Nuessel, F. Jr. "Resource Guide: Sexism in Language Texts." *Language Sciences*, 1977, 46, 22–23.

Sontag, S. "The Double Standard of Aging." *The Saturday Review,* September 23, 1972, pp. 29–38.

Ward, R. *The Aging Experience: An Introduction to Social Gerontology.* J. B. Lippincott Company, New York, 1979.

Guidelines for Age-Neutral or Nonageist Language

Ageism is defined as any prejudice or discrimination against or in favor of an age group, for example, older persons, teenagers, young adults, or youth in general. Probably the greatest negative stereotyping is that directed at the older generation.

Ageist language is the use of terms and expressions that oppress a particular age group, most notably older persons, by young adults and middle-age adults.

Rule 1. Do not refer to a person's age unless it is relevant.

Rule 2. Refrain from describing older people in ageist terms.

Terms such as "the elderly," "the aged," "old-timers," "the old folk," "geriatric," or "the oldsters" describe older persons as a homogeneous group. Older people come from different backgrounds, are members of different ethnic communities, hold different beliefs, and have different interests. Labeling them as "old" implies a nameless, faceless group of individuals.

Rule 3. When referring to an Individual who is recognized as older (a relative notion), use the age-neutral term "older person."

Not a hard and fast rule, we often identify someone as older when he or she reaches his or her forties or middle age. Once an older person reaches sixty-five, he or she is recognized as a "senior" or "senior citizen." "Senior" is a more relative term than "senior citizen." Not all older adults accept their passage into senior citizenhood smoothly, however, so "senior" or "senior citizen" in some instances may be offensive.

Rule 4. Do not use patronizing expressions to describe older adults.

Instead of addressing an older person as "good girl," "attaboy," "young lady/man," "sweetie," "dearie," "hon," "sweetheart," and "frisky" use his or her given name or title.

Rule 5. Avoid set expressions that refer to getting old.

Expressions such as "over the hill," "out to pasture," "old as the hills," "old as time," and "old as Methuselah" reflect the cultural assumption that older persons are no longer vital, productive forces in society.

Rule 6. Avoid all ageist expressions.

Female terms: hag, old maid, old spinster, wrinklies, grannies, blue rinse set, blue hair, old biddy, old cow, old bag, old witch, dowager, shrew, widow lady
Male terms: dirty old man, old boy, lech/letch, geezer, old codger, old fogey, grampa, gramps
Female and male ageist terms: gerries, coot, crone, geezer, hag, has-been, old buzzard, old crock, old duffer, old fogey, old goat, old fuddy-duddy, old fangled, old-fashioned, old-timer

Rule 7. Stereotyping the younger generation.

Because we are a culture that values youthfulness, not many negative connotations exist for the younger generation. "Girl" and "boy" are commonly used until an individual reaches puberty. "Youth," "young person," "young adult," "young man," "young woman," "teenager," and "adolescent" are neutral terms that apply to an individual of either sex. Youth-biased language includes "juvenile," "hoodlum," and "punks." Referring to or addressing a younger person as "sonny," "sister," "sis," "kid," and "teenybopper" discounts the youth as immature and irresponsible.

Language
and Ableism

The best and most beautiful things in the world cannot be seen or even touched. They must be felt.

HELEN KELLER

In the past couple of decades, the United States has experienced a dramatic change with respect to the rights, needs, and cultures of citizens with disabilities. Federal and state laws have been passed to guarantee that persons with disabilities have the same legal rights and protection as persons without disabilities by removing physical, educational, employment, housing, and other barriers for the purpose of enhancing the quality of life for children and adults with disabilities. The passage of the most significant civil rights legislation, the Americans with Disabilities Act (ADA) signed into law on January 26, 1990, closed a chapter on the discrimination of 53 million individuals in the United States with disabilities. Such legislation was designed to prevent discrimination against individuals with disabilities in the private sector, employment opportunities or situations, public services, public accommodations, transportation, and telecommunications. As a result, employers could no longer discriminate against individuals with disabilities in their hiring and firing, and advancement practices; airplanes, trains, and buses were required to provide accessibility to all persons with disabilities; and restaurants, hotels, and other public service buildings were mandated to remove all physical barriers that impeded patrons with disabilities from entering and using the premises. Due to this kind of legislation, persons with disabilities now have access to an enhanced quality of life.

Although persons with disabilities are legally protected, the long history of segregation, prejudice, and stigma still remains in the perceptions and attitudes of society. Due to the general public's lack of understanding of persons with disabilities, the practice of demeaning and stigmatizing this population persists in the words and images we use to describe people with disabilities. Much of our language still views people with disabilities as unfortunate, suffering, helpless victims of tragedies. We describe persons with disabilities as "handicapped." Children insult each other with an exchange of words like "spaz," "retardo," and "lame." We often unfairly compare persons with disabilities with normal, healthy, able-bodied persons and describe persons with disabilities as "crippled," "gimpy," and "deformed" and label them as "dumb-mute" and "retarded." To eliminate such insensitive labels, proponents for linguistic change advocate a language with a positive view of persons with disabilities. The antiableist language movement has been underway to change the attitudes and perceptions about people with disabilities by putting "people first" in language.

In this chapter we explore the language of *ableism*, the stereotyping of and negative attitudes toward people based on a physical or mental disability or illness resulting in prejudice. Ableist language is characterized by derogatory labeling, negative stereotyping, depersonalizing the individual, and emphasizing the disability rather than the person. In order for persons with disabilities to be perceived as valuable participating members of society, efforts have been made to change the way we view persons with disabilities through language. The first selection "Sexism, Ageism, and 'Disability': (Re) Constructing Agency through (Re) Writing Personal Narrative" is a personal narrative by Professor Maia Boswell, who acknowledges her hearing loss as a deficit but describes it as a gift by recounting memorable struggles as a child and later as an adult. Like Boswell, Nancy Mairs, who lost the use of her arms and legs to degenerative multiple sclerosis, in the next piece "On Being a Cripple" offers us insight into life as a "cripple." With writing as the liberating force, she finds a voice as a woman, writer, and person with a disability. Sucheng Chan in "You're Short, Besides" recounts the discrimination she endured throughout her childhood and adult life as an Asian-American woman with a physical disability and as someone "vertically challenged" as well. In the fourth selection "AIDS: The Linguistic Battlefield," AIDS activist Michael Callen explains how the language of AIDS became a battleground for political and social debate.

Following the readings, suggested "Guidelines for Avoiding Ableist Language" are provided to help you redefine the way the English language describes children and adults with disabilities. Embracing a *people-first language* policy, these guidelines focus on the person-first and the disability or illness last. Just as language changes, so do perceptions and attitudes: Through linguistic change, society's acceptance and respect for persons with disabilities will become a reality.

Discussion Questions

1. How do the oppressions of ableism, ageism, sexism, heterosexism, and racism intersect?

2. How are attitudes toward individuals with disabilities similar to those toward racial and ethnic minority groups? How are they different?

3. Do you think that gay males and lesbians with disabilities, women with disabilities, or ethnic minorities with disabilities experience double discrimination?

4. Do you think the deaf culture should be considered a linguistic minority group or a disability group? Explain your rationale.

5. How does language perpetuate the image that women, older adults, and persons with disabilities are immature and childlike? Does language treat persons who are not white, male, heterosexual, and English-speaking differently?

6. What assumptions do we have about norms and "ability" that define our place in society? What is "normal"?

7. We tend to position everything as opposites: normal-abnormal, heterosexual-homosexual; female-male; abled-disabled; old-young, etc. Do you think that there will be a time when these binary categories no longer exist?

8. Do persons without disabilities treat persons with disabilities differently in the United States? How? Provide specific examples to support your answer.

Projects and Other Writing Activities

1. Most often absent in mainstream programming, persons with disabilities have identified ten commonly recurring disabling stereotypes in the mass media: the disabled person as pitiable and pathetic, as an object of cu-

riosity or violence, as sinister or evil, as the super cripple, as atmosphere, as laughable, as his or her own worst enemy, as a burden, as nonsexual, and as being unable to participate in daily life. These stereotypes are particularly evident on television, in the press, and in advertising. Provide examples of each stereotype from television or film. Choose a medium and study how persons with disabilities generally are portrayed in it.

2. Interview an individual with a disability or illness. Ask him or her about his or her experiences with discrimination. Write an essay describing or narrating a particular time when he or she was treated unfairly due to their particular disability or illness.

3. Trace the history of the disabilities rights movement. Show that the battles fought and the rights gained by the disabilities activists are similar to the history of the gay rights, civil rights, and women's movements in the United States.

4. Not until the mid-1970s were children with disabilities permitted to attend public schools. Write a paper reporting on the history of children receiving special education services in the United States and how parents and disabilities advocates successfully argued for equal education for all children.

5. The Americans with Disabilities Act (ADA) of 1990 was one of the most important pieces of civil rights legislation in the history of the United States. Describe an historical event or personal experience that gives insight into the reasons why the ADA was signed.

6. Write an essay describing whether life has changed since the signing of the ADA in 1990 for the millions of persons with disabilities in the United States.

7. Interview an individual with a disability and write a paper presenting that person in a positive way. This approach does not mean, however, that the person's disability should be omitted or ignored in your interview.

8. View one of the following films. Discuss the representation of a particular disability in the film.

Born on the 4th of July, starring Tom Cruise and Kyra Sedgwick; directed by Oliver Stone (1989)

Children of a Lesser God, starring Marlee Matlin and William Hurt; directed by Randa Haines (1986)

My Left Foot—The Story of Christy Brown, starring Daniel Day-Lewis; directed by Jim Sheridan (1989)

The Elephant Man, starring John Hurt and Anthony Hopkins; directed by David Lynch and Jonathan Sanger (1980)

The Waterdance, starring Eric Stoltz and Wesley Snipes; directed by Neal Jimenez and Michael Speinberg (1992)

What's Eating Gilbert Grape, starring Johnny Depp; directed by Lasse Hallstrom (1994)

The Other Sister, starring Juliette Lewis; directed by Garry Marshall (1999)

Molly, starring Elisabeth Shue and Aaron Eckhart; directed by John Duigan (2000)

9. Consult one of the following national disabilities organizations and write a report reviewing its mission and advocacy on issues related to specific disabilities and illnesses, disabilities rights, equitable employment, job training, child development services, public awareness, and other programs and activities.

American Association of People with Disabilities (AAPD), www.aapd.com

American Foundation for the Blind (AFB), www.afb.org

Disability Rights Education & Defense Fund (DREDF), www.dredf.org

Disabled American Veterans (DAV), www.dav.org

Easter Seals, www.easter-seals.org

U.S. Equal Employment Opportunity Commission (EEOC), www.eeoc.gov

National Association of the Deaf (NAD), www.nad.org

National Organization on Disability (NOD), www.nod.org

Sexism, Ageism, and "Disability": (Re)Constructing Agency Through (Re)Writing Personal Narrative

MAIA BOSWELL

Maia Boswell teaches in the Department of Women's Studies at the State University of New York at Albany. Published in the journal *Women and Language*, "Sexism, Ageism, and 'Disability': (Re)Constructing Agency Through (Re)Writing Personal Narrative" examines the author's unusual birth and hearing loss within the context of paradoxes. Boswell describes her "disability" as both a deficit and gift, and "feminisms" as both perpetuators and liberators. She challenges feminists and others to analyze their own oppressive behaviors and to "unlearn their privilege" as they continue to forge healthy environments for all.

1. This article is an academic paper written for the journal *Women and Language.* Who is the audience? What is the thesis of this paper? What makes this paper challenging to read?
2. What is a paradox? Provide examples of a paradox. What are the paradoxes surrounding Boswell's disability that she addresses in this paper?
3. What does the author mean when she says, "having a hearing impairment has to do, not only with one's ability to hear, but also with one's ability to be heard, to speak and find one's voice encountered by listeners"?
4. From infancy, how was Boswell treated "differently"? By whom?
5. What does Boswell mean when she says her difference "gives me insight and allows me to see myself as someone who has some affinity with the 'others' "?
6. How does ableism relate to ageism, sexism, heterosexism, and elitism?
7. What is *paternalism*? What persons does Boswell associate with being paternalistic?
8. What messages did Boswell receive when her father said to her, "You just don't understand" and "You're in the dark"? How did her father's use of language "situate" her?
9. Do you think that women with disabilities experience a double disadvantaged status?

Writing Assignments

1. Boswell writes that "language and writing have emerged as central to the process of re-constructing and negotiating healthy change." What does she mean by this? Write a narrative of self-discovery.
2. Is there something about you that marks you as "different"? Write about a significant "difference" that has shaped your life.

3. Write a paper to an audience of people who are "abled" "differently" than you. Try to "unthink" your privilege.

4. Two fairy tales that are based on *lookism* or prejudice against people based on their appearance are *Cinderella* and the *Ugly Duckling*. Can you think of other childhood rhymes, tales, or myths that are based on lookism? Choose a childhood story that you have read or that was recited to you and rewrite it to conform to nonbiased language and attitude.

5. Write a paper addressing the isms in childhood rhymes and fairy tales. What messages do they send to little girls and little boys? Are they harmful?

———————— ✦ ————————

Abstract: This paper examines paradoxes involved in living with "disability," arguing that such paradoxes arise from a complex interaction among a set of habitually expressed oppressions. It also discusses how feminisms, ostensibly devoted to dismantling these isms, sometimes perpetuates dominant discourses instead. The paradoxes discussed are "disability" as both deficit and gift, and feminisms as both perpetuators and liberators. In addition, I show how hearing "disabilities" often have as much to do with loss of voice as they do with loss of hearing, and conclude with a plea to develop a new social construct of differently abled.

Having been born three months premature, with a twenty-percent hearing impairment, I live with several paradoxes stemming from my "disability" status. It is paradoxical that I sometimes perceive myself to be "different"— somehow "wrong" or "limited" —while I also embrace my "loss" as a "gift," as a mark of special awareness, a portal into an "other" space offering "other" perceptual encounters and insights. I understand that for me, and I suspect for many others, having a hearing impairment has to do, not only with one's ability to hear, but also with one's ability to be heard, to speak and find one's voice encountered by listeners. A second paradox resides in other losses, in the interstices connecting women's issues and "disability" issues. Recognition of ableism, like racism, ageism, classism, heterosexism, and other forms of habitually imposed ethnocentric oppressions, constitutes a central component of feminists' struggle against patriarchal dominance. Yet, those who resist

ableism, like advocates fighting other "isms," often call feminist movements to task, and argue that these movements sometimes perpetuate the dominant discourses they seek to dis-
lodge, by themselves closing out the "others." Mirroring my
experience of gender issues, my experience of "disability" issues has both a personal and a political component; indeed, it
dislodges the arbitrary distinction between the two, reminds us
that we must remain aware of our own internalized oppressive
behaviors, and models a way for us to bring greater sensitivity
and conviction to our work as feminists.

My awareness of my "difference" has sometimes reflected a
limited self-conceptualization, where I have appropriated notions
of "normalcy," "ability," and "power" from voices that seek to impose their world-view on me. At other times I have seen my "difference" as an entry into a range of perspectives that have situ-
ated themselves, through struggle, so as to shift discursive
meaning in a direction that justice, understanding, and responsibility become defining points of decision-making. Surveying a
range of situations surrounding my hearing loss, I will suggest,
here, that by re-weaving memories, and re-inscribing articulations which have sought to position me in limited ways, I have
been able to embrace the paradox of "loss," and to (re)construct
my "disability" not only as a mark of awareness, insight, and vision, but also as a catalyst for positive change. I have come to understand that, from the very beginning, my negotiation of my
(dis)ability has been closely linked to my interaction with hegemonic structures of meaning, identity, and agency.

Early on my father attempted to contain me and to situate
me within his world-conception; this has meant that for much of
my life, limited hearing has been conflated with limited understanding and a voice to be silenced unless it spoke the appropriate words. Increasingly the paradoxes surrounding my "disability" have become part of the process of (re)mapping my
developing relationship with a patriarchal system of norms; they
also suggest ways for us, as members of a complex social network, to become more creative in how we choose to articulate
difference.

5   For me, language and writing have emerged as central to the
process of re-constructing and negotiating healthy change. As Helene Cixous suggests, "writing is precisely the very possibility of
change, the space that can serve as a springboard for subversive

thought, the precursory movement of a transformation of social and cultural structures" (149).

"DIFFERENT" AND "SPECIAL": HEARING IMPAIRMENT AS A "DEFICIT" AND A "GIFT"

Hearing impairment as both deficit and gift is the first paradox of which I write. Even when I was a very small child I was aware that I was "different," that I somehow deviated from the "norm." Feeling a certain affinity with the toys on the "Island of the Rejected Toys," from the popular children's Christmas special, I internalized notions of "normalcy," and accepted my positioning as "other." I am what people call a "preemie"; born twelve weeks before full gestation, and weighing under two pounds, I made an appearance in the local papers which marveled over my tiny size and my fighting spirit. Throughout my childhood, adults often commented on what a little "struggler" I was, or on how I had all of them scared that I was going to die. Indeed, I am told that the doctors did not stamp my inked foot on my birth certificate until I was over a week old, because of the trauma of rushed medical intervention, and my almost certain impending death.

Because of my "preemie" status and its consequences, I was treated "differently" early on, and saw myself as "different." When I was about five years old, my mother, explaining that the doctors wanted to do some "tests" on me, reluctantly let go of my hand as the audiologist assured her that things would be "just fine." The tall man in the white coat put pillows in a big looming chair, so I could see over the deep mahogany desk, and instructed me to "punch the button whenever you hear a noise." Later, his voice, sounding through the huge headphones that had been placed over my tiny, nearly hairless head (preemies are "late" in many developmental ways) instructed me to "make sure you punch the button—even if you think you hear something," thus making apparent how much I deviated from the "norm." Without a doubt, this experience has shaped my life and my sensibilities.

In representing the situation to myself, a series of significant moments present themselves. I remember how, during first grade, the teacher separated me from the class when phonetics hour arrived. Marched into a pre-fab building with blocks and rods, chalk and chalkboards, I dutifully performed the tasks requested of me; repeating the alphabet backwards, working with language and numbers, I understood that my hearing impairment came with other indicators that something was amiss. Paradoxically, though, I did not always feel as though my "difference" meant that something was "wrong" with me; in my child's freshness of vision, it sometimes served as a mark of privilege, a sign that I was "special." Adults turned their attention towards me in ways that gave me a certain "legitimacy." And now that I wear hearing aids, and teach and write about various forms of discrimination, my "loss" positions me somehow outside my privileged status as a white, middle class heterosexual woman; it gives me insight and allows me to see myself as someone who has some affinity with the "others." Empathizing with those who do not fit within the "norm," I can claim what bell hooks calls "marginality as a site of resistance."

At this point, the only visible result of my early birth is that I wear hearing aids; but I continue the struggle to situate my hearing loss, and to embrace it as a gift and a catalyst for interrogating inherited structures of agency, identity, and meaning. In spite of wearing the devices, I still struggle to hear in a wide range of situations, and I still confront the frustration of missing key points in spoken discourse. Sometimes I also have nightmares where a white-haired professor, lecturing to a class I am attending, moves his lips, but leaves me in insular silence, frustration and rage. I scream at him that I cannot hear, and yet he continues his silent lecture. Increasingly, though, I have "interpreted" my memories of my birth and my resulting hearing loss so that they comprise a "mirror" into where I am at any given point, and how I chose to situate my agency in a system with a particular hegemonic system of normalcy and privilege. I am constantly aware of my "disability" and how it, though minor, affects many aspects of my life. Indeed, the narrative surrounding my "disability" has become a template for registering my engagement with various oppressive structures; ageism, sexism, and the categorization of "disability" come together in the story of my unusual birth and hearing loss.

10   For example, my experience of my hearing impairment has had to do, in a very palpable way, with ageism. Sexism, and the privileging of "experts," especially medical "experts" over mothers and lay people also participate in this dynamic. Never speaking directly to me about my "disability," but only to my parents, the doctors left it to my father to decide not to procure hearing aids for me; I believe my father's decision stemmed from his desire

that I should not be made to feel "different." Classism and racism also come into play, here. Having been raised in a privileged, upper-middle class family in the South, where school segregation means that in many districts only 2% of public-school children are "white," I was placed in an expensive, progressive private school, where open-classrooms meant that even if I sat in the front of the class, I oftentimes was unable to hear the lessons. And sexism, similarly impacted the scene. Given my socialization as a girl, I did not question my father's decision until much later. Consequently, I never wore hearing aids until one semester in graduate school, when I imagined that I was either mentally deficient, or going crazy. It eventually occurred to me that I happened to have one professor that semester who would swallow the ends of words, and another who would sit amongst the students, so that I could not read his lips. I had to face implications of my hearing loss then. And I embraced the partial help made available through hearing aids. I do want to note that other ageist assumptions greatly impact the experiences of older people with hearing loss. And I too, will face this other set of assumptions that justify our culture's dismissal of elderly people, especially those with limited hearing. Because our culture privileges youth, many elderly people fear to get hearing aids, and get lost in a silent, insular world where their ability to hear and to be heard gets curtailed. Again, work to re-configure "disability" necessarily involves work to re-configure ageist, classist, racist, and other assumptions.

HEARING IMPAIRMENT AFFECTS ONE'S ABILITY TO BE HEARD, TO SPEAK

A major effect of the hearing "disability" paradox is that it affects not only one's ability to hear, but also one's ability to be heard, to speak. My father, an older father, an orthopedic surgeon, and a Texan who clearly uses power to his "advantage" used to say to me, repeatedly, about a series of incidents "You just don't understand." Sometimes he would also say the words, or perhaps he just implied them— "You're in the dark." My interpretations of these moments have become key to my assessment of many of the structural features of our social fabric. When I reflect on my development, I know that there were certainly times in my life when I acted on the belief, filtered through my father, that the patriarchy was "right," and that I, having a hearing loss, and being born a female, was doubly "wrong." Believing sometimes that I was "in the dark," I lived sometimes "in the dark"— especially when my hearing prevented me from encountering conversations in full. The programming silenced me in many ways, and it has taken many years of work for me to feel comfortable assuming a voice, and proclaiming the right to use all of my power to say things that matter. But I have created successes. Indeed, as I sort through memories of my past, it now strikes me that even as a small child I had some impression that when my father told me "you don't understand" or "you're in the dark," that he was telling me as a command, as though he, as "author" or father, pronounces the perspective that is always right, the standard. I do remember thinking, with a child's ability to hold two seemingly contrasting views at once, that his proclamation that he possessed greater "understanding," held some truth; but at the same time, I remember thinking that he had some ulterior, perhaps unacknowledged motive in working to limit my confidence in my perspective.

A large part of the genealogy, here, involves language—in particular, the language my father used to situate me, and the language we, as a culture use to address "disability." Memories offer me an understanding of different forms of oppression. And they provide space for me to contemplate a range of possible responses to the cultural landscapes which we inhabit. I remember that my father would pronounce those words "you're in the dark" in particular contexts in my early childhood—usually when I was being "too big for your britches, young lady!" bell hooks's discussion of "Talking Back," where adults discourage or punish young African-American girls for "talking back," offers commentary on a similar instance of repression. My experience of these words from my father connects with my hearing loss in that while I have often perceived myself to be "different" and "limited," and while this meant having limited hearing, it also became tied up with the status of having the limited "sight" or "vision" implied in the statements "you're in the dark," "you don't understand."

Helene Cixous, pointing out that "it must be said that in spite of the enormity of the repression that has kept [women] in the 'dark'—that dark which people have been trying to make them accept as their attribute" —suggests that my struggle against being positioned as "in the dark" is a struggle that has a gender component. Most women living in a sexist social framework can relate to Cixous's lament, "And I, too, said nothing showed nothing, I didn't open my mouth, I didn't repaint my half of the world" (246). With her we can ask "Where is the ebullient, infinite woman who, immersed as she was by her naivete, kept in the dark about herself, led into self-disdain by the great arm of parental-conjugal phallogocentrism, hasn't been ashamed of her strength?" But remembering one's shame, and the ways one has allowed oneself to be positioned according to others' arbitrary and self-interested proclamations is a necessary first step to re-writing inherited trajectories of difference. Cixous points out that "In woman, personal history blends together with the history of all women, as well as national and world history" (253). Accurate as Cixous' generalizations may be, we need to remember, as bell hooks reminds us, that the silencing and dismissal many white and heterosexual women continue to struggle against operate in more pronounced ways for women of color, lesbians, poor women, the elderly, and others shut out of privileged norms.

Many of the dynamics I encountered as a child continue to-day. But increasingly, I seek to become more and more aware of social and political implications of events and situations, and to raise the awareness of those around me, and to raise my own awareness of how I participate in perpetuating patterns of injus-tice. This semester, for example, I had a student in one of my classes who has a fifty-percent hearing impairment. I learned to annunciate more clearly, to repeat student comments, and to limit using films without subtitles. And now, when I cannot hear, I ask (when feasible) for speakers to repeat themselves with more clarity. And when people get irritated over having to repeat them-selves, or say things like "what are you, deaf?" I hold my ground and seize the opportunity to bring greater awareness and sensitiv-ity to people's habitual modes of interaction.

CONFRONTING SEXISM & ABLEISM: PARALLEL OPPRESSIONS

In my task of recuperation, several dynamics of control play out in my memories. The ageism I experienced as a result of the med-ical establishment's failure to treat children as capable of making decisions on their own is perpetuated today, not only for children with "disability," but also for adults labeled as "mentally incom-petent." Only slowly are health-care workers beginning to under-stand that many people communicate and process language in al-ternative ways, and are thus capable of making decisions for themselves—even if they appear, initially, unable to do so. The case of Sharon Kowalski, a lesbian in a committed relationship whose partner Karen Thompson was denied access to her when Sharon sustained head injuries in an auto accident, illustrates the debilitating results of the complex workings of sexism, heterosexism, and ableism. Joan Griscom points out that the court and the medical and legal establishments conspired to deny Sharon the right to make her own decisions about her treatment. Assuming that her inability to speak in the "normal" way meant that she had nothing to communicate, the court denied Sharon the right to choose her own rehabilitation and living situation, thus severely limiting her recovery. While some "did not speak to Sharon," some "raised their voices as if she were deaf, . . . spoke to her as if she were a child," or spoke about her in her presence "as if she were not there"; a reporter described the "eerily silent daughter" lying trapped in her "twisted body" (31).

Similar denial of voice is seen in treatment of children who do not fit culturally sanctioned binarized sex categories. These helpless infants are denied the opportunity to decide whether cutting will take place, and are "assigned" a gender by doctors, reflecting the persistent oppressive interaction of ableism, ageism, sexism, heterosexism. (Coventry 52–59). In this case, assumptions about "normalcy" have meant genital surgery on "approximately 2,000 children a year in the U.S." (56).

My work in women's studies, teaching about gender, "disability" and related issues, writing, and analyzing interlocking systems of oppression have been central to my process of representing my hearing loss to myself. In proclaiming "you just don't understand," my father assumed that he understood, that he was "right," while I was "wrong," had gotten things "wrong." I sometimes internalized this and fell into line with the role that was being scripted for me. Very shy for most of my early life, I have worked to come to a position where I less often give my power away and play out limiting roles constructed for me by various systems of oppression. For many years I did not question the Patriarchy; as a child it was unsafe, and later, other situations meant that gaining strength required struggle, and work that sometimes proved to be too challenging, or lonely. My hearing loss, my memories of my status as a child, and my experiences of living in a male-dominated system of power all converge to suggest that one can draw a link between various forms of oppression, including sexism, ableism, racism, classism, heterosexism. Occasionally, my father would shake my shoulders and interrogate me in a loud voice when I said things that constituted boundary crossing, when I assumed too much power by critiquing his sometimes childish behavior when I was still a child, and a girl-child, one with a disability, too. But my negotiation of my hearing loss points beyond the conventions that govern relations between fathers and daughters and between the "normally abled" and the "disabled." It points to social and language-based constructions of identity and meaning, suggesting that for change to occur, we need to interrogate existing paradigms, which often get positioned as "natural." The challenge of feminists and those who work for social justice is to analyze our own oppressive behaviors, to "unlearn our privilege" as we continue to forge healthy environments for all.

CONCLUSION: "DIFFERENTLY ABLED" AS A SOCIAL CONSTRUCT

Ableist, sexist, and ageist assumptions meant, in the past, that I was treated as though I resided "in the dark." And so I resided there for many years, in what was sometimes a silent, imageless space; there I learned to relinquish my power, and did so again and again, having internalized the belief that I existed apart from others who "knew." Paradoxically, my struggle became transformed into a gift, and a catalyst for writing, thinking, and working for change. Tori Amos's popularized lines "silent all these years," and "she's been everybody else's girl, maybe someday she'll be her own" remind me of the moments of struggle, and suggest to me that it is not only ageism and assumptions about norms and "ability" that have often defined my struggle to become "my own." Sexism has played a major role in the mechanisms by which others have sought to silence me and to position me in a voiceless space.

I remember countless moments in which I existed, in a very literal way, outside the charmed circle of "normalcy." In restaurants, bars, parties, discussion-sessions—any event where many voices and sounds fill the air—I still have to relinquish my tendency to feel "out of control," or "lost" when I cannot hear the articulations at hand. (These are situations in which my hearing aids offer no help.) I have come to recognize that something else can be gained from being positioned as "other" or "different." My empathy for the "others," and my recognition that claiming my power involves refusing to allow others to undermine me, both have been direct results of my "disability." While being unable to hear has frequently meant being positioned as unable to, or not worthy of, speaking, this dynamic has initiated a space where writing and speaking, in spite of the silencing, assume greater meaning. The language of "darkness" and "light" implied in my father's articulations participate, today, in my work with linguistic and social structures; interrogating the implications of maintaining a host of inherited binarized categories, I have assumed the power to re-script notions of agency, of essentialism, and of difference. And this struggle must continue—for me personally, and for many others—because work remains to be done.

20   Indeed, while public policies advocating for "disability" rights still need to rely on categorizing people—at least until more responsible socialization makes such policy no longer necessary—such categorizing also has severe limitations. For example, while I suffer the consequences of having a twenty-percent hearing loss—feeling shut out of discursive engagements, constantly risking irritated responses when I have to ask people to repeat themselves—I gain none of the "policy" benefits. For example, I do not qualify for special treatment in admissions or hiring. And I get little help in paying for the aids (I receive $1,000 for a five-year period, the "standard" life of the devices, which cost around $4,000 for a digital pair). Such funds come from my union. They are not a benefit of the Americans with Disabilities Act (ADA), since I use the aids both on the job and at other times. Socializing people differently and altering the environments in which we live and work seem to me to be the desired goals; and while the ADA has its limits, it is, at least, a step in the right direction.

As I have pursued work in Women's Studies, I have come to see my negotiation of my "disabled" status to be linked to my negotiation of my status as a woman in a sexist society — and this is a complex process, with many overlapping issues which sometimes require complex responses. One thing seems clear to me, though—we need to become conscious of how our interactions can become part of a growing movement for justice. One way we can do this is to realize that the categories are arbitrary and constructed. In "Disability Beyond Stigma: Social Interaction, Discrimination, and Activism," Michelle Fine and Adrienne Asch point out that people commonly assume that "the disadvantaged are the ones who need to be changed, rather than the people and institutions who have kept the disadvantaged in a submerged position" (208). Using analytical tools from postmodern linguistic studies, they lodge a critique of essentialized conceptions of "disability," suggesting that work remains to be done to bring people to see "disability" as a social construct, rather than as a given, biological situation.

Not unrelated is the realization that paradox, too, can be reread in such a light. According to Camille R. LaBossiere, "For all the aspiration to ontological wholeness that it bespeaks, though, paradoxy so practiced does not display features familiar to students of contemporary theory, deconstruction in particular" (603). Interrogating assumptions of ontological wholeness, and quoting Colie, LaBossiere points out that "The paradoxical form, . . . by its very nature 'denies commitment': breaking out of imprisonment by disciplinary forms and the regulations of schools, it denies limitation, defies 'sitting' in any specific philosophical position." At once self-destructive, and self-regarding, self-contained . . . self-confirming, the paradox offers a way out of the impasses presented by my status as a hearing-impaired person (604).

Helene Cixous claims that "we are at the beginning of a new history, or rather a process of becoming in which several histories intersect with one another" (253).

For Cixous, woman writing " 'un-thinks' the unifying, regulating history that homogenizes and channels forces . . . She foresees that her liberation will do more than modify power relations or toss the ball over to the other camp; she will bring about a mutation in human relations, in thought, in all praxis . . . [a] staggering alteration in power relations and in the production of individualities" (253). Cixous suggests, "writing is precisely the very possibility of change, the space that can serve as a springboard for subversive thought, the precursory movement of a transformation of social and cultural structures" (149).

While it is a small step, I always ask the students in my classes confronting "disability" issues to use the blank space of their journals to engage, on an emotional level, with people who are "abled" "differently" than themselves. Writing, I have found, helps people to "unthink" their privilege. My hope is that "disabled" will become "differently abled," which will, in turn, become just plain "abled," where the arbitrary, binarized, and divisive categories which we adopt to simplify our experiences will be shattered, as we step away from the world as we know it, 25 and into a more just social fabric where we transform living environments into enabling healthy spaces.

References

Cixous, Helene. "The Laugh of the Medusa." *New French Feminisms: An Anthology.* Eds. Elaine Marks and Isabelle de Courtivron. New York: Schocken, 1980. 245–264

Fine, Michelle and Adrienne Asch. "Disability Beyond Stigma: Social Interaction, Discrimination, and Activism." *The Meaning of Difference: American Constructions of Race, Sex and Gender, Social Class, and Sexual Orientation.* Eds. Karen E. Rosenblum and Toni-Michelle C. Travis. Second Edition. Boston: McGraw Hill, 1996. 201–209.

Griscom, Joan. "The Case of Sharon Kowalski and Karen Thompson: Ableism, Heterosexim, and Sexism." *Race, Class, and Gender in the United States.* Ed. Paula S Rothenberg. New York: 1995. 346–357.

hooks, bell. "Talking Back." *Out There: Marginalization and Contemporary Cultures.* Eds. Russel Ferguson, Martha Gever, Trinh T. Minh-ha, and Cornel West. New York: MIT Press, 1990. 337–340.

LaBossiere, Camille R. "Paradox." *Encyclopedia of Contemporary Literary Theory: Approaches, Scholars, Terms.* Ed. Irena R. Makaryk. Toronto: University of Toronto Press, 1993. 602–603.

On Being a Cripple
NANCY MAIRS

Nancy Mairs, born in 1943, grew up north of Boston. She earned an M.F.A. in creative writing in 1975 and a Ph.D. in English literature in 1984, both from the University of Arizona. A poet, a short story writer, and an essayist, Mairs published her first work in 1986, a collection of essays entitled *Plaintext: Deciphering a Woman's Life.* At the age of thirty, she was diagnosed with disabling multiple sclerosis (MS). In her book *Waist-High in the World: A Life among the Nondisabled,* Mairs chronicles her life of setbacks: rape, depression, attempted suicide, agoraphobia, MS, death of a parent, and a period of residency in a mental institution. "On Being a Cripple," which is taken from the *Plaintext* collection, shows the power of narrative to bring meaning to one's life at moments of great physical and emotional crisis.

1. Why does Mairs choose to be called "cripple" over the terms "handicapped" and "disabled"? Why is she especially critical of the term "differently abled"?
2. Precisely describe Mairs and her condition as a "cripple"? What is her prognosis?
3. How do Mairs's husband and children behave toward her?
4. What does Mairs mean when she says, "I am not a disease."
5. Do you agree with Mairs's view that "there are worse things than dying"?

Writing Assignments

1. Look up the etymologies of the words "cripple," "handicapped," and "disabled." Write a comparison of the history of these three terms.
2. Interview someone who has a disability. Explore the psychological, emotional, and relational aspects of conditions such as cancer, heart disease, disability, alcoholism, AIDS, and mental illness.
3. Interview a nondisabled person who is fearful or apprehensive around people with disabilities? Explore why some people fear or feel uncomfortable around people with disabilities.
4. Explore what it is really like to experience serious illness, or even to face the possibility of death, by interviewing someone who has experienced illness or by reading autobiographies, memoirs, and personal accounts.

———————————— ✦ ————————————

To escape is nothing. Not to escape is nothing.

LOUISE BOGAN

The other day I was thinking of writing an essay on being a cripple. I was thinking hard in one of the stalls of the women's room in my office building, as I was shoving my shirt into my jeans and tugging up my zipper. Preoccupied, I flushed, picked up my book bag, took my cane down from the hook, and unlatched the door. So many movements unbalanced me, and as I pulled the door open I fell over backward, landing fully clothed on the toilet seat with my legs splayed in front of me: the old beetle-on-its-back routine. Saturday afternoon, the building deserted, I was free to laugh aloud as I wriggled back to my feet, my voice bouncing off the yellowish tiles from all directions. Had anyone been there with me, I'd have been still and faint and hot with chagrin. I decided that it was high time to write the essay.

First, the matter of semantics. I am a cripple. I choose this word to name me. I choose from among several possibilities, the most common of which are "handicapped" and "disabled." I made the choice a number of years ago, without thinking, unaware of my motives for doing so. Even now, I'm not sure what those motives are, but I recognize that they are complex and not entirely flattering. People—crippled or not—wince at the word "cripple," as they do not at "handicapped" or "disabled." Perhaps I want them to wince. I want them to see me as a tough customer, one to whom the fates/gods/viruses have not been kind, but who can face the brutal truth of her existence squarely. As a cripple, I swagger.

But, to be fair to myself, a certain amount of honesty underlies my choice. "Cripple" seems to me a clean word, straightforward and precise. It has an honorable history, having made its first appearance in the Lindisfarne Gospel in the tenth century. As a lover of words, I like the accuracy with which it describes my condition: I have lost the full use of my limbs. "Disabled," by contrast, suggests any incapacity, physical or mental. And I certainly don't like "handicapped," which implies that I have deliberately been put at a disadvantage, by whom I can't imagine (my God is not a Handicapper General), in order to equalize chances in the great race of life. These words seem to me to be moving away from my condition, to be widening the gap between word and reality. Most remote is the recently coined euphemism "differently abled," which partakes of the same semantic hopefulness that transformed countries from "undeveloped" to "underdeveloped," then to "less developed," and finally to "developing" nations. People have continued to starve in those countries during the shift. Some realities do not obey the dictates of language.

Mine is one of them. Whatever you call me, I remain crippled. But I don't care what you call me, so long as it isn't "differently abled," which strikes me as pure verbal garbage designed, by its ability to describe anyone, to describe no one. I subscribe to George Orwell's thesis that "the slovenliness of our language makes it easier for us to have foolish thoughts." And I refuse to participate in the degeneration of the language to the extent that I deny that I have lost anything in the course of this calamitous disease; I refuse to pretend that the only difference between you and me are the various ordinary ones that distinguish any one person from another. But call me "disabled" or "handicapped" if you like. I have long since grown accustomed to them; and if they are vague, at least they hint at the truth. Moreover, I use them myself. Society is no readier to accept crippledness than to accept death, war, sex, sweat, or wrinkles. I would never refer to another person as a cripple. It is the word I use to name only myself.

I haven't always been crippled, a fact for which I am soundly   5
grateful. To be whole of limb is, I know from experience, infinitely more pleasant and useful than to be crippled: and if that knowledge leaves me open to bitterness at my loss, the physical soundness I once enjoyed (though I did not enjoy it half enough) is well worth the occasional stab of regret. Though never any good at sports, I was a normally active child and young adult. I climbed trees, played hopscotch, jumped rope, skated, swam, rode my bicycle, sailed. I despised team sports, spending some of the wretchedest afternoons of my life, sweaty and humiliated, behind a field-hockey stick and under a basketball hoop. I tramped alone for miles along the bridle paths that webbed the woods behind the house I grew up in. I swayed through countless dim hours in the arms of one man or another under the scattered shot of light from mirrored balls, and gyrated through countless more as Tab Hunter and Johnny Mathis gave way to the Rolling Stones, Creedance Clearwater Revival, Cream. I walked down the aisle. I pushed baby carriages, changed tires in the rain, marched for peace.

When I was twenty-eight I started to trip and drop things. What at first seemed my natural clumsiness soon became too pronounced to shrug off. I consulted a neurologist, who told me that I had a brain tumor. A battery of tests, increasingly disagreeable, revealed no tumor. About a year and a half later I developed a blurred spot in one eye. I had, at last, the episodes "disseminated in space and time" requisite for a diagnosis: multiple sclerosis. I have never been sorry for the doctor's initial misdiagnosis, however. For almost a week, until the negative results of the tests were in, I thought that I was going to die right away. Every day for the past nearly ten years, then, has been a kind of gift. I accept all gifts.

Multiple sclerosis is a chronic degenerative disease of the central nervous system, in which the myelin that sheathes the nerves is somehow eaten away and scar tissue forms in its place, interrupting the nerves' signals. During its course, which is unpredictable and uncontrollable, one may lose vision, hearing, speech, the ability to walk, control of bladder and/or bowels, strength in any or all extremities, sensitivity to touch, vibration, and/or pain, potency, coordination of movements—the list of possibilities is lengthy and, yes, horrifying. One may also lose one's sense of humor. That's the easiest to lose and the hardest to survive without.

In the past ten years, I have sustained some of these losses. Characteristic of MS are sudden attacks, called exacerbations, followed by remissions, and these I have not had. Instead, my disease has been slowly progressive. My left leg is now so weak that I walk with the aid of a brace and a cane; and for distances I use an Amigo, a variation on the electric wheelchair that looks rather like an electrified kiddie car. I no longer have much use of my left hand. Now my right side is weakening as well. I still have the blurred spot in my right eye. Overall, though, I've been lucky so far. My world has, of necessity, been circumscribed by my losses, but the terrain left me has been ample enough for me to continue many of the activities that absorb me: writing, teaching, raising children and cats and plants and snakes, reading, speaking publicly about MS and depression, even playing bridge with people patient and honorable enough to let me scatter cards every which way without sneaking a peek.

Lest I begin to sound like Pollyanna, however, let me say that I don't like having MS. I hate it. My life holds realities—harsh ones, some of them—that no right-minded human being ought to accept without grumbling. One of them is fatigue. I know of no one with MS who does not complain of bone-weariness; in a disease that presents an astonishing variety of symptoms, fatigue seems to be a common factor. I wake up in the morning feeling the way most people do at the end of a bad day, and I take it from there. As a result, I spend a lot of time *in extremis* and, impatient with limitation, I tend to ignore my fatigue until my body breaks down in some way and forces rest. Then I miss picnics, dinner parties, poetry readings, the brief visits of old friends from out of town. The offspring of a puritanical tradition of exceptional venerability, I cannot view these lapses without shame. My life often seems a series of small failures to do as I ought.

10   I lead, on the whole, an ordinary life, probably rather like the one I would have led had I not had MS. I am lucky that my predilections were already solitary, sedentary, and bookish—un-

like the world-famous French cellist I have read about, or the young woman I talked with one long afternoon who wanted only to be a jockey. I had just begun graduate school when I found out something was wrong with me, and I have remained, interminably, a graduate student. Perhaps I would not have if I'd thought I had the stamina to return to a full-time job as a technical editor; but I've enjoyed my studies.

In addition to studying, I teach writing courses. I also teach medical students how to give neurological examinations. I pick up freelance editing jobs here and there. I have raised a foster son and sent him into the world, where he has made me two grandbabies, and I am still escorting my daughter and son through adolescence. I go to Mass every Saturday. I am a superb, if messy, cook. I am also an enthusiastic laundress, capable of sorting a hamper full of clothes into five subtly differentiated piles, but a terrible housekeeper. I can do italic writing and, in an emergency, bathe an oil-soaked cat. I play a fiendish game of Scrabble. When I have the time and the money, I'd like to sit on my front steps with my husband, drinking Amaretto and smoking a cigar, as we imagine our counterparts in Leningrad and make sure that the sun gets down once more behind the sharp childish scrawl of the Tucson Mountains.

This lively plenty has its bleak complement, of course, in all the things I can no longer do. I will never run again, except in dreams, and one day I may have to write that I will never walk again. I like to go camping, but I can't follow George and the children along the trails that wander out of a campsite through the desert or into the mountains. In fact, even on the level I've learned never to check the weather or try to hold a coherent conversation: I need all my attention for my wayward feet. Of late, I have begun to catch myself wondering how people can propel themselves without canes. With only one usable hand, I have to select my clothing with care not so much for style as for ease of ingress and egress, and even so, dressing can be laborious. I can no longer do fine stitchery, pick up babies, play the piano, braid my hair. I am immobilized by acute attacks of depression, which may or may not be physiologically related to MS but are certainly its logical concomitant.

These two elements, the plenty and the privation, are never pure, nor are the delight and wretchedness that accompany them. Almost every pickle that I get into as a result of my weakness and clumsiness—and I get into plenty—is funny as well as maddening and sometimes painful. I recall one May afternoon when a friend and I were going out for a drink after finishing up at school. As we were climbing into opposite sides of my car, chatting, I tripped and fell, flat and hard, onto the asphalt parking lot, my abrupt departure interrupting him in mid-sentence. "Where'd you go?" he called as he came around the back of the car to find me hauling myself up by the door frame. "Are you all right?" Yes, I told him, I was fine, just a bit rattly, and we drove off to find a shady patio and some beer. When I got home an hour or so later, my daughter greeted me with "What have you done to yourself?" I looked down. One elbow of my white turtleneck with the green froggies, one knee of my white trousers, one white kneesock were blood-soaked. We peeled off the clothes and inspected the damage, which was nasty enough but not alarming. That part wasn't funny: The abrasions took a long time to heal, and one got a little infected. Even so, when I think of my friend talking earnestly, suddenly, to the hot thin air while I dropped from his view as though through a trap door, I find the image as silly as something from a Marx Brothers movie.

I may find it easier than other cripples to amuse myself because I live propped by the acceptance and the assistance and, sometimes, the amusement of those around me. Grocery clerks tear my checks out of my check book for me, and sales clerks find chairs to put into dressing rooms when I want to try on clothes. The people I work with make sure I teach at times when I am least likely to be fatigued, in places I can get to, with the materials I need. My students, with one anonymous exception (in an end-of-the-semester evaluation), have been unperturbed by my disability. Some even like it. One was immensely cheered by the information that I paint my own fingernails; she decided, she told me, that if I could go to such trouble over fine details, she could keep on writing essays. I suppose I became some sort of bright-fingered muse. She wrote good essays, too.

15   The most important struts in the framework of my existence, of course, are my husband and children. Dismayingly few marriages survive the MS test, and why should they? Most twenty-two- and nineteen-year-olds, like George and me, can vow in clear conscience, after a childhood of chicken pox and summer colds, to keep one another in sickness and in health so long as they both shall live. Not many are equipped for catastrophe: the dismay, the depression, the extra work, the boredom that a degenerative disease can insinuate into a relationship. And our society, with its

emphasis on fun and its association of fun with physical performance, offers little encouragement for a whole spouse to stay with
a crippled partner. Children experience similar stresses when
faced with a crippled parent, and they are more helpless, since
parents and children can't usually get divorced. They hate, of
course, to be different from their peers, and the child whose
mother is tacking down the aisle of a school auditorium packed
with proud parents like a Cape Cod dinghy in a stiff breeze jolly
well stands out in a crowd. Deprived of legal divorce, the child
can at least deny the mother's disability, even her existence, forgetting to tell her about recitals and PTA meetings, refusing to accompany her to stores or church or the movies, never inviting
friends to the house. Many do.

But I've been limping along for ten years now, and so far
George and the children are still at my left elbow, holding tight.
Anne and Matthew vacuum floors and dust furniture and haul
trash and rake up dog droppings and button my cuffs and bake
lasagna and Toll House cookies with just enough grumbling so I
know that they don't have brain fever. And far from hiding me,
they're forever dragging me by racks of fancy clothes or through
teeming school corridors, or welcoming gaggles of friends while
I'm wandering through the house in Anne's filmy pink babydoll
pajamas. George generally calls before he brings someone home,
but he does just as many dumb thankless chores as the children.
And they all yell at me, laugh at some of my jokes, write me funny
letters when we're apart—in short, treat me as an ordinary human being for whom they have some use. I think they like me.
Unless they're faking. . . .

Faking. There's the rub. Tugging at the fringes of my consciousness always is the terror that people are kind to me only because I'm a cripple. My mother almost shattered me once, with
that instinct mothers have—blind, I think, in this case, but unerr-
ing nonetheless—for striking blows along the fault-lines of their
children's hearts, by telling me, in an attack on my selfishness,
"We all have to make allowances for you, of course, because of
the way you are." From the distance of a couple of years, I have to
admit that I haven't any idea just what she meant, and I'm not
sure that she knew either. She was awfully angry. But at the time,
as the words thudded home, I felt my worst fear, suddenly realized. I could bear being called selfish: I am. But I couldn't bear
the corroboration that those around me were doing in fact what
I'd always suspected them of doing, professing fondness while

silently putting up with me because of the way I am. A cripple. I've been a little cracked ever since.

Along with this fear that people are secretly accepting shoddy goods comes a relentless pressure to please—to prove myself worth the burdens I impose, I guess, or to build a substantial account of good will against which I may write drafts in times of need. Part of the pressure arises from social expectations. In our society, anyone who deviates from the norm had better find some way to compensate. Like fat people, who are expected to be jolly, cripples must bear their lot meekly and cheerfully. A grumpy cripple isn't playing by the rules. And much of the pressure is self-generated. Early on I vowed that, if I had to have MS, by God I was going to do it well. This is a class act, ladies and gentlemen. No tears, no recriminations, no faint-heartedness.

One way and another, then, I wind up feeling like Tiny Tim, peering over the edge of the table at the Christmas goose, waving my crutch, piping down God's blessing on us all. Only sometimes I don't want to play Tiny Tim, I'd rather be Caliban, a most scurvy monster. Fortunately, at home no one much cares whether I'm a good cripple or a bad cripple as long as I make vichyssoise with fair regularity. One evening several years ago, Anne was reading at the dining-room table while I cooked dinner. As I opened a can of tomatoes, the can slipped in my left hand and juice spattered me and the counter with bloody spots. Fatigued and infuriated, I bellowed, "I'm so sick of being crippled!" Anne glanced at me over the top of her book. "There now," she said, "do you feel better?" "Yes," I said, "yes, I do." She went back to her reading. I felt better. That's about all the attention my scurviness ever gets.

20   Because I hate being crippled, I sometimes hate myself for being a cripple. Over the years I have come to expect—even accept—attacks of violent self-loathing. Luckily, in general our society no longer connects deformity and disease directly with evil (though a charismatic once told me that I have MS because a devil is in me) and so I'm allowed to move largely at will, even among small children. But I'm not sure that this revision of attitude has been particularly helpful. Physical imperfection, even freed of moral disapprobation, still defies and violates the ideal, especially for women, whose confinement in their bodies as objects of desire is far from over. Each age, of course, has its ideal, and I doubt that ours is any better or worse than any other. Today's ideal woman, who lives on the glossy pages of dozens of magazines, seems to be between the ages of eighteen and twenty-

five; her hair has body, her teeth flash white, her breath smells minty, her underarms are dry; she has a career but is still a fabulous cook, especially of meals that take less than twenty minutes to prepare; she does not ordinarily appear to have a husband or children; she is trim and deeply tanned; she jogs, swims, plays tennis, rides a bicycle, sails, but does not bowl; she travels widely, even to out-of-the-way places like Finland and Samoa, always in the company of the ideal man, who possesses a nearly identical set of characteristics. There are a few exceptions. Though usually white and often blonde, she may be black, Hispanic, Asian, or Native American, so long as she is unusually sleek. She may be old, provided she is selling a laxative or is Lauren Bacall. If she is selling a detergent, she may be married and have a flock of strikingly messy children. But she is never a cripple.

Like many women I know, I have always had an uneasy relationship with my body. I was not a popular child, largely, I think now, because I was peculiar: intelligent, intense, moody, shy, given to unexpected actions and inexplicable notions and emotions. But as I entered adolescence, I believed myself unpopular because I was homely; my breasts too flat, my mouth too wide, my hips too narrow, my clothing never quite right in fit or style. I was not, in fact, particularly ugly, old photographs inform me, though I was well off the ideal; but I carried this sense of self-alienation with me into adulthood, where it regenerated in response to the depredations of MS. Even with my brace I walk with a limp so pronounced that, seeing myself on the videotape of a television program on the disabled, I couldn't believe that anything but an inchworm could make progress humping along like that. My shoulders droop and my pelvis thrusts forward as I try to balance myself upright, throwing my frame into a bony S. As a result of contractures, one shoulder is higher than the other and I carry one arm bent in front of me, the fingers curled into a claw. My left arm and leg have wasted into pipe-stems, and I try always to keep them covered. When I think about how my body must look to others, especially to men, to whom I have been trained to display myself, I feel ludicrous, even loathsome.

At my age, however, I don't spend much time thinking about my appearance. The burning egocentricity of adolescence, which assures one that all the world is looking all the time, has passed, thank God, and I'm generally too caught up in what I'm doing to step back, as I used to, and watch myself as though upon a stage. I'm also too old to believe in the accuracy of self-image. I know that I'm not a hideous crone, that in fact, when I'm rested, well dressed, and well made up, I look fine. The self-loathing I feel is neither physically nor intellectually substantial. What I hate is not me but a disease.

I am not a disease.

And a disease is not—at least not singlehandedly—going to determine who I am, though at first it seemed to be going to. Adjusting to a chronic incurable illness, I have moved through a process similar to that outlined by Elizabeth Kübler-Ross in *On Death and Dying*. The major difference—and it is far more significant than most people recognize—is that I can't be sure of the outcome, as the terminally ill cancer patient can. Research studies indicate that, with proper medical care, I may achieve a "normal" life span. And in our society, with its vision of death as the ultimate evil, worse even than decrepitude, the response to such news is, "Oh well, at least you're not going to *die*." Are there worse things than dying? I think that there may be.

25   I think of two women I know, both with MS, both enough older than I to have served me as models. One took to her bed several years ago and has been there ever since. Although she can sit in a high-backed wheelchair, because she is incontinent she refuses to go out at all, even though incontinence pants, which are readily available at any pharmacy, could protect her from embarrassment. Instead, she stays at home and insists that her husband, a small quiet man, a retired civil servant stay there with her except for a quick weekly foray to the supermarket. The other woman, whose illness was diagnosed when she was eighteen, a nursing student engaged to a young doctor, finished her training, married her doctor, accompanied him to Germany when he was in the service, bore three sons and a daughter, now grown and gone. When she can, she travels with her husband; she plays bridge, embroiders, swims regularly; she works, like me, as a symptomatic-patient instructor of medical students in neurology. Guess which woman I hope to be.

At the beginning, I thought about having MS almost incessantly. And because of the unpredictable course of the disease, my thoughts were always terrified. Each night I'd get into bed wondering whether I'd get out again the next morning, whether I'd be able to see, to speak, to hold a pen between my fingers. Knowing that the day might come when I'd be physically incapable of killing myself, I thought perhaps I ought to do so right away, while I still had the strength. Gradually I came to understand that the Nancy who might one day lie inert under a bedsheet, arms and legs paralyzed, unable to feed or bathe herself, unable to reach out for a gun, a bottle of pills, was not the Nancy I was at present, and that I could not presume to make decisions for that future Nancy who might well not want in the least to die. Now the only provision I've made for the future Nancy is that when the time comes—and it is likely to come in the form of pneumonia, friend to the weak and the old—I am not to be treated with machines and medications. If she is unable to communicate by then, I hope she will be satisfied with these terms.

Thinking all the time about having MS grew tiresome and intrusive, especially in the large and tragic mode in which I was accustomed to considering my plight. Months and even years went by without catastrophe (at least without one related to MS), and really I was awfully busy, what with George and children and snakes and students and poems, and I hadn't the time, let alone the inclination, to devote myself to being a disease. Too, the richer my life became, the funnier it seemed, as though there were some connection between largesse and laughter, and so my tragic stance began to waver until, even with the aid of a brace and a cane, I couldn't hold it for very long at a time.

After several years I was satisfied with my adjustment. I had suffered my grief and fury and terror, I thought, but now I was at ease with my lot. Then one summer day I set out with George and the children across the desert for a vacation in California. Part way to Yuma I became aware that my right leg felt funny. "I think I've had an exacerbation," I told George. "What shall we do?" he asked. "I think we'd better get the hell to California," I said, "because I don't know whether I'll ever make it again." So we went on to San Diego and then to Orange, up the Pacific Coast Highway to Santa Cruz, across to Yosemite, down to Sequoia and Joshua Tree, and so back over the desert to home. It was a fine two-week trip, filled with friends and fair weather, and I wouldn't have missed it for the world, though I did in fact make it back to California two years later. Nor would there have been any point in missing it, since in MS, once the symptoms have appeared, the neurological damage has been done, and there's no way to predict or prevent that damage.

The incident spoiled my self-satisfaction, however. It renewed my grief and fury and terror, and I learned that one never finishes adjusting to MS. I don't know now why I thought one would. One does not after all, finish adjusting to life, and MS is simply a fact of my life—not my favorite fact, of course—but as ordinary as my nose and my tropical fish and my yellow Mazda station wagon. It may at any time get worse, but no amount of worry or anticipation can prepare me for a new loss. My life is a lesson in losses. I learn one at a time.

30   And I had best be patient in the learning, since I'll have to do it like it or not. As any rock fan knows, you can't always get what you want. Particularly when you have MS. You can't for example, get cured. In recent years researchers and the organizations that fund research have started to pay MS some attention even though it isn't fatal; perhaps they have begun to see that life is something other than a quantitative phenomenon, that one may be very much alive for a very long time in a life that isn't worth living. The researchers have made some progress toward understanding the mechanism of the disease: It may well be an autoimmune reaction triggered by a slow-acting virus. But they are nowhere near its prevention, control, or cure. And most of us want to be cured. Some, unable to accept incurability, grasp at one treatment after another, no matter how bizarre; megavitamin therapy, gluten-free diet, injections of cobra venom, hypothermal suits, lymphocytopharesis, hyperbaric chambers. Many treatments are probably harmless enough, but none are curative.

The absence of a cure often makes MS patients bitter toward their doctors. Doctors are, after all, the priests of modern society, the new shamans, whose business is to heal, and many an MS patient roves from one to another, searching for the "good" doctor who will make him well. Doctors too think of themselves as healers, and for this reason many have trouble dealing with MS patients, whose disease in its intransigence defeats their aims and mocks their skills. Too few doctors, it is true, treat their patients as whole human beings, but the reverse is also true. I have always tried to be gentle with my doctors, who often have more at stake in terms of ego than I do. I may be frustrated, maddened, depressed by the incurability of my disease, but I am not diminished by it, and they are. When I push myself up from my seat in the waiting room and stumble toward them, I incarnate the limitation of their powers. The least I can do is refuse to press on their tenderest spots.

This gentleness is part of the reason that I'm not sorry to be a cripple. I didn't have it before. Perhaps I'd have developed it anyway—how could I know such a thing?— and I wish I had more of it, but I'm glad of what I have. It has opened and enriched my life enormously, this sense that my frailty and need must be mirrored in others, that in searching for and shaping a stable core in a life wrenched by change and loss, change and loss, I must recognize the same process, under individual conditions, in the lives around me. I do not deprecate such knowledge, however I've come by it.

All the same, if a cure were found, would I take it? In a minute. I may be a cripple, but I'm only occasionally a loony and never a saint. Anyway, in my brand of theology God doesn't give bonus points for a limp. I'd take a cure; I just don't need one. A friend who also has MS startled me once by asking, "Do you ever say to yourself, 'Why me, Lord?' " "No, Michael, I don't," I told him, "because whenever I try, the only response I can think of is 'Why not?' " If I could make a cosmic deal, who would I put in my place? What in my life would I give up in exchange for sound limbs and a thrilling rush of energy? No one. Nothing. I might as well do the job myself. Now that I'm getting the hang of it.

You're Short, Besides!

Sucheng Chan

Professor emeritus of history and Asian American studies at the University of California, Santa Barbara, Sucheng Chan helped create one of the first academic departments in North America dedicated to the field of Asian American studies. Chan is the author or editor of nine books, author of dozens of articles on the social history of Asian American diaspora communities, and recipient of many prestigious awards in recognition of her work on the Asian American experience. In "You're Short, Besides!" having been stricken with pneumonia and polio at the age of four, Chan describes the discrimination she felt growing up physically challenged as well as the prejudices she experienced as an Asian American woman.

1. How does Chan experience double discrimination?
2. The concept of *karma* implies that every human action, thought, word, or deed leads to results. A very old doctrine in East Asian religions and philosophies, karma deals with causality. Why does Chan link her illness to karma? Do you believe that our previous actions determine our condition in this life?

3. What incidents in Chan's life led to her discovery that the way others perceive her is not the same way that she thinks about herself?
4. Chan moved from China to Hong Kong to Malaysia, then to the United States. How did each culture react to her and her disability?
5. Chan claims that people in the United States pretend not to notice people who are physically challenged. How does this attitude compare to yours?

Writing Assignments

1. Write an essay describing the way that you think about yourself as different from the way others perceive you.
2. Go to the library and explore how other cultures view persons with disabilities.
3. Research the notion of karma and rebirth.

✦

When asked to write about being a physically handicapped Asian American woman, I considered it an insult. After all, my accomplishments are many, yet I was not asked to write about any of them. Is being handicapped the most salient feature about me? The fact that it might be in the eyes of others made me decide to write the essay as requested. I realized that the way I think about myself may differ considerably from the way others perceive me. And maybe that's what being physically handicapped is all about.

I was stricken simultaneously with pneumonia and polio at the age of four. Uncertain whether I had polio of the lungs, seven of the eight doctors who attended me—all practitioners of Western medicine—told my parents they should not feel optimistic about my survival. A Chinese fortune teller my mother consulted also gave a grim prognosis, but for an entirely different reason: I had been stricken because my name was offensive to the gods. My grandmother had named me "grandchild of wisdom," a name that the fortune teller said was too presumptuous for a girl. So he advised my parents to change my name to "chaste virgin." All these pessimistic predictions notwithstanding, I hung onto life, if only by a thread. For three years, my body was periodically pierced with electric shocks as the muscles of my legs atrophied.

Before my illness, I had been an active, rambunctious, preco-
cious, and very curious child. Being confined to bed was thus a
mental agony as great as my physical pain. Living in war-torn
China, I received little medical attention; physical therapy was
unheard of. But I was determined to walk. So one day, when I was
six or seven, I instructed my mother to set up two rows of chairs
to face each other so that I could use them as I would parallel
bars. I attempted to walk by holding my body up and moving it
forward with my arms while dragging my legs along behind. Each
time I fell, my mother gasped, but I badgered her until she let me
try again. After four nonambulatory years, I finally walked once
more by pressing my hands against my thighs so my knees
wouldn't buckle.

My father had been away from home during most of those
years because of the war. When he returned, I had to confront the
guilt he felt about my condition. In many East Asian cultures,
there is a strong folk belief that a person's physical state in this
life is a reflection of how morally or sinfully he or she lived in previous lives. Furthermore, because of the tendency to view the
family as a single unit, it is believed that the fate of one member
can be caused by the behavior of another. Some of my father's relatives told him that my illness had doubtless been caused by the
wild carousing he did in his youth. A well-meaning but somewhat
simple man, my father believed them.

Throughout my childhood, he sometimes apologized to me
for having to suffer retribution for his former bad behavior. This
upset me; it was bad enough that I had to deal with the anguish of
not being able to walk, but to have to assuage his guilt as well was
a real burden! In other ways, my father was very good to me. He
took me out often, carrying me on his shoulders or back, to give
me fresh air and sunshine. He did this until I was too large and
heavy for him to carry. And ever since I can remember, he has told
me that I am pretty.

After getting over her anxieties about my constant falls, my   5
mother decided to send me to school. I had already learned to
read some words of Chinese at the age of three by asking my parents to teach me the sounds and meaning of various characters in
the daily newspaper. But between the ages of four and eight, I received no education since just staying alive was a full-time job.
Much to her chagrin, my mother found no school in Shanghai,
where we lived at the time, which would accept me as a student.
Finally, as a last resort, she approached the American School

which agreed to enroll me only if my family kept an *amah* (a servant who takes care of children) by my side at all times. The tuition at the school was twenty U.S. dollars per month—a huge sum of money during those years of runaway inflation in China—and payable only in U.S. dollars. My family afforded the high cost of tuition and the expense of employing a full-time *amah* for less than a year.

We left China as the Communist forces swept across the country in victory. We found an apartment in Hong Kong across the street from a school run by Seventh-Day Adventists. By that time I could walk a little, so the principal was persuaded to accept me. An *amah* now had to take care of me only during recess when my classmates might easily knock me over as they ran about the playground.

After a year and a half in Hong Kong, we moved to Malaysia, where my father's family had lived for four generations. There I learned to swim in the lovely warm waters of the tropics and fell in love with the sea. On land I was a cripple; in the ocean I could move with the grace of a fish. I liked the freedom of being in the water so much that many years later, when I was a graduate student in Hawaii, I became greatly enamored with a man just because he called me a "Polynesian water nymph."

As my overall health improved, my mother became less anxious about all aspects of my life. She did everything possible to enable me to lead as normal a life as possible. I remember how once some of her colleagues in the high school where she taught criticized her for letting me wear short skirts. They felt my legs should not be exposed to public view. My mother's response was, "All girls her age wear short skirts, so why shouldn't she?"

The years in Malaysia were the happiest of my childhood, even though I was constantly fending off children who ran after me calling, "*Baikah! Baikah!*" ("Cripple! Cripple!" in the Hokkien dialect commonly spoken in Malaysia). The taunts of children mattered little because I was a star pupil. I won one award after another for general scholarship as well as for art and public speaking. Whenever the school had important visitors my teacher always called on me to recite in front of the class.

10   A significant event that marked me indelibly occurred when I was twelve. That year my school held a music recital and I was one of the students chosen to play the piano. I managed to get up the steps to the stage without any problem, but as I walked across the stage, I fell. Out of the audience, a voice said loudly and clearly, "Ayah! A *baikah* shouldn't be allowed to perform in pub-

lic." I got up before anyone could get on stage to help me and, with tears streaming uncontrollably down my face, I rushed to the piano and began to play. Beethoven's "Für Elise" had never been played so fiendishly fast before or since, but I managed to finish the whole piece. That I managed to do so made me feel really strong. I never again feared ridicule.

In later years I was reminded of this experience from time to time. During my fourth year as an assistant professor at the University of California at Berkeley, I won a distinguished teaching award. Some weeks later I ran into a former professor who congratulated me enthusiastically. But I said to him, "You know what? I became a distinguished teacher by *limping* across the stage of Dwinelle 155!" (Dwinelle 155 is a large, cold, classroom that most colleagues of mine hate to teach in.) I was rude not because I lacked graciousness but because this man, who had told me that my dissertation was the finest piece of work he had read in fifteen years, had nevertheless advised me to eschew a teaching career.

"Why?" I asked.

"Your leg . . ." he responded.

"What about my leg?" I said, puzzled.

"Well, how would you feel standing in front of a large lec-   15
ture class?"

"If it makes any difference, I want you to know I've won a number of speech contests in my life, and I am not the least bit self-conscious about speaking in front of large audiences . . . Look, why don't you write me a letter of recommendation to tell people how brilliant I am, and let *me* worry about my leg!"

This incident is worth recounting only because it illustrates a dilemma that handicapped persons face frequently: those who care about us sometimes get so protective that they unwittingly limit our growth. This former professor of mine had been one of my greatest supporters for two decades. Time after time, he had written glowing letters of recommendation on my behalf. He had spoken as he did because he thought he had my best interests at heart; he thought that if I got a desk job rather than one that required me to be a visible, public person, I would be spared the misery of being stared at.

Americans, for the most part, do not believe as Asians do that physically handicapped persons are morally flawed. But they are equally inept at interacting with those of us who are not able-bodied. Cultural differences in the perception and treatment of handicapped people are most clearly expressed by adults. Children, regardless of where they are, tend to be openly curious about people who do not look "normal." Adults in Asia have no hesitation in asking visibly handicapped people what is wrong with them, often expressing their sympathy with looks of pity, whereas adults in the United States try desperately to be polite by pretending not to notice.

One interesting response I often elicited from people in Asia but have never encountered in America is the attempt to link my physical condition to the state of my soul. Many a time while living and traveling in Asia people would ask me what religion I belonged to. I would tell them that my mother is a devout Buddhist, that my father was baptized a Catholic but has never practiced Catholicism, and that I am an agnostic. Upon hearing this, people would try strenuously to convert me to their religion so that whichever God they believed in could bless me. If I would only attend this church or that temple regularly, they urged, I would surely get cured. Catholics and Buddhists alike have pressed religious medallions into my palm, telling me if I would wear these, the relevant deity or saint would make me well. Once while visiting the tomb of Muhammad Ali Jinnah in Karachi, Pakistan, an old Muslim, after finishing his evening prayers, spotted me, gestured toward my legs, raised his arms heavenward, and began a new round of prayers, apparently on my behalf.

20   In the United States adults who try to act "civilized" towards handicapped people by pretending they don't notice anything unusual sometimes end up ignoring handicapped people completely. In the first few months I lived in this country, I was struck by the fact that whenever children asked me what was the matter with my leg, their adult companions would hurriedly shush them up, furtively look at me, mumble apologies, and rush their children away. After a few months of such encounters, I decided it was my responsibility to educate these people. So I would say to the flustered adults, "It's okay, let the kid ask." Turning to the child, I would say, "When I was a little girl, no bigger than you are, I became sick with something called polio. The muscles of my leg shrank up and I couldn't walk very well. You're much luckier than I am because now you can get a vaccine to make sure you never get my disease. So don't cry when your mommy takes you to get a polio vaccine, okay?" Some adults and their little companions I talked to this way were glad to be rescued from embarrassment; others thought I was strange.

Americans have another way of covering up their uneasiness: they become jovially patronizing. Sometimes when people spot my crutch, they ask if I've had a skiing accident. When I answer that unfortunately it is something less glamorous than that, they say, "I bet you *could* ski if you put your mind to it!" Alternately, at parties where people dance, men who ask me to dance with them get almost belligerent when I decline their invitation. They say, "Of course you can dance if you *want* to!" Some have given me pep talks about how if I would only develop the right mental attitude, I would have more fun in life.

Different cultural attitudes toward handicapped persons came out clearly during my wedding. My father-in-law, as solid a representative of middle America as could be found, had no qualms about objecting to the marriage on racial grounds, but he could bring himself to comment on my handicap only indirectly. He wondered why his son, who had dated numerous high school and college beauty queens, couldn't marry one of them instead of me. My mother-in-law, a devout Christian, did not share her husband's prejudices, but she worried aloud about whether I could have children. Some Chinese friends of my parents, on the other hand, said that I was lucky to have found such a noble man, one who would marry me despite my handicap. I, for my part, appeared in church in a white lace wedding dress I had designed and made myself—a miniskirt!

How Asian Americans treat me with respect to my handicap tells me a great deal about their degree of acculturation. Recent immigrants behave just like Asians in Asia; those who have been here longer or who grew up in the United States behave more like their white counterparts. I have not encountered any distinctly Asian American pattern of response. What makes the experience of Asian American handicapped people unique is the duality of responses we elicit.

Regardless of racial or cultural background, most handicapped people have to learn to find a balance between the desire to attain physical independence and the need to take care of ourselves by not overtaxing our bodies. In my case, I've had to learn to accept the fact that leading an active life has its price. Between the ages of eight and eighteen, I walked without using crutches or braces but the effort caused my right leg to become badly misaligned. Soon after I came to the United States, I had a series of operations to straighten out the bones of my right leg; afterwards though my leg looked straighter and presumably better, I could no longer walk on my own. Initially my doctors fitted me with a brace, but I found wearing one cumbersome and soon gave it up.

I could move around much more easily—and more important, faster—by using one crutch. One orthopedist after another warned me that using a single crutch was a bad practice. They were right. Over the years my spine developed a double-S curve and for the last twenty years I have suffered from severe, chronic back pains, which neither conventional physical therapy nor a lighter work load can eliminate.

25   The only thing that helps my backaches is a good massage, but the soothing effect lasts no more than a day or two. Massages are expensive, especially when one needs them three times a week. So I found a job that pays better, but at which I have to work longer hours, consequently increasing the physical strain on my body—a sort of vicious circle. When I was in my thirties, my doctors told me that if I kept leading the strenuous life I did, I would be in a wheelchair by the time I was forty. They were right on target; I bought myself a wheelchair when I was forty-one. But being the incorrigible character that I am, I use it only when I am *not* in a hurry!

It is a good thing, however, that I am too busy to think much about my handicap or my backaches because pain can physically debilitate as well as cause depression. And there are days when my spirits get rather low. What has helped me is realizing that being handicapped is akin to growing old at an accelerated rate. The contradiction I experience is that often my mind races along as though I'm only twenty while my body feels about sixty. But fifteen or twenty years hence, unlike my peers who will have to cope with aging for the first time, I shall be full of cheer because I will have already fought, and I hope won, that battle long ago.

Beyond learning how to be physically independent and, for some of us, living with chronic pain or other kinds of discomfort, the most difficult thing a handicapped person has to deal with, especially during puberty and early adulthood, is relating to potential sexual partners. Because American culture places so much emphasis on physical attractiveness, a person with a shriveled limb, or a tilt to the head, or the inability to speak clearly, experiences great uncertainty—indeed trauma—when interacting with someone to whom he or she is attracted. My problem was that I was not only physically handicapped, small, and short, but worse, I also wore glasses and was smarter than all the boys I knew! Alas, an insurmountable combination. Yet somehow I have managed to have intimate relationships, all of them with extraordinary men. Not surprisingly, there have also been countless men who broke my heart—men who enjoyed my company "as a friend," but who never found the courage to date or make love with me, although I am sure my experience in this regard is no different from that of many able-bodied persons.

The day came when my backaches got in the way of having an active sex life. Surprisingly that development was liberating because I stopped worrying about being attractive to men. No matter how headstrong I had been, I, like most women of my generation, had had the desire to be alluring to men ingrained into me. And that longing had always worked like a brake on my behavior. When what men think of me ceased to be compelling, I gained greater freedom to be myself.

I've often wondered if I would have been a different person had I not been physically handicapped. I really don't know, though there is no question that being handicapped has marked me. But at the same time I usually do not *feel* handicapped—and consequently, I do not *act* handicapped. People are therefore less likely to treat me as a handicapped person. There is no doubt, however, that the lives of my parents, sister, husband, other family members, and some close friends have been affected by my physical condition. They have had to learn not to hide me away at home, not to feel embarrassed by how I look or react to people who say silly things to me, and not to resent me for the extra demands my condition makes on them. Perhaps the hardest thing for those who live with handicapped people is to know when and how to offer help. There are no guidelines applicable to all situations. My advice is, when in doubt, ask, but ask in a way that does not smack of pity or embarrassment. Most important, please don't talk to us as though we are children.

So, has being physically handicapped been a handicap? It all 30 depends on one's attitude. Some years ago, I told a friend that I had once said to an affirmative action compliance officer (somewhat sardonically since I do not believe in the head count approach to affirmative action) that the institution which employs me is triply lucky because it can count me as nonwhite, female, and handicapped. He responded, "Why don't you tell them to count you four times? . . . Remember, you're short, besides!"

AIDS: The Linguistic Battlefield
Michael Callen

Singer, songwriter, AIDS activist, and author Michael Callen (1956–1993) is recognized as one of the first advocates of safe sex, a cofounder of the People with AIDS self-empowerment movement, and a proponent of community-based AIDS research. Diagnosed with gay-related immune deficiency (GRID) in 1982, Callen continued to make significant contributions to the gay and lesbian movement before succumbing to the disease in December 1993. Fighting what he felt was the linguistic maneuvering and censorship practiced by the media, the Public Health Service, and mainstream AIDS organizations, Callen coined the term "people with AIDS" (PWAs) to replace the earlier semantically loaded term "AIDS victims." His influential writings and songs, his appearances in numerous films and documentaries, and his work with national gay and lesbian organizations attest to Callen's dedication to the shaping of the United States response to AIDS and his own struggles for gay identity and self-hood. In "AIDS: The Linguistic Battlefield," Callen calls attention to how the language of AIDS became a powerful tool in its recognition as a non-gay-male disease.

1. Trace the history of the name GRID's replacement by AIDS. Do you think AIDS is a more neutral-sounding, cheerful, palatable label?
2. Callen describes the highly charged political controversy between the United States and France on which country first identified the AIDS virus. How was the legal dispute settled regarding who identified AIDS first? Do you think that this dispute was a delaying tactic to detract public attention away from the issue of gay males dying?
3. What is the difference between labeling someone as an "AIDS victim" and labeling someone as "person with AIDS"?
4. What is AIDSpeak? Do you think that this new language was an attempt to minimize the tragedy of AIDS, as writer Randy Shilts suggested?

Writing Assignments

1. Read Randy Shilts's *And the Band Played On* or view the 1993 film version directed by Roger Spottiswoode, starring Alan Alda, Matthew Modine, and Lily Tomlin. Chronicling the history of AIDS' first five years in the United States, the film depicts the research community's struggles to understand this new disease, the spread of public fear and insensitivity, and

the in-fights among government agencies, gay and lesbian
groups, and the medical community. Write a review of it.

2. Write a report on the gay and lesbian movement. Examine
   the forces of resistance that led to a collective social identity
   among gay males and lesbians in the United States.

———————————— ✦ ————————————

AIDS is the moment-to-moment management of uncertainty.
It's like standing in the middle of the New York Stock
Exchange at midday, buzzers and lights flashing, everyone yelling,
a million opinions. AIDS is about loss of control—of one's bowels,
one's bladder, one's life. And so there is often a ferocious drive by
those of us with AIDS to exert at least *some* control over it. When
I was diagnosed in 1982, I decided that I'd have to pay close attention to the language of AIDS—to keep my wits about me in order
to see beyond the obfuscating medical mumbo-jumbo meant to
dazzle me into a deadly passivity.

AIDS is a sprawling topic. War is being waged on many
fronts. From the beginning of this epidemic, there have been a
number of important battles over how we speak about AIDS
which have had subtle but profound effects on how we think
about—and respond to—AIDS. These linguistic battles have also
affected how those of us diagnosed as having AIDS experience
our own illness.

In the early seventies, the gay liberation movement won a
smashing victory when it forced the American Psychiatric Association to declassify homosexuality as an illness. But with the creation of a new disease called G.R.I.D., or gay-related immune deficiency, as AIDS was first termed, in an instant, those of us
whose primary sexual and affectional attraction is to members of
our own sex once again became medicalized and pathologized—
only now we were considered literally, as opposed to merely
morally, contagious.

Soon, gay-related immune deficiency was discovered in nongay
people and a new name for this disease had to be found. All factions
were poised for a political battle over the new name. Instinctively,
those empowered to create and police the definition of AIDS (and
those who would be profoundly affected by it) were aware that the
new name would affect how the epidemic would be handled by the
federal government and the "general" (meaning, generally, the non-
homosexual, non-IV-drug-using, rest-of-you) public.

5   In the end, a neutral sounding, almost cheerful name was chosen: A.I.D.S. Words can resonate with other words and take on subtle, sympathetic vibrations. AIDS: as in "health and beauty aids" or, to retain some of the sexual connotations of the disease, "marital aids." Or AIDS: as in "aid to the Contras." Or, "now is the time for all good men to come to the aid of their country." "AIDS" sounded like something . . . well, helpful.

My highly trained eye can now spot the letters A-I-D on a page of newsprint at lightning speed. It's amazing how often those three letters appear in headlines: afrAID, mislAID, medic-AID, pAID—even bridesmAIDS. Every time I would hear a newscaster say "The president's aide reported today . . .," I'd be momentarily disoriented by the linkage of "president" and "AIDS."

It's interesting to speculate, by the way, what the public response to AIDS might have been had the name proposed by a group from Boston prevailed: *herpes virus reactivation syndrome*. Prior to AIDS, the American public—general or otherwise—had been barraged by *Time* magazine cover stories about another fearsome, sexually transmitted epidemic: herpes. If those with the power to name the current plague had linked its name to the herpes epidemic, getting the American public to take AIDS seriously might not have been quite so difficult. One important consequence (some would say cause) of the profound immune disturbance we now call *AIDS* is that latent herpes viruses are reactivated, leading to a vicious cycle of immune suppression. Had the name *herpes virus reactivation syndrome,* or *HVRS,* been selected instead of *AIDS,* it might not have taken so long to convince Americans to support research into a disease which, by name at least, everyone was theoretically at risk for. But perhaps because *HVRS,* as an acronym, does not roll tripplingly off the tongue, the more neutral sounding *AIDS,* was chosen.

WHAT THE "L" IS GOING ON HERE?

The most momentous semantic battle yet fought in the AIDS war concerned the naming of the so-called AIDS virus. The stakes were high; two nations—France and the United States—were at war over who first identified (and therefore had the right to name) the retrovirus presumed to cause AIDS. Hanging in the balance was a Nobel prize and millions of dollars in patent royalties.

U.S. researcher Dr. Robert Gallo had originally proposed that HTLV-I (human T-cell leukemia virus) was the cause of AIDS. Meanwhile, scientists at the Pasteur Institute isolated a novel retrovirus, which they named *LAV*, to stand for "Lymphadenopathy Associated Virus." The U.S. scoffed at French claims, arrogantly asserting that HTLV-I or HTLV-II must be the cause of AIDS. When it became obvious that neither HTLV-I nor II could possibly be the cause, if for no other reason than because Japan (where HTLV-I and II are endemic) was not in the midst of an AIDS epidemic, the U.S. had to find some way to steal both LAV itself as well as the credit for having discovered it first, while covering over the embarrassing fact that they had proposed the wrong virus as "the cause" of AIDS.

What to do? In an election year (1984), it was simply unthinkable that the French could so outshine U.S. medical research. The United States hit upon a brilliant solution. Gallo simply renamed LAV "HTLV-III" and Secretary of Health and Human Services Margaret Heckler staged a preemptive press strike. She declared that another achievement had been added to the long list of U.S. medical breakthroughs: "The probable cause of AIDS has been found—HTLV-III, a variant of a known, human cancer virus. . . ."

The ploy was certainly ballsy. And looking back, amazingly successful.

But what was going on here? The *L* in HTLV-I and II stands for leukemia, since it proposed that HTLV-I and II account for a particular form of leukemia. Unfortunately for the perpetrators of this massive fraud, it just so happens that leukemia is one of the few diseases which is *not* a complication of AIDS. So, in order to retain the symmetry of nomenclature, Gallo quietly proposed that the *L* in HTLV-III and HTLV-IV now stand for *lymphotropic* instead of *leukemia*.

It is now widely acknowledged that HIV is not a member of the HTLV family at all. It is a lentivirus. But the consequences of Gallo's bold attempt at semantic damage control are still with us. The *Index Medicus* listing for AIDS still refers to HTLV-III, not HIV. The legal dispute was eventually settled by the state department; the presidents of the U.S. and France signed an agreement whereby their nations would share credit and royalties, a settlement potentially worth billions. But what was the cost in human lives lost from research delays caused by the willful misclassification of HIV? . . .

WHO HAS THE POWER TO NAME?

The question of who has the power to name is an ongoing turf battle between people with AIDS and those who insist on defining us as victims. I was at the founding of the people with AIDS self-empowerment movement in Denver, Colorado, in 1983. When the California contingent insisted that we make part of our manifesto the demand that we be referred to as "people with AIDS" (or the inevitable acronym "PWAs") instead of "AIDS victims," I must confess that I rolled my eyes heavenward. How California, I thought.

15   But time has proven them right. Americans, whose ability to think has been dessicated by decades of television and its ten-second-sound-bite mentality, think in one-word descriptors. Someone on the TV screen must be labeled: a feminist, a communist, a homosexual, an AIDS victim. The difference between the descriptors *person with AIDS* and *AIDS victim* seems subtle until one watches oneself on reruns on TV. To see oneself on screen and have the words *AIDS victim* magically flash underneath has a very different feel about it than when the description *person with AIDS* appears. Its very cumbersomeness is startling and makes the viewer ask: "Person? Why person? Of course he's a person. . . ." In that moment, we achieve a small but important victory. Viewers are forced to be conscious, if only for a moment, that we *are* people first.

The founding statement of the PWA self-empowerment movement (known as the "Denver Principles") is quite eloquent on this point:

> We condemn attempts to label us as "victims," which implies defeat; and we are only occasionally "patients," which implies passivity, helplessness and dependence upon the care of others. We are "people with AIDS."

This statement was further refined in the founding Mission Statement of the National Association of People with AIDS (NAPWA):

> We are people with AIDS and people with AIDS-Related Complex (ARC) who can speak for ourselves to advocate for our own causes and concerns. We are your sons and daughters, your brothers and sisters, your family, friends and lovers. As people now living with AIDS and ARC, we have a unique and essential

contribution to make to the dialogue surrounding AIDS and we will actively participate with full and equal credibility to help shape the perception and reality surrounding the disease.

We do not see ourselves as victims. We will not be victimized. We have the right to be treated with respect, dignity, compassion and understanding. We have the right to lead fulfilling, productive lives—to live and die with dignity and compassion.

In a gratuitous aside in his best-selling AIDS epic, *And the Band Played On*, Randy Shilts attacked the right of people with AIDS to choose how they wished to be referred to. Completely twisting the empowering impulse of people with AIDS to wrest some control of our lives, Shilts accused us of attempting to minimize the tragedy of AIDS:

AIDSpeak, a new language forged by public health officials, anxious gay politicians, and the burgeoning ranks of "AIDS activists." The linguistic roots of AIDSpeak sprouted not so much from the truth as from what was politically facile and psychologically reassuring. Semantics was the major denominator of AIDSpeak jargon, because the language went to great lengths never to offend.

A new lexicon was evolving. Under the rules of AIDSpeak, for example, AIDS victims could not be called victims. Instead, they were to be called People with AIDS, or PWAs, as if contracting this uniquely brutal disease was not a victimizing experience. "Promiscuous" became "sexually active," because gay politicians declared "promiscuous" to be "judgmental," a major cuss word in AIDSpeak. The most-used circumlocution in AIDSpeak was "bodily fluids," an expression that avoided troublesome words like "semen."

. . . Thus, the verbiage tended toward the intransitive. AIDSpeak was rarely empowered to motivate action; rather, it was most articulately pronounced when justifying inertia. Nobody meant any harm by this; quite to the contrary, AIDSpeak was the tongue designed to make everyone content. AIDSpeak was the language of good intentions in the AIDS epidemic; AIDSpeak was a language of death.

Shilts notwithstanding, there is now a movement to further emphasize hope. In some quarters PLWAs and PLWArcs have entered the language: Persons *Living* With AIDS and Persons *Living* with ARC, respectively. There is also a new movement to organize all individuals suffering from conditions related to immune deficiency. Acronym conscious, its leaders say they are "PISD" (pronounced "pissed"), which stands for "Persons with Immune System Disorders."

20   The *New York Times*, whose editorial policies influence other newspapers, has been drawn into the battle being waged by people with AIDS to reclaim some small amount of linguistic control over their lives—a battle similar to one being waged by gay people over the *Times's* intransigent use of *homosexual* instead of *gay*. The following exchange concerns the *Times's* obituary of the first president of the New York People with AIDS Coalition:

December 1986

We protest the New York Times' not listing Kenneth Meeks' surviving life-mate of over ten years, Mr. Jack Steinhebel. Upon calling your office, I spoke to "Fred," who told me that it was the policy of the Times "not to include lovers" as survivors. That policy is totally inappropriate in that it lacks sensitivity and basic respect. "Fred" also informed me that in his "six years at the Times and with hundreds of phone calls the policy had not changed" and that we should "not expect it to change in the future." How sad.

    Finally, the labeling of People with AIDS as "victims" in Ken's obit was incorrect and more so in light of Ken's extensive work to end such practices. We are greatly disappointed by such journalism.

> Sincerely,
> Michael Hirsch
> Executive Director
> People with AIDS Coalition

The *New York Times* responded:

No slurs were intended, but I can well understand your feelings about Kenneth Meeks's obituary. We are reviewing our obituary conventions regarding mention of intimates other than blood relatives and spouses. I cannot predict what we will decide to do, but think you have contributed to consciousness-raising.

As for the word "victim," I cannot agree that it is pejorative. Along with most of society, we have long written about "stroke victims," "heart attack victims," and "cancer victims." The logic is equally applicable to AIDS, and I am uncomfortable about drying [*sic*] idiom for any cause, no matter how meritorious.

Sincerely,
Alan M. Siegel
News Editor
New York Times

In the ensuing three years, there has been no change in the *Times*'s policy of refusing to acknowledge the status of "intimates other than blood relatives and spouses" (now, there's a mouthful) in the obituaries of lesbian and gay people. If a change of policy so obviously just and easy to accommodate cannot be made by the *Times*, one holds out little hope that they'll ever use a descriptor other than *victim* when referring to PWAs. . . .

Is there anyone who can talk about AIDS and emerge from the battle unscathed? Probably not. We all want to control AIDS somehow, and at times language seems to be our only weapon. But we must not try to master AIDS by crushing its complexities, mysteries, and terrors into convenient labels that roll trippingly and with false authority off the tongue. We must always speak fully and carefully about AIDS, even if that often requires a mouthful—cumbersome constructions full of words strung together by hyphens—to say precisely what we mean. The stakes are simply too high to do otherwise.

Guidelines for Avoiding Ableist Language

Ableism is defined as stereotyping and negative attitudes toward people with a physical or mental disability or illness that result in discrimination and/or prejudice. *Disability* is defined as a physical or mental restriction or lack of ability that substantially limits an individual's performance of one or more major life activities: seeing, hearing, speaking, walking, working, and learning. A disability is not a handicap. *Handicap* is defined as an obstacle or barrier to the freedom and independence of people with disabilities. *Impairment* is defined as a physiological disorder affecting one or more of a number of body systems or a mental or psychological disorder.

Ableist language is the use of words or labels that disparages persons with disabilities as abnormal, unhealthy, and unable. Ableist language depersonalizes and stereotypes persons with disabilities by emphasizing the disability over the person.

Rule 1. Do not refer to a person's disability unless it is relevant.

The most widely preferred term for a person with a disability is "disabled" although alternative expressions such as "physically or mentally different," "physically or mentally challenged," "differently abled," "exceptional," and "special needs" are commonly used.

Use these expressions cautiously because they often function as euphemisms and disparaging labels. Use the current terminology "person with a disability" or name the specific disability; do not use "handicapped persons" or "the handicapped" to refer to persons with disabilities.

Rule 2. Use *person first language* to describe persons with disabilities.

Person First Rule

According to the Americans with Disabilities Act, always describe the person over the disability: Name the person first and only when relevant, then follow with pertinent descriptors such as the particular disability or illness. Rather than calling someone "an AIDS sufferer" or "an AIDS victim," refer to that person, not the condition, and call him or her "a person living with AIDS." Use "person who has polio" not "polio victim." Use "person who uses a wheelchair" not "wheelchair bound."

Ableist	Preferred Terminology
autistic child	child who has autism
cerebral palsy	person with cerebral palsy
epileptic	person with epilepsy
Mongoloid	child with Down's syndrome

Rule 3. Use adjectives to describe persons with disabilities rather than nouns.

Calling a person "a cripple," "a deaf mute," "an arthritic," or "a quadriplegic" reduces the individual to a disease and stereotypes that individual as helpless, weak, and dependent. Rather than using a noun to refer to an individual with a disability, use adjective forms such as "person who is hard of hearing," "someone with arthritis," or "a person who is blind." Avoid adjectives that arouse pity such as "poor," "helpless," and "unfortunate."

Rule 4. Avoid describing persons with disabilities in emotional or sympathetic terms.

Avoid using sensationalistic expressions such as "suffers from," "afflicted with," "stricken with," or "victim of" or nouns such as "invalid," "patient," or "case." Such terms dehumanize the person and emphasize weakness and powerlessness.

Rule 5. Do not use patronizing expressions to describe persons with disabilities.

Avoid expressions such as "a courageous being," "doing so well given the circumstances," and "brave." Avoid ableist expressions such as "was blind, but now I see."

Rule 6. Cautiously use common expressions that refer to disabilities: "blind as a bat," "deaf as a doornail," "crazy as a loon," "a mental midget."

Avoid discriminatory jokes about people with disabilities; such humor is offensive.

Rule 7. Use alternative neutral forms to describe persons with disabilities.

Ableist	Preferred Terminology
able-bodied/normal	person without disabilities/a typical person
birth defect/affliction	congenital disability/birth anomaly
blind/deaf-mute	person who is blind or visually impaired/person who is deaf
deaf and dumb	person who is hard of hearing, person who is deaf
Down's person/Mongoloid	person with Down's syndrome
epileptic	person who has epilepsy, person with seizure disorder
epileptic fit	person with epileptic episodes/events/seizure disorder
mentally retarded	person who has mental retardation
feeble-minded/slow	person with developmental delay/a developmental disability
mentally ill/crazy	person who has mental illness/person with an emotional disorder
midget	little person, person of short stature, short-statured person, person with dwarfism
mute, speechless, stammerer, lisp, stutterer	person with a communication disability
psycho/mental case	person with an emotional disorder

Bosmajian, Haig A. "Defining the 'American Indian': A Case Study in the Language of Suppression," from *The Speech Teacher*, March 1973: 89–99. Reprinted with the permission of the publisher.

Boswell, Maia. "Sexism, Ageism and Disability: (Re)Constructing Agency Through (Re)Writing Personal Narrative" from *Women and Language* 24.2:47–51. Reprinted by permission of the author.

Callen, Michael. "AIDS: The Linguistic Battlefield" from *The State of the Language*, Christopher Ricks and Leonard Michaels, eds. Copyright © 1989 The Regents of the University of California. Reprinted by permission.

Chan, Suchen. "You're Short, Besides!" from *Making Waves* by Asian Women United. Copyright © 1989 by Suchen Chan. Reprinted by permission of the author.

Cole, James W. "Prejudice Quiz" from *Beyond Prejudice*, Homepage, www.eburg.com/~cole/Quiz.html. Reprinted by permission of the author.

Crystal, David. "The Sapir-Whorf Hypothesis" from *The Cambridge Encyclopedia of Language*. Reprinted with the permission of Cambridge University Press.

Das, Kamala. "An Introduction" from *In Their Own Voice: The Penguin Anthology of Contemporary Indian Women Poets*, compiled and edited with an introduction by Dr. Arlene R. K. Zide (New Delhi: Penguin Books, 1993), pp. 45–47. Reprinted by permission of Dr. Arlene R. K. Zide.

Davis, Ossie. "The English Language Is My Enemy!" from *Negro History Bulletin*, 3.4. April 1967: 18. Reprinted by permission of the author.

Dhongde, Ashwini. "Small Ads: Matrimonials" from *In Their Own Voice: The Penguin Anthology of Contemporary Indian Women Poets*, compiled and edited with an introduction by Dr. Arlene R. K. Zide (New Delhi: Penguin Books, 1993), p. 62. Reprinted by permission of Dr. Arlene R. K. Zide.

Faderman, Lillian. "Queer" from the *Boston Globe*, July 28, 1991. Reprinted by permission of the author.

Friedmann, Thomas. "Heard Any Good Jews Lately?" from *Speaking of Words* by James MacKillop and Donna Woolfolk Cross (Holt, Rinehart and Winston, 1982), pp. 254–258.

260